CLASS
WARS

The Story of the Washington Education Association 1965~2001

Class Wars
The Story of the Washington Education Association
1965–2001

by Steve Kink and John Cahill

Designed by Marie McCaffrey, Crowley Associates, Inc.
Edited by Priscilla Long and Walt Crowley

First printing, July 2004

Printed in the USA at Graphic Arts Center, Seattle

ISBN: 0-295-98463-5

Published by the Washington Education Association
PO Box 9100
Federal Way, WA 98063-9100

253-941-6700 (800-622-3393 toll-free)
www.wa.nea.org

Produced by History Ink

Distributed by University of Washington Press

A HistoryLink Book

To learn more, visit www.wa.nea.org or www.historylink.org

TABLE OF CONTENTS

Foreword

As the President of the Washington Education Association, I am proud to recommend *Class Wars: The Story of the Washington Education Association, 1965–2001*. This book offers a personal and historical perspective of the struggle by teachers and other education personnel to improve public education for the children of our state. *Class Wars* is told in the words of those who lived and shaped this story.

To write this book the WEA commissioned the authors, Steve Kink and John Cahill, to interview over sixty people who were part of Association governance and staff between 1965 and 2001. They also researched the major external events, internal policies and program activities that influenced the direction and history of the WEA. The authors, who were themselves major players in the events during this time period, combined the interviews and the research to write this book for the Association membership and others who have an interest in the WEA's intriguing history.

Class Wars is a coming-of-age story about the Washington Education Association set against the backdrop of the turbulent 1960s and 1970s. It is a candid, inside account of a revolution that transformed the role that teachers and other education personnel would play to shape education policy in Washington. It is the story of how classroom activists seized control of their own organization and came to wield power within state education.

I am proud of WEA's past and present efforts to make public education the best it can be for students, their parents and public education employees. I believe that it is extremely important to remember the efforts of those who came before us and built the foundation on which we proudly stand today. This story is an inspiration for those of us who follow and who will shape Association history in years to come.

Charles Hasse, President
Washington Education Association

Introduction

This book is a storied history of the Washington Education Association from 1965 to 2001 as told by those who lived it. Known as the WEA by many, the Association has a history filled with precedent-setting successes and some failures. This history involves a cast of characters who took personal risks to improve the public education profession.

Chapter 1 describes the traditional, administrator-dominated professional association of the 1960s. However, with passage of the Professional Negotiations Act in 1965, the winds of change begin a transition in the WEA to a teacher-controlled professional union.

Chapter 2 chronicles the gale-force revolution in WEA called UniServ. Through the UniServ Program, the power within the WEA is shifted from state and urban association control to broad-based local association control. With UniServ, WEA makes the transition to a union.

Chapter 3 describes how UniServ organizes the first teacher strikes and gains dominance in the battle to achieve authentic teacher collective bargaining. As WEA power grows, it gains a new collective bargaining law and begins to challenge the political establishment of the state.

Chapter 4 takes WEA to the peak of its power. The collective power of WEA affiliates and membership is demonstrated through collective bargaining gains, an impressive political action program, legal victories and pro-education legislation.

Chapter 5 describes conditions and events that moved WEA a step backward. External challenges and internal conflicts plague WEA for the decade of the 1980s.

Chapter 6 shows WEA coming back into focus and once again moving forward. An unprecedented statewide Multi-Local Strike leads off the decade of the 1990s. WEA redefines itself, expands its base as an advocate for public education, takes its message to the public and ends the decade by passing an important school employee pay initiative.

This book chronicles eight "perfect storm" events that had catalytic impacts on WEA's history: the 1965 Professional Negotiations Act, the UniServ Program, the 1972 Aberdeen strike, the 1973 Evergreen strike, the 1978 campaign to defeat August Mardesich, the 1980 Precinct Caucus Program, the 1991 Multi-Local Strike and the 2000 Initiative 732 campaign.

Not only are we the authors of this portion of WEA's long history, we were active participants in most of the events establishing this history. We have, without reservation, hesitation or modesty, shared our perspectives. We spent hundreds of hours interviewing over sixty association activists to pull from them their recollections and stories, which we have woven into the fabric of this history.

We want to acknowledge those we interviewed. They are the heart and soul of this history. We also want to acknowledge the management and support staff of WEA, the UniServ and their support staff, plus the local, council and state governance leaders who played crucial parts in this history. Without a courageous WEA membership throughout this period of time, none of this would have happened.

We want to thank Walt Crowley, Marie McCaffrey and Priscilla Long of HistoryLink for their expertise, encouragement and support in the publication process, Armand Tiberio for his leadership in providing financial support and finally Joann Kink Mertens and Andrea Dahl for their motivation, time, computer assistance and putting up with us!

Steve Kink, Seattle
John Cahill, Gig Harbor
February 2004

CLASS WARS

The Story of the Washington Education Association 1965~2001

BY STEVE KINK
AND JOHN CAHILL

CHAPTER ONE

Origins: The 1960s

In 1965 the Washington Education Association (WEA) had all but finished sweeping up the balloons and confetti from its Diamond Jubilee celebration the previous year and was looking to its future with great optimism. The organization had seen its membership grow from 124 educators in April 1889 to over 34,000 teachers and school administrators in 1965. The WEA was one of fifty state organizations affiliated with the National Education Association (NEA), founded in 1857. In turn, local associations in most of the 397 school districts in the state of Washington were affiliated with the WEA.

WEA's success was legend. Early in the century the Association helped secure a firm financial footing for Washington schools through passage of two so-called "Barefoot Schoolboy Laws," which provided a foundation of state funds for local school districts. WEA had raised teacher standards by strengthening teacher certification and teacher education. In the depths of the Great Depression, WEA formed a coalition of organizations to pass an income tax initiative to fund schools, only to have the state Supreme Court strike it down 5 to 4. WEA bounced back from that defeat to secure passage of sales and business and occupation taxes. By 1947 WEA achieved passage of state-funded teacher pensions of $100 per month for thirty years' service. Improved pensions would continue to be a legislative goal. In 1957, through legislative enactment and a plebiscite of the state's teachers, WEA brought them coverage under the Social Security system. In 1959 statewide sick leave was achieved for teachers, replacing various district-provided benefits.

The WEA was well established in downtown Seattle in a modern three-story office building at 910 Fifth Avenue, built in 1956. The building was to serve the Association's needs until it outgrew it in 1979.

Few in the WEA at that time saw reason for any dramatic changes in the way the Association did business. To most members and observers WEA was a strong and well-respected name in state education. Yet, two vital ingredients were missing. Teachers were not vitally involved and in control of their organization. And teachers lacked a strong voice in the school districts where they taught. The year 1965 would prove to be an historic divide between the old "professional" WEA and the new "teacher union" that would emerge dramatically in the 1970s.

The "old WEA" was dominated by its administrative members. Most WEA Presidents had been school administrators content to serve in a largely ceremonial role. Since 1940 WEA had been run by one dominant school superintendent–like figure, its highly respected Executive Secretary, Joe Chandler. Chandler was a short, square-shouldered, charismatic leader who had built the WEA into a powerful education lobby in Olympia. His employees at WEA called him "Mr. Chandler." He was known to educators and the public alike across the state as "Mr. Education." Chandler was a spellbinding speaker who delivered flawless speeches from a handful of note cards with brief notations typed on them. He was the genius behind WEA's legislative achievements. Chandler had the power to summon the Governor to his office on short notice in the middle of a legislative session.

But the winds of change were blowing. Chandler retired in 1965 and turned the reins of Executive Secretary over to his hand-picked successor, Cecil Hannan, who had been WEA Field Services Director and had replaced a tiring Chandler as WEA's point person in Olympia.

Hannan was a young, handsome, wavy-haired man with the charisma and speaking ability of Joe Chandler. In addition, he was very energetic. He had been a vice principal in Longview and WEA President in 1957. He was well connected in the National Education Association (NEA). When he became only the third Executive Secretary in WEA's history, it did not seem to signal any change in the organization — just a continuation of the same successes.

Teacher members were still basking in the importance education was accorded nationally in the post-Sputnik era. The United States was in a race with the Soviet Union to "put a man on the moon." President Johnson's stepped-up involvement in Vietnam was not yet very controversial. It was an optimistic time for education. Teachers felt they had an important mission to carry out.

The 1960s was a time when have-not groups in society were beginning to rise up and assert themselves. Teachers, too, were feeling it was time for them to stand up and assume leadership of their organization. Administrative dominance of the WEA was apparently a visible issue because WEA's seventy-five-year history, written as a report to the 1964 annual Representative Assembly, stressed, "eleven years have gone by since a superintendent has been elected President. . . . this shift to classroom teacher leadership is also reflected in other areas of Association leadership. Only two city superintendents were delegates to the 1963 Representative Assembly. This year's committee membership is 66 percent classroom teachers, and the Board of Directors currently includes no city superintendent, but 16 classroom teachers."

Though a preponderance of Washington teachers were not seeking to change WEA into a teacher union, the rise of the American Federation of Teachers (AFT) in the East and the 1962 Al Shanker-led strike in New York City added fuel to the growing notion that classroom teachers should have an authentic voice in their profession and in the policies of their districts. The AFT's aggressive union posture appealed particularly to urban teachers' growing sense of powerlessness. The AFT openly espoused collective bargaining for teachers and, in head-to-head competition with the NEA, had won exclusive bargaining rights in most of the large cities of the East and Midwest. AFT locals in Seattle, Tacoma, Bremerton and elsewhere in Washington were plenty vocal about teacher unionism but could never gain bargaining rights in any Washington school district.

The WEA President in 1965 was a Puyallup teacher named Frank "Buster" Brouillet, who would go on to be elected State Superintendent of Public Instruction in 1972. He couldn't even chair his Representative Assembly, held at the Masonic Temple in Tacoma on April 9 and 10, because the Legislature was still in session, and he was a State Representative. The new Executive Secretary, Cecil Hannan, also was in Olympia shepherding WEA legislation.

One of the pieces of legislation Brouillet and Hannan supported was a WEA-sponsored Professional Negotiations Act that would mark 1965 as a watershed year for the organization. "Professional Negotiations" was an NEA-coined euphemism for teacher collective bargaining but couched in professional, non-union jargon. Hannan was an energetic advocate for the PN Act. With his eye on a position with the NEA, he was fulfilling one of NEA's goals and helping to fend off AFT takeovers of large city school districts. Few members, including those from the state's urban districts, which had pressured WEA to sponsor such a bill, envisioned that it would change WEA from a "tea and crumpets" organization into the state's largest and most powerful public employee labor union.

The two-day Representative Assembly, in 1965, passed a budget with a $2 dues increase and elected Seattle teacher Gladys Perry President-elect. It heard reports from a host of standing committees including Public Relations, Legislation, Professional Rights and Responsibilities, Teacher Education and Professional Standards, Professional Accreditation Study, Citizenship and School Lands. Necrology, chaired by Ermol Howe, sang the Lord's Prayer in memory of teachers who had died that year. The minutes of that meeting made no mention of the Professional Negotiations Act!

The Seattle Impact on Professional Negotiations

The Professional Negotiations Act, which gave teachers the right to negotiate a wide range of school district policies with their school boards, did not simply fall from the sky. Several pressures and influences came together in the mid-1960s to mandate WEA to seek its passage. Foremost among them was pressure from the WEA's urban affiliate associations, notably Seattle and

Tacoma, which sought authentic input into their district's educational policy making. In short, they wanted to negotiate with their school boards. The Urbans, as they were called, had offices and executive secretaries of their own and were an independent-minded power within the Chandler WEA.

Leading the way was the Seattle Teachers Association, which had sought a negotiations relationship with its school board only to be rebuffed.

According to chief negotiator and later Seattle Teachers Association President Wes Ruff, Seattle's relationship with the WEA was contentious. The Seattle Teachers Association was a teacher-only organization. Excluding administrators ran afoul of Joe Chandler, who staunchly favored an all-inclusive organization. Tacoma, too, was a similar teacher-only local association.

WEA felt a negotiations relationship was a concept for local associations to work out with their school boards. Seattle clamored for legislation giving them the right to negotiate with their school board, a cause that was promoted initially more by the National Education Association (NEA) than by the WEA.

Wes Ruff and the Seattle Teachers Association

The key figure in this movement for a Professional Negotiations Act in Washington was Seattle teacher Wes Ruff. Ruff was a short, stocky man with a professorial demeanor and a quick mind and tongue to match. He began his teaching career at Seattle's old Warren Avenue Elementary School, which was razed in 1959 to make way for the construction of the 1962 Seattle World's Fair. Ruff ended up at Ballard High School and James Monroe Junior High.

As a political science major he was well aware of the labor movement. "I asked if there was a union I could join," recalled Ruff. "I was told there were five! There was the Seattle Association of Classroom Teachers, the Grade Club for elementary teachers, the AFT and two others. I joined the Seattle Association of Classroom Teachers."

Ruff got to know others in that organization as well as in the AFT. "All agreed something had to be done. The school board would play off one organization against the other." Ruff and his colleagues Gladys Perry, Maynard Mathison, Ralph Stevens, John Doty and Dave Broderick conspired to "kill the Grade Club" and form a single organization, affiliated with the WEA, that would negotiate with the school board. "Lavern Girky, President of the Grade Club, never forgave us," said Ruff. "The AFT members were always mouthing off, but they had no loyalty to the labor movement. They were more interested in upward mobility. They always complained that we were not aggressive enough." According to Ruff, the Seattle Teachers Association was formed in 1957. Gladys Perry was the first President, Stan McEchren the second and Ruff was the third.

A young Sharples Junior High science teacher in the late 1950s, Warren Henderson, recalled how frustrated he felt about the Seattle Association of Classroom Teachers. "I joined and attended several meetings but was frustrated there was little the Association could do to improve teaching conditions," said Henderson. "I spoke out at several meetings. I wanted each of my students to have their own textbooks. We had only room sets, and students had to check out the text if I gave homework."

Later, in the mid-1960s, Henderson became involved in the Association after he took a stand against salaries that had been set by the District. "At a Representative Assembly meeting," recalled Henderson, "the President presented the salary that had been set by the school district. The President was trying to get the assembly to take a positive vote in favor of the outcome — although the vote would have no impact on the board's decision. For the first time I spoke out at the RA, saying the salary was disgustingly low and did not deserve our consideration. The next day I was visited in my classroom by Dave Broderick asking me if I would serve on STA's salary committee."

Ruff and other Seattle teacher leaders had a vision that the Seattle Teachers Association would have genuine teacher input into legislation and district policy. For them genuine input was input unfiltered by school administrators.

Seattle's pressure to get the parent WEA to sponsor negotiations legislation, according to Ruff, grew out of a failed attempt to get the Seattle School Board to negotiate voluntarily with the local association. "We got the school board to sit down with us every other Thursday for three months," said Ruff. "We sat down and talked to the board about having genuine, authentic teacher input. WEA was against us."

Seattle found a ready ally in its national affiliate, the National Education Association. The NEA eagerly embraced Professional Negotiations as a strategy for stemming the tide of urban defections to the AFT. Seattle was a key NEA urban affiliate.

The NEA lent the Seattle local the assistance of two top labor attorneys. "We brought them in the back door to talk to the board about what negotiations would be like. Superintendent Ernie Campbell was livid. He said we 'conned' the school board into listening to us."

That's when the Seattle School Board balked. "Then the fateful day came. I was the chief negotiator. School board President Frances Owen, or Mrs. Henry B. Owen as she was referred to then, said, 'Now Mr. Ruff, we have been talking to each other and we have a suggestion.'"

Ruff replied that he was always interested in suggestions. He was stunned by what followed. "We think you should get a very large trunk," said Owen, "and then take this whole concept and all your notes and all your discussions and all your promises and all your visions and put them into the bottom of that trunk and close the trunk and put it in storage and go about your job of teaching."

That ended the discussion. "Gladys cried," Ruff said. "I was overwhelmed. Ralph was angry. We left with our tails between our legs."

According to Ruff, the next step was to become politically powerful and to pressure WEA for negotiations legislation. It was heavy pressure Seattle brought on WEA. "We got active in all Seattle political races. We interviewed candidates. We doorbelled all over the city. The upshot was we became such good friends with Seattle legislators and such supporters that before any legislation of consequence to teachers was passed, the Seattle legislators would check with us. Guess what? WEA could not pass any legislation we did not want passed!"

But Seattle could not go it alone. Ruff said they looked to coalitions with other like-minded local associations. "We then started the King County Coordinating Council so we could work with Bellevue, Issaquah and the others on legislation we wanted passed for urban districts. It became so overwhelming that WEA could not pass any legislation without the King County Coordinating Council being on board."

"The NEA Convention was in Seattle in 1964. Without WEA knowing about it, we rented the penthouse on top of the Edmond Meany Hotel and talked to all the urban people we knew from Minneapolis, Denver and so on." According to Ruff, that was the beginning of the National Council of Urban Education Associations (NCUEA). NCUEA became a potent force in the NEA.

"Professional Negotiations" may have been an euphemism for collective bargaining, but it had a far wider appeal to most of the nation's teachers, who were not yet ready to don the "union label." Ruff credits Hannan with "seeing the handwriting on the wall and getting behind a PN law." Hannan had replaced Chandler as WEA's lead lobbyist in Olympia. He also had his eye on a bigger prize, a position in the NEA, which he achieved in 1967. Passing a PN law in Washington, which was accomplished in 1965, had helped his chances. "We had good support from Tacoma, Bellingham and Bremerton [which had the state's first contract dating back to AFT days in 1954]."

Ruff said that Seattle had a good friend in State Superintendent of Public Instruction Louis Bruno and his assistant Lew Griffith. "They not only saw the handwriting on the wall, they supported genuine teacher involvement."

The PN Act covered both K–12 teachers and Community College instructors. Community Colleges were then a part of their respective school districts. When the community colleges were split off from public school systems a few years later, separate but virtually identical laws were codified.

The one part of the PN Act that did not fit Seattle's plans was that it specified bargaining units must include all administrators except district superintendents. "We could not get rid of it in the Legislature. We felt we could work it out later. When we tried to negotiate as a teacher-only association, there was a court battle, and WEA went up against STA. STA and Tacoma could not operate alone. So we formed the Seattle Alliance of Educators — an umbrella organization with token administrative participation." Tacoma followed suit by forming the Tacoma Alliance of Educators.

Ruff said that the PN Act led to Superintendent Campbell's early retirement. "Ernie Campbell, both at a school board meeting and to me personally, said, 'You are ruining the schools and I will not be a party to it.'" He resigned.

Support for a PN law was not entirely an urban effort. Don Johnson, hired in 1963 to head up WEA's Professional Rights and Responsibilities activities, said that there was support within the WEA field staff for Professional Negotiations. And WEA's Eastern Washington Field Representative Don Murray recalled that Joe Chandler and Cecil Hannan unveiled WEA's legislation at a statewide meeting of local Presidents. Dale Troxel from Vancouver, later hired by WEA in 1967, recalled making several trips to Olympia to lobby for the bill.

Once passed, the challenge was to make the PN Act the vehicle for authentic teacher input into education policies that Ruff and his colleagues at STA had envisioned when they originally sat down with the Seattle School Board years before.

The Professional Negotiations Act

This law — the law on which Seattle and other state teachers pinned their hopes for a greater teacher voice in education — was only one page long. (See Appendix 1.) It did not look particularly like a collective bargaining law, but it was a big leap in that direction.

The law's stated purpose was "to strengthen methods of administering employer-employee relations through orderly methods of communication between certificated employees and the school districts by which they are employed." It called for representation by a single organization chosen by a secret ballot. Unlike "meet and confer" laws that passed in some other states, the PN Act gave the elected teacher organization the right to "meet, confer, and negotiate with the board of directors of the school district or a committee thereof to communicate the considered professional judgment of the certificated staff prior to the final adoption by the board of proposed school policies. . . ."

Those who began to work with this new law, however, began to understand its similarities to traditional collective bargaining and how it gave teachers the potential to exercise great power for the first time. "The word 'negotiate' is a wonderful ambiguity," said Ruff, who in 1967 would be hired by WEA as its first field staff person for Professional Negotiations.

Unlike traditional collective bargaining laws that specified a contract agreement as the final product of negotiations, the PN Act made school policy the final product. Even though a later Attorney General's opinion ruled that the law permitted the bargaining of contracts, boards were not required by the Act to do so. That proved to be a problem in later years.

Whereas traditional collective bargaining laws specify the scope of bargaining as "wages, hours and terms and conditions of employment," the

PN Act seemed to have a much broader scope. Its scope included "school policies relating to, but not limited to, curriculum, textbook selection, in-service training, student teaching programs, personnel, hiring and assignment practices, leaves of absence, salaries and salary schedules and non-instructional duties." This broad scope or "laundry list," combined with the phrase "but not limited to," gave teachers what they thought was the right to bargain all school district policies.

Many school boards, on the other hand, would claim that the Act merely specified "orderly methods of communication." They felt they only had an obligation to sit down and talk, and then could do as they pleased. It was a wonderful formula for conflict!

One of the problem areas of the law was its inclusion of all administrators or school managers in the bargaining units. The lone exception was the superintendent. Anyone familiar with traditional bargaining knows that the inclusion of managers in the bargaining unit ultimately is an untenable conflict of interest. Superintendents and school boards pulled school middle management one way and the teachers at first pulled them the other. Eventually, teachers began to doubt the loyalties of their principals. Principals and other middle managers followed superintendents right out of the WEA.

The law had a curious mechanism for dispute resolution. There was no equivalent agency to the current Public Employment Relations Commission to administer the law. Dispute resolution was left to the ill-equipped Office of the State Superintendent of Public Instruction.

The Act specified, "In the event that any matter being jointly considered by the employee organization and the board of directors of the school district is not settled by means provided in this act, either party, twenty-four hours after serving written notice of their intended action to the other party, may request the assistance and advice of a committee composed of educators and school directors appointed by the state superintendent of public instruction." This "impasse committee" was to hear the parties and make written recommendations within twenty days. The recommendations were not binding on either party.

The Act was careful not to use labor jargon. Was the purpose of this committee "fact finding," "mediation" or something else? The lack of effective dispute resolution was to be one of the downfalls of the Act in the 1970s.

One of Wes Ruff's first assignments at WEA was to work out a set of negotiation guidelines including rules on how impasses would work. Impasse committees were to consist of two teachers, two school directors and a so-called neutral superintendent who would chair the committee.

Another curious feature of the law was the authority school boards were given to "adopt reasonable rules and regulations for the administration of employer-employee relations." In most districts associations sat down with boards and worked out these rules and set them down in procedural agreements. In a few places like Edmonds, even though the board did work with the local on developing rules, they insisted they were not negotiating them and had every right to adopt whatever rules they wanted.

In Lake Washington, past-President Jake Rufer wrote in a 1969 article in *Washington Education*, "When negotiations started last year, no procedural agreement existed with the school board (and there is none to this date). Instead, the board unilaterally set procedural rules and consistently applied those rules to its own satisfaction." That same year Lake Washington had two impasse committees come and go with no result, a failed attempt to secure a restraining order against the board's unilateral adoption of a new salary schedule, an inconclusive "stacking of contracts," which entailed the union collecting and holding individual teacher service contracts until an agreement with management could be reached, and a lack of WEA and NEA commitment to sanction the district. The term "surface bargaining" had now become common. Surface bargaining was the appearance of bargaining without a good faith attempt by management to reach any agreement.

This frustrating lack of satisfaction with the "professional negotiations" process was the forerunner of ever-greater conflicts that radicalized teachers and helped lead to passage of a full-blown collective bargaining act in 1975.

One of the strengths of the law was the requirement of an exclusive bargaining representative chosen by an election. When the Act was under consideration by the Legislature, the WEA wanted the law to state simply that the school board could designate the exclusive bargaining agent. But fortunately, wiser heads prevailed in the Legislature. Imagine the mischief school boards could have perpetrated on the bargaining process if they could unilaterally select the bargaining representative and change it when they saw fit!

Exclusive representation was far superior to the process in California's Winton Act, which set up a very awkward system of proportional representation among competing teacher organizations. Exclusive representation also settled once and for all that WEA would be the dominant K–12 teacher organization in the state. The much smaller AFT was defeated in all of those elections and to this day has never held teacher bargaining rights in a single school district in Washington. Later on it did gain control of some of the community colleges that were a lower priority to WEA.

When Cecil Hannan announced his resignation as Executive Secretary at the Representative Assembly in April 1966, he said this of Professional Negotiations:

> Professional negotiations is the only mechanism that makes it possible for the associations to exercise leadership in the business of education. There is a need for grievance machinery which will operate effectively. Apathy and lack of involvement on the part of local associations must be overcome.

That same Representative Assembly passed the following commendation:

To the members of the 1965 Legislature and Governor Evans for their wisdom and foresight in establishing the nation's first Professional Negotiations law for the teaching profession and for legislation making it possible for teachers to transfer sick leave and seniority benefits within the state of Washington.

Whatever this one-page act said on paper, it ushered in a completely new era of teacher-school management relations. School board and administrative determination to render the PN Act impotent frustrated teacher expectations of authentic participation in educational decision-making.

Local Association Organizing: The Yakima Story

At the time the PN Act was passed, most local associations in the state had salary committees that met with their school boards each year to "negotiate" improved salaries. Certain individuals and locals made pioneering efforts to achieve authentic bargaining rights in Washington. Ken Landeis and Doug Suhm in Yakima exemplified the spirit that would catch hold across the state.

In the years prior to 1965, WEA had but two field staff to organize and work with local associations. Cecil Hannan serviced Western Washington, and Don Murray covered all of Eastern Washington. Murray recalled meeting with Chandler Monday mornings each week. In these meetings Chandler would go through his stack of mail and dole the letters out to his staff. These became the assignments for the field staff. Murray got his assignments, got to a phone, made appointments for the week, and headed out in his car to Eastern Washington. Typically, he didn't return until late Friday or Saturday. Often he had to sleep in his car when no motels were available. Murray had to report to WEA by phone each morning by 8 a.m. and was expected by Chandler, a lead-foot driver himself, to average 60 miles per hour on the road. Murray spent much of his time building coalitions of locals, bringing them salary data they could use in early salary negotiations and solving member problems.

Even before the PN Act passed, two activist members in Yakima showed the rest of the state what good organizing, the willingness to take great risks and teacher power could produce in a negotiations setting.

Of average height, Ken Landeis stood straight with his neatly trimmed straight dark hair. With a friendly but no-nonsense demeanor, he was focused, always in control and spoke right to the point. Landeis would go on to be elected WEA President and would represent and bargain for the teachers of Southeast Washington until 1990. An expert carpenter, he was an industrial arts teacher who had started his career in Renton in 1956. "I moved to Yakima because it paid $50 more . . . per year. I made 50 cents less per hour than a carpenter."

Doug Suhm started out as a junior high school teacher in Yakima in 1955 and by 1963 ended up at Davis High School as a counselor. Suhm partnered well with Landeis. His approach was more spirited. He could use passion and emotion to good effect. He was slender and athletic and was as much at home paddling a canoe on the Boundary Lakes of Minnesota as he was counseling students. "It was the Superintendent, Milt Martin, who asked, or really required, me to join the Association."

Neither Landeis nor Suhm were active in the local Association in their early years. Landeis felt the Association didn't do anything worthwhile.

In the early 1960s Ken Landeis and his wife, Ginny, had an infant son who contracted a terminal disease. Local doctors said they could do nothing for him and said he would have to see a specialist at the University of Washington Hospital. Landeis used his sick leave and took off for Seattle on a Thursday and Friday and returned on a Monday.

"When I arrived back at Franklin Junior High," Landeis relates, "I was greeted by my principal, who was told to tell me that I would lose two day's pay because of inappropriate use of sick leave. My son died a few months later. In all the years I had taught, I had used but one-half day sick leave until this emergency with my son." That was a defining moment for Landeis. "I decided this was never going to happen again." He got involved in the Yakima Education Association.

First, Landeis became a Building Representative at Franklin. Then, in 1962, he ran for and was elected Vice President. Landeis thought the current President was disorganized and didn't do much of anything. "I held an executive committee meeting without the President and they agreed to ask him for his resignation." He felt the President was glad it happened. Ken Landeis became President of the Yakima Education Association.

By about 1964 or 1965, Doug Suhm ended up as Vice President and a member of their bargaining team. He remembers meeting WEA's Eastern Washington Field Representative Don Murray when Murray was traveling the region promoting salary negotiations prior to passage of the PN law.

In 1965 the local had a three-person bargaining team consisting of Landeis, Suhm and Art James. They organized the executive committee around the bargaining issues and went to every school to explain them. Among the issues were salaries and a salary schedule. At the time, Yakima did not have a salary schedule or matrix based on years of teaching and degrees and college credits. According to Suhm, Superintendent Martin said, "In this district the superintendent and the board set the salaries!"

They got other districts' salaries and schedules and compared them with Yakima's. Bargaining was going nowhere, so they invited the chair of the school board and the superintendent to a general membership meeting. The local asked them to give a presentation as to why the District's proposal should be accepted by the membership. Even though Martin was a member of the Association, he and the board chair were then asked to leave.

At that point, the bargaining team gave its report and explained why the District's proposal was so unfair. The bargaining team recommended that they "stack contracts," a process by which the association collects and holds the members' personal services contracts until negotiations are resolved. The membership voted 223 to 6 to stack contracts.

"We scrambled to get an attorney to draft language giving the Association power of attorney to represent each individual contract," said Landeis. Suhm recalled collecting 495 contracts or about 95 percent.

Landeis then called Martin to give him the news of their successful action. Upon hearing the results, Martin commented, "That sure makes the point!" At the next bargaining session the District agreed to the Association's latest proposal.

Suhm recalled that the newly bargained salary schedule had its share of consequences. While most members benefited by having an indexed schedule based on years of service and degrees and college credits, some of the older teachers who had never earned a BA could not advance, and many ended up leaving teaching.

Both Vancouver and Bellevue also successfully stacked contracts. In 1969 Highline's 1,400 members, including district principals, used a version of contract stacking they called a "trusteeship" to gain a successful settlement. Lake Washington attempted contract stacking that same year but backed down when it appeared the board was preparing to replace some or all of the staff. It was a risky process because a determined board could attempt to selectively fire teachers who did not turn in a signed contract by a specified deadline.

At Suhm's urging and with his support, Landeis went on to run for WEA President-elect in 1968. He was successful and served as President in 1969–1970.

Local Association Organizing: The Vancouver Story

Jim Raines is another teacher who went on to have a major influence on the development of the modern WEA.

Tall, husky and slightly hunched over, Raines had a gruff exterior and a salty vocabulary to match. He was a tough and intimidating bargainer. He had done some contract bargaining before becoming a teacher, and he was union through and through. He started teaching in Vancouver in 1958 as a speech and hearing therapist. In 1964 the Vancouver School District lost a school levy election and was the first district to do a major Reduction In Force, or RIF as it came to be known. The 900-teacher District cut 125 jobs.

The Vancouver Education Association had bargained a salary raise before passage of the PN Act. The Legislature did not come through with enough money to fund it. District administrators wanted to save jobs at the expense of the raises. Instead, the board honored the agreement with VEA to pay the salaries.

Principals were given a number of staff in each building to cut. They could do it any way they wanted. There was no contract specifying how layoffs were to take place. Vancouver became a "poster boy" for how school district management would behave with no contract to make sure it acted fairly and equitably. The high school principal used this mandate to get rid of AFT members. Other principals saved their "favorites."

Raines thought the local should have done more to protect the teachers. He decided to get involved. He was on the bargaining team with two other members, Dale Troxel and Jack Beyers. Both would go on to work for the WEA. Raines became the local Association President in 1967. That year the local had a difficult bargain. Raines organized teachers to stack personal services contracts. Nearly 91 percent of the teachers turned them over to the Vancouver Education Association, and the District quickly came to a satisfactory settlement.

Raines then convinced the members to raise dues from $12 per year to $57 to hire an executive director and open an association office. He got an office in the credit union for $25 a month rent. Teachers helped to furnish and fix it up.

Raines was through as President and was waiting to see if he would get the usual offer from the District for an administrative internship, as had happened for every President since 1941. At that time, elevating local association Presidents to administrative positions was common in school districts across the state. But Raines had a union outlook on the practice. He believed that as President it was a conflict of interest to advocate for his members and aspire to a management position at the same time. He was not one to "sell his soul" to management. When he got the offer, he turned it down.

His local began its search for an executive director. The Association developed some interview questions and asked Raines to do a test run for them. He did, and it turned out to be a real interview. He was offered the job.

During his time as the local Executive Director, he was proud that Vancouver was named NEA's local of the month in April 1968.

The WEA asked him to do bargaining training many times. In 1970 WEA Executive Director Bob Addington offered him the job of Field Representative for Professional Negotiations, and Jim Raines joined Wes Ruff in that role of growing importance.

Early Negotiations Under the PN Act

In much of the state, the passage of the Professional Negotiations Act went largely unnoticed at first. Local salary committees continued to meet with school boards to make their cases for higher salaries, which in 1965 averaged about $5,000 a year for a beginning teacher.

In the October 1969 issue of *Washington Education*, Wes Ruff summed up the early history of negotiations under the PN Act:

The school year 1965–66 can be characterized as the year of local education associations' elections to establish the right of associations to negotiate. The school year 1966–67 was the year when associations vigorously pursued procedural agreements and started negotiations on wages, hours, and working conditions while some associations were still holding elections...

The school year 1967–68 brought school directors and associations throughout the state into direct confrontation on a particular item which school directors refused to surrender to the negotiations arena — negotiating the local levy . . .

During 1967–68, highly motivated and insistent local associations were successful in negotiating policies relating to wages, hours, and working conditions and adding items classified as rights while including limited items in the category of improvement of instruction.

By 1967 WEA's new Executive Secretary, Bob Addington, recognized it was necessary to professionalize the process and bring all locals on board. According to Representative Assembly minutes, "He stressed the need for statewide training in the area of professional negotiations — local units must begin to move from informal negotiating methods to 'professional negotiating techniques.'"

Salaries as well as salary schedules and various policies were brought to the table. "Rationale" became the buzzword of the day. Associations, reflecting the mentality of their teacher members, felt that reason ought to be persuasive. Notebooks bulging with data and rationale were brought to the table. Teachers felt this new right to negotiate would usher in authentic teacher input into district policy and create true collegiality.

In some districts, like Shoreline and Puyallup, enlightened superintendents engaged in negotiations and avoided tactics that would inflame their teachers. Those districts benefited, and for years Puyallup was known as "Happy Valley."

In other large suburban districts, teacher negotiation teams met with unexpected resistance that was to radicalize otherwise professionally minded teachers and bring about a movement for a true collective bargaining law.

North Shore was the first local in the state to declare an impasse, in 1967. The North Shore Education Association bargaining chair, Bob Bell, was an astute natural negotiator. With a husky build and light red hair, he was always confident of his ability to cut a good deal. Bell went on to become a WEA Director of Research and later Deputy Executive Director in the late 1970s and early 1980s.

In Edmonds, Superintendent Harold Silvernail and his school board smelled a rat in this PN Act and decided it posed a threat to their authority to run the district as they saw fit. Silvernail was as anachronistic as his 1950s flat-top haircut.

One of the early issues was the Edmonds Education Association's desire to get an evenly indexed salary schedule. The board saw this as a challenge to their authority to set salaries. While board members agreed to such a schedule, they insisted on their right to change one cell of the salary matrix by a few dollars just to make their point.

Negotiations soon became contentious. One of the first Edmonds Education Association negotiators, Harry Robinson, recalled that the board would make a point of talking to all hours of the morning and then send school administrators around to their classrooms the next day to make sure they were busily teaching and not dozing off. On another occasion, Robinson said one board member, a Mountlake Terrace attorney named Levy Johnson, got miffed at the Association team and turned his chair around to face away from them for the remainder of the session.

Superintendent Harold Silvernail once explained his philosophy to local Association President Bob Brown and Executive Director John Cahill. He did not like written school district policy any more than he liked written contract agreements. "When the school board writes down policy, it limits my liberty as a superintendent," said Silvernail.

In Seattle, Warren Henderson recalled that the District remodeled a room in its administration center for Professional Negotiations. It had one-way glass in it.

Seattle, Tacoma, Renton and Yakima Valley College set out to bargain full-blown collective bargaining agreements, then called Master Contracts, or Agreements to avoid labor jargon and to distinguish them from teachers' personal services contracts. Tacoma was the first to achieve a full-blown contract under the old PN Act in 1968. Seattle, Renton and Yakima Valley College followed the next year. When completed, Seattle's agreement was actually entitled "Collective Bargaining Agreement." "It made quite a stir at WEA because, among other things, its title," recalled Henderson. However, the honor of being first in the state still goes to Bremerton, whose contract well predated the PN Act.

In Bellevue negotiations took a different turn. Staying well within the spirit of the PN law, the Bellevue Education Association and the District signed the District's complete policy book just as parties would sign a contract. Was it a contract? The question was never answered.

Other local associations met with more resistance to bargaining contracts. Most school boards were determined to confine the spread of bargaining and insisted on restricting it to district policy that was subject to change at any time.

Professional Negotiations and Impasses

When the Act was written, the impasse procedure, as the Act's dispute resolution procedure quickly came to be known, was really an attempt to keep such disputes "within the education family." Education was not ready for any outside agency that "knew nothing about education" to tell it how to run its schools!

An impasse committee usually consisted of two teachers recommended by the WEA, two school directors chosen by the Washington State School Directors' Association (WSSDA) and a superintendent who chaired the panel. Lew Griffith from the Office of the State Superintendent of Public Instruction usually advised the panel. Wes Ruff and later other WEA staff would assist the association. Usually Ruff, who had handpicked the two teacher members, would meet with them ahead of time. "We chose teachers like Dick Iverson, Roger Cantaloube and John Ward to be on the committees."

Early impasses, beginning about 1967, were "very successful," according to Wes Ruff. They had a big impact on districts and assisted the associations in making substantial gains. Usually school boards were caught off guard. They were frequently embarrassed because their bargaining behavior was exposed to the light of day. School districts, by their nature, disliked controversy, but with impasses the local newspaper would get hold of the juicy story and expose the dispute to the community. "Where we had particularly egregious policies, like Mukilteo," explained Ruff, "the Association could do nothing wrong in impasse."

"Most school districts," Ruff continued, "would not take them seriously until they had one." Associations, in line with their practice in negotiations, were well prepared with elaborate notebooks laying out all the issues and their rationale and a detailed history of the failed negotiations. They were also armed with a heightened sense of righteousness. The school board was not playing fair, and they were going to expose their terrible behavior to the committee.

Ruff assisted Tacoma in one of the first impasses. Unlike most impasses that were held behind closed doors, this one was public. "We had 700 people present," recalled Ruff. At one point during the proceedings, "one school board member took out a crayon and wrote on the front of his notebook, 'WE'VE HAD IT!' We agreed to go back into negotiations and kept the committee on hold. It was a helluva pressure. It was a powerful weapon."

Impasses were not restricted to the large locals. In 1968 Ron Scarvie, a tall, young science teacher in Royal City, was also his Association's bargainer. Scarvie would go on to become a UniServ Representative in the Bellingham and Puyallup regions of the state. Negotiations over salaries in Royal City broke down soon after one of the board members declared that he figured teachers should be paid about what he paid his farm hands! Scarvie recalled that Bob Fisher, a newly hired member of the WEA Governmental Relations staff, came to Royal City to help the Association. He was filling in for Ruff, who was helping with another impasse.

The early success of impasses gradually gave way to increasing teacher frustration with the process. School boards and WSSDA soon got their act together and took advantage of their three-to-two majority on the committees. Impasse reports got watered down as management representatives kept anything embarrassing to the district out of the report.

Ken Landeis was one of the first to question the adequacy of the Professional Negotiations Act, in particular the impasse procedure. Soon after it was passed, he attended a bargaining conference at which a Canadian labor speaker convinced him that the PN Act was not enough and that Washington needed a true collective bargaining act. Ken served on several impasse panels and came away more convinced than ever of the need for a new law.

When he became WEA President in 1969, Landeis set about promoting a new collective bargaining law. He spoke to the issue in every speech he gave across the state. He was convinced that the impasse process was not working and that a labor law defining "wages, hours, and terms and conditions of employment," plus a better resolution process with binding arbitration and union security were a better deal than to continue to "hang our hat on the PN Act's 'but not limited to' language."

In his report to the 1970 Representative Assembly Landeis insisted, "There is a need to define in law what is 'good faith negotiations.' " (In an earlier court case a superior court judge had said the PN Act did not require "good faith negotiations.") He went on:

> Negotiations entailed compromise, settlement and ultimately an agreement which is signed by and binding upon both parties — the school board and the representative organization. The law should provide for fact-finding and mediation.

On Jim Raines' first day on the job with WEA in 1970, he worked an impasse in Federal Way. He eventually worked many impasses every year. He said he soon figured out that if the administration stuck together in the impasse process, teachers would lose every time. It was also recognition that teachers needed to look to their own power rather than to a legal process that was stacked against them.

Raines soon recognized that a major battle was brewing inside the WEA over the issue of the PN Act versus the need for a new hard-line collective bargaining law. Raines recalled that some urban executive directors including Seattle's Dallas Shockley, plus WEA President Jackie Hutcheon, Myra Lupton from Bellevue and Wes Ruff, advocated maintaining the current system. On the other side of the issue, Landeis advocated for a new law, as did many of the WEA field staff, with Jim Raines now leading the charge.

The WEA Professional Negotiations Commission, advised by Wes Ruff, supported the current law. When Marysville's John Ward and Grandview's Mike Schoeppach got on the committee, the tide began to turn.

Raines did a lot of training and used it to organize around the issue of the bargaining impasse. He worked to create an awareness of the PN law's flaws, arguing that changes were needed. He also trained WEA members and leaders to participate on the impasse committees and to use the process to advocate for teachers. Many of those he trained also came to realize the process was stacked against them. Jim Raines and Wes Ruff came to represent the two sides of the issue of bargaining laws.

Dick Iverson, Spokane President in 1968 and local bargainer, said the debate centered on the issue of "are we a union or a professional organization?" This debate, he notes, "still goes on today within the Association." The union vs. professional conflict erupted in controversy over the nature of WEA publications, whether they should be professional journals or advocacy newspapers. (Iverson later chaired the PN Commission and was hired as a WEA field representative in 1972.)

In the early 1970s a superior court judge dealt a severe blow to those arguing that the PN law's laundry list of bargainable subjects, beginning with the phrase "but not limited to," provided for wide-open bargaining. The court ruled that "but not limited to" must be read within the scope and limitations of the laundry list. Supporters of the PN Act lost much of their remaining argument for keeping the Act as it was.

In retrospect, the PN Act of 1965 was a monumental leap forward in giving Washington teachers an authentic voice in education policy making. It was all that teachers and school districts could have expected in 1965. It awakened teachers to the harsh realities of negotiations. It raised their expectations. At the same time their experience, once at the bargaining table, made them realize just how far they still had to go. School boards and administrators, on the other hand, were caught off guard at first. By the end of the decade they had learned how to use the Act to their advantage, particularly in the impasse procedure.

In short, the PN Act had a very effective but limited shelf life, and by the early 1970s support for a true collective bargaining law had gained strong momentum within WEA.

The issue of what legislation would eventually govern teacher collective bargaining in Washington was not resolved until the passage of the Educational Employment Relations Act, a standard collective bargaining law, in 1975.

Legislation and Political Action in the 1960s

School legislation had been WEA's dominant activity since 1889. In 1965 it moved into a changing world of politics and assumed an even higher priority.

Joe Chandler had turned the Olympia work over to Cecil Hannan. Hannan believed that WEA needed to become even more politically active, including supporting candidates for office. The lobby staff expanded in the middle and late 1960s, first with Wally Johnson and then Dave Broderick as chief lobbyists, and with Bob Fisher and Maynard Mathison, a school budget expert out of Seattle. When Cecil Hannan became Executive Secretary in 1965, Wally Johnson became the chief lobbyist.

In 1965 Hannan and Wally Johnson led the way in forming WEA's first political action committee. It was named the Political Unity of Leaders in State Education, or PULSE. Adopted as a recommendation of the Legislation

Committee at the 1966 Representative Assembly, it was set up as a separate corporation. Annual dues were $10. At a 1967 Representative Assembly special awards luncheon, PULSE Chair Dale Leavitt promoted PULSE membership, and as an incentive offered sixteen months of membership for the price of twelve months.

The first PULSE member was Spokane principal and NEA Board member Gerald Saling. PULSE membership in the early years was strictly voluntary, and in that time before the Public Disclosure Commission, WEA did not disclose, even to its own members, how much money went to candidates for the legislative or statewide offices. It was felt that disclosure would make legislators less inclined to support WEA on education legislation.

The Legislature was itself becoming more political and some, like Senator Martin Durkin, dropped strong hints that if WEA wanted to remain in the ball game, it would have to start supporting candidates financially.

In 1967 Spokane teacher Bob Fisher had just been elected SEA President. At that summer's leadership training program, WEA's new Executive Secretary, Bob Addington, persuaded him to become a WEA lobbyist.

Fisher's first assignment for Wally Johnson was to travel the state and personally interview every legislator, using a written questionnaire. The questionnaire was part of Johnson's work to gain his doctorate at WSU. Fisher saw this as a great opportunity to introduce himself, gain credibility and learn about legislators.

While Professional Negotiations would eventually go on to change the face of the WEA, the dominant and most visible program of the Association, particularly at the state level, was legislation. Appointment to the WEA Legislation Committee was considered the plum appointment for members.

In 1968 legislation was to assume even greater importance in WEA. Local Association leaders and local school district needs would become more of a driving force than ever before. Vancouver's levy failed in 1964, and this was not an isolated occurrence. Other districts began to fail levies or just squeak by with close votes. Levies faced tough hurdles. They not only required a 60 percent vote for passage, the voter turnout had to equal at least 40 percent of the turnout in the last general election. In those days general elections were held only in even-numbered years, when US presidents, governors or legislators were on the ballot, and voter turnout was much larger than in odd-numbered years. Unlike today, when levies can be run for up to four years, they had to be run every year. Levies were also becoming a larger percentage of district budgets as school costs were rising faster than the Legislature would increase school funding.

Washington teachers saw a very real school-funding crisis unfolding. The 1968 WEA Representative Assembly held in Seattle and presided over by President Stan Jeffers passed the following action as part of the Legislative Committee Report:

That the Washington Education Association shall take action to develop and promote a program to achieve reform of the total tax structure of the state of Washington; such a program shall be developed by August 1, 1968, and following adoption at a Special Representative Assembly meeting, be introduced at the 1969 Legislature.

This was the very tax structure that had its beginnings in 1932, when WEA's income tax initiative was passed by the voters only to be struck down 5-4 by the state Supreme Court. The Legislature, at WEA's urging, then enacted the sales tax and the business and occupation tax we have today.

The WEA hired the Stanford Research Institute to do a study of Washington's tax structure and to come up with recommendations that would provide a stable and reliable source of funding for schools.

The Special Representative Assembly was held December 7, 1968, in the HUB Auditorium at the University of Washington. The Stanford Research Institute report to the delegates, complete with colored slides of charts concerning Washington's tax structure, left no doubt that the tax structure needed a complete reform with revenues balanced among property, sales and a new personal and corporate income tax.

The 452 delegates adopted a thirteen-point Principles of Taxation and passed a motion (see Appendix 3) directing the WEA Legislation Committee to prepare legislation to enact a personal income tax, a single-rate corporate income tax, and reductions in the sales tax and in the business and occupations tax.

Several motions for statewide sanctions and a statewide strike if the Legislature did not pass such a package were offered, though they were either tabled or defeated. This special Representative Assembly clearly had a level of activism not seen during the days of Joe Chandler.

WEA's tax package was taken to the 1969 Legislature as mandated by the Representative Assembly. The task was politically daunting for the Legislature. It was a two-step process. First, the Legislature, by a two-thirds vote of both houses, had to pass a constitutional amendment for a vote of the people in November. It would amend the state constitution to authorize an income tax in order to get around the 1933 state Supreme Court decision. Second, by a simple majority the Legislature had to pass the specific tax legislation that would go into effect if the constitutional amendment were to pass at the polls in November.

WEA was successful in getting both measures passed by the Legislature, but come November, HJR 42, the constitutional amendment, failed badly when voters defeated it in a 60-40 vote. The very complexity of the companion tax measure plus a growing distrust of government, even in those relatively innocent days, doomed it. Despite wide support from many groups, it was defeated largely by people who would have benefited most, including low-income and blue-collar workers.

Another special Representative Assembly was held in November 1970 to adopt a plan of action for alternatives to tax reform. It gave a mandate to WEA lobbyists. Again calls for sanctions and school closures were proposed but set aside.

Two other attempts at tax reform were made in the early 1970s, but they suffered the same fate at the polls. As a result, for thirty years the Legislature has not ventured to raise the issue of an income tax.

WEA continued to move ahead in the late 1960s to establish a modern and aggressive lobbying program. Prior to 1969, WEA rented a house in Olympia for the session. There was a lot of hectic driving between Seattle and Olympia. During Stan Jeffers' term, the WEA purchased land in Olympia for a permanent office. Jeffers turned over the first shovel of dirt, and the office opened in 1969. Fisher learned that the office was built on the site of the first meeting of the Washington Territorial Legislature.

During the late 1960s and early 1970s, WEA lobbyists worked primarily on salary and retirement legislation. Negative legislation like merit pay kept them busy as well. Generally Democrats supported WEA retirement legislation and Republicans opposed it.

When Wally Johnson left to become the Florida Executive Director in 1969, Dave Broderick was moved over from Public Relations to be chief lobbyist. One of Fisher's first assignments was to check with the Chief Clerk's Office each day of the session to review any bills related to education. This gave Fisher great insight into how the process worked and in what ways various bills could affect education.

Joe Chandler had never allowed WEA lobbyists to buy drinks for legislators in local bars. According to Bea Carlberg, who was hired in 1960 to set up WEA's rented lobbying office in Olympia, "Chandler would not allow WEA, as the representative of the children of the state, to use dues money to buy alcohol for legislators." Carlberg went on, "However, when WEA started renting a house as its lobby headquarters, it hired a cook and served alcohol in the privacy of the house." By 1969, when WEA opened its own full-time office building in Olympia, Chandler's no-alcohol policy was all but forgotten.

Fisher describes the lobbying style by the late 1960s as "wine and dine." Lobbyists stayed up at night, mostly in local bars, trying to get legislators to see their side of the issues. Bob said he could not hold a candle to other lobbyists who did the bar scene almost every night. He remembers several occasions when the WEA credit card was given to legislators to host various functions. WEA would often supply legislative functions with food and beverages. They had a budget category called "legislative promotion" that was used for these expenditures. That is how lobbying was done in Olympia in those days.

According to Fisher, once a lobbyist was able to get a commitment from a legislative leader, that leader could deliver the votes necessary to pass, kill or bury a piece of negative legislation. Once a deal was made, it stood up.

As the decade of the sixties drew to a close, the WEA, with a prominent Olympia office and four full-time lobbyists, had an imposing presence in the Legislature.

Individual Teacher Rights in the 1960s

As Professional Negotiations gradually caught on with local associations across the state, the most prominent area of growth in WEA was advocacy for teachers' employment rights. WEA field staff became heavily involved in protecting individual teachers who were threatened with various forms of discipline by their administrators.

West Valley High School Principal Don Johnson, of Spokane, was hired in 1963 to assist Loren Troxel, from Vancouver, in what was called Professional Rights and Responsibilities (PR&R). That division not only passed judgment on teachers and administrators threatened with discipline or dismissal, it also reviewed ethics cases.

The process was very formal and cumbersome in the mid-1960s. An accused member would apply to WEA for legal assistance. The WEA PR&R staff would investigate and make a recommendation to the full PR&R Committee. PR&R would then pass judgment on the member's case. If it approved support, the committee's recommendation would then go to the WEA Board for funding.

At that time Washington had one of the toughest laws protecting teachers from unfair dismissal in the country. It was and still is called the Continuing Contract Law. The NEA played down its importance because it was not labeled "tenure." But it did all of the things a tenure law would do, only better. The myth of tenure laws is that districts "can't fire bad teachers." Tenure laws are really "due process" laws. Washington's Continuing Contract Law afforded all certificated school employees the strongest due process protections in the country.

A teacher automatically was presumed to be rehired for the following year unless the district notified him or her by April 15 of deficient performance or some other cause, such as a levy failure. The teacher then had ten days to appeal to the school board. An attorney, usually a WEA attorney, could represent him or her. If the teacher did not prevail at that level, and one usually did not, he or she could appeal to superior court, which would hear the entire case from scratch, or de novo. This process was euphemistically called "non-renewal."

A companion statute provided for outright dismissal at any time for conduct that rendered a teacher unfit to teach. Again, a district would have to prove its case to the satisfaction of a superior court judge.

According to Don Johnson, WEA's growing willingness to take on more non-renewal and dismissal cases was more than WEA Attorney George Mack and the firm Roberts and Sheffelman could handle. Under Mack's direction WEA formed a network of attorneys around the state to handle rights cases.

According to Johnson, it grew to twenty attorneys in two years' time. School law was not a recognized specialty. Mack would, therefore, hold periodic conferences with the network attorneys to discuss cases and the emerging body of law on the subject.

Johnson recalled that in the mid-1960s teacher rights evolved from WEA "judging" a teacher to a process of automatic WEA support. "The most advocacy then was in teacher rights," said Johnson.

Dale Troxel, who came to work in the teacher rights area in 1967 when Don Johnson, along with Wally Johnson, were on sabbatical leave at WSU, said PR&R came to support a member's "appeal rights," not necessarily the individual.

Much staff work then involved "problem solving." There were few specific district policies and virtually no negotiated provisions defining teacher rights. Often teachers were subject to the whim and caprice of local administrators and school boards, and it could be very arbitrary.

Don Johnson and other WEA staff would go to a district where a teacher was in trouble and talk to the superintendent or principal and "jawbone" with them. Johnson recalled that about 1965 he went to Spokane to help out a young high school teacher, Dick Iverson, who had been accused by a parent of treason for teaching about the Soviet Union, Communism and Cuba. "The principal and the superintendent took it seriously," laughed Johnson. "I met with them and said, 'You've got to be kidding!' They dropped it. It was not a formal process. We just talked to them." Sometimes WEA staff would make presentations to school boards at their regular meetings.

"I had another case in Colville," said Johnson. "The District tried to fire a teacher because he bought a six-pack of beer in a local store." Again Johnson prevailed and the teacher kept his job.

Johnson said a lot of cases dealt with dress codes that many districts still had in policy. When Stan Jeffers came to be the first Executive Director of the Edmonds Education Association in 1968, he recalled getting a phone call from Mountlake Terrace High School science teacher Ken Bumgarner, who was sent home for wearing a turtleneck, not a standard shirt and tie. After some discussion, the district dropped it. Such advocacy was another way teacher rights were expanded.

The PR&R process proved to be too cumbersome, and it gave way to teachers being referred directly to a network attorney who assessed the winnability of the case and, with WEA staff approval, moved ahead.

Joint State Studies and Sanctions

Two Chandler-era WEA institutions faded away by the early 1970s. The first was joint state studies. The WEA and the Washington State School Directors' Association (WSSDA) would team up to investigate and report back to communities major problems plaguing particular districts. Often, the problem was a pattern of bad administration resulting in poor morale or community turmoil. Teachers and education generally suffered as a result, especially if that result was the community voting down a school levy.

According to both Johnson and Troxel, WEA staffed the studies. Usually, a panel of some five teachers, administrators and school board members would hold a formal hearing and take testimony from anyone having anything to do with the situation. The next step was to write a report that would be presented back to the community. Because WEA had a staff, the reports were written by WEA.

Troxel recalled a joint state study in Mount Vernon in the late 1960s. "The only problem was getting the report approved by Elmer Stanley." Stanley was the Executive Director of WSSDA. He tried to soften the blow of a report that was critical of a superintendent or school board.

When battle lines became more sharply drawn between WEA and WSSDA over negotiations, WSSDA no longer participated in joint state studies.

Sanction was the other institution that saw its last days in the early 1970s. The process of sanctions was much the same as joint state studies. The major difference was the absence of WSSDA and other administrative groups. WEA would assemble a panel of WEA members advised by WEA staff people like Johnson and Troxel. The panel took testimony and issued a report to the community and to the WEA Board. If the report recommended sanctions, the WEA Board would determine whether or not to sanction a district. For instance, sanction in Yakima in 1971 helped jolt the community to pass a school levy after having voted one down.

Sanctions very publicly alerted a community that educational conditions were unsatisfactory and that sanctions would remain in effect until the conditions were remedied. One of the hammers was notice to the state's colleges and universities to alert education graduates not to seek employment in those districts.

Egregious cases of bad administration or levy failures were most often reasons for issuing sanctions. Once strikes became a viable option in 1972, sanctions were abandoned as an instrument of WEA policy.

Teacher Certification, Improvement of Instruction and Professional Practices in the 1960s

Teacher activism in the late 1960s included attempts to control entry into and out of the profession. This appealed particularly to WEA members who valued the "professional" side of the Association and felt that teachers, like attorneys and doctors, should control their own profession. Some interest in this aspect of professionalism has remained until today, but the institutions created at the time for this purpose have not survived.

In 1966 the Lake Washington Education Association proposed a constitutional amendment to establish in WEA an Office of Certification and Accreditation (OCA) with a board of its own elected from five director regions in the state. It was passed at the 1967 Representative Assembly (see Appendix 4).

By 1970 the WEA Representative Assembly sought the cooperation of the Office of the State Superintendent of Public Instruction in formulating certification standards. A resolution asked for discussions between the WEA and the Office of the State Superintendent of Public Instruction for the purpose of reaching agreement on the basis for certification and the standards for preparation leading to it in the state of Washington. WEA wanted a substantive role in setting teacher certification standards.

Another attempt at professional self-governance was WEA's effort to pass a Professional Practices Act. Even before 1965, the WEA Teacher Education and Professional Standards Commission (TEPS) brought to the Representative Assembly a recommendation for such legislation. It would have created a board of practicing educators, replacing the State Board of Education, to set standards for teachers and to have the authority to remove a teacher's certificate when he or she was found to have violated those standards. Established education forces like the lay State School Board opposed it, and opposition came from an unexpected source — teachers themselves.

By the late 1960s just enough teachers had come to understand the adversarial nature of negotiations and the protection of teacher rights that they did not want a system in which peers would sit in judgment of peers. That judgment, they argued, should come from the management side of the table. Teachers felt that the Association's role was to advocate for teachers threatened with discipline. They testified in the Legislature against the proposed act. The Legislature was not going to pass something of this magnitude as long as the WEA itself appeared divided.

WEA Governance in the 1960s

Structurally, the WEA was one of fifty state education associations affiliated with the National Education Association. Typically, local associations in school districts were affiliated with both the WEA and the NEA. Affiliation left both state and local associations fairly autonomous. In fact, it was not until the 1960s that NEA was able to impose "unification" on all state and local affiliates. Unification meant that members had to belong to and pay dues to the NEA, the state organization and the local.

Like the WEA, the NEA had a President elected for one year as a President-elect and for one year as President. It had an Executive Secretary who was the dominant figure and answerable to a large board of directors representing all of the states. All state affiliates were more or less structured like the NEA.

Membership consisted of teachers, school administrators and other school professionals like counselors and librarians who were required to have state certification.

The governance structure in place in WEA at the time Joe Chandler retired in 1965 would remain in place with little change through the 1960s.

It was a structure that ensured that administrators would continue to be represented far in excess of their numbers. The notion of one-person-one-vote was not yet a guiding principle of the Association.

Chandler's first priority had been to keep all parts of the education family under one umbrella. And to do so, administrators had to have significant representation in the Association.

In some ways, the overall structure of a Representative Assembly, a Board of Directors and an Executive Secretary (later Executive Director) is the same as today. The differences, however, are significant.

The WEA consisted of three departments: the Department of Classroom Teachers, the Department of Administration and Supervision and the Department of College and University Faculties (later renamed the Department of Higher Education). The Student Washington Education Association was given department status in 1966. Each department had its own committees and held annual meetings. They then brought their interests to the WEA Representative Assembly. Because of its size the Department of Classroom Teachers held annual meetings that looked like Representative Assemblies in all respects.

The Board of Directors was the dominant power among Governance groups. And here is where real imbalances showed up. In addition to the officers and board members elected from the fifteen director districts, each department President sat on the board as well as a county superintendent and two school district superintendents elected by the Washington School Superintendents Association. In addition, the State Superintendent of Public Instruction was a guest member of the board. Each director-district had at least one director and an additional director for each additional 1,200 members. The Executive Committee consisted of all directors in their third year of their three-year term. The Board of Directors held two very important powers. The first was to hire the Executive Secretary and other staff, and the second was to develop and approve the annual budget. Dues increases had to be passed by the Representative Assembly.

The President and the President-elect had much less power than do today's officers. Terms of office were limited to one year, and it was not until 1968 that the RA gave the President full-time release from his or her regular employment.

Within the WEA a large number of standing committees and commissions met three or four times a year and generated much of WEA policy. The President appointed the members with the approval of the WEA Board. Each had a WEA staff consultant.

The 1965 WEA Representative Assembly minutes list the following committees and commissions giving reports that year:

1. Citizenship Committee
2. Conference Center Committee
3. Improvement of Instruction Commission

4. Insurance and Special Services Committee
5. Legislation Committee
6. Federal Relations Committee
7. Professional Accreditation Study Committee
8. Professional Rights and Responsibilities Commission
9. Public Relations Committee
10. Retirement Committee
11. Salaries, School Finance, and Taxation Committee
12. School Lands Committee
13. Teacher Education and Professional Standards Commission
14. Teacher Selection and Recruitment Committee

The plum committee assignment then was the Legislation Committee. The 1966 committee had seventeen members including two administrators, twelve classroom teachers and three local association executive secretaries from Spokane, Seattle and Highline.

From 1965 to 1970 the level of delegate activism increased noticeably. Early in this period, business was carried out in a routine manner. Reports were made and motions proposed and passed with few amendments. But as time passed, it seemed that no item of business before the Representative Assembly passed without many attempts by the delegates to change it in some way. At times delegates would offer complete rewrites of proposed resolutions. Delegates challenged decisions of the chair, and often the chair was sustained by the thinnest of margins.

As the school funding crises deepened and tax reform became urgent, delegate passions led many to attempt to pass motions from the floor for statewide strikes or sanctions. These motions, usually made by younger delegates, were always defeated, but it illustrated the growing level of member unrest that was to spill over into the 1970s with the advent of UniServ and the first teacher strikes.

The 1970 RA ended on a most bitter note for President Ken Landeis. With the assembly's business not yet finished, a proposal from the floor for a dues increase was being hotly debated. It was Saturday evening and as always happened, many delegates had left early. The Tacoma Association of Classroom Teachers delegation was opposed to the dues increase. They hit on a novel plan to defeat it. A member of this sizable delegation went to the microphone and called for a quorum count. Before the count could begin, they exited the San Juan Room at the Seattle Center. When the count showed a lack of a quorum under the rules at the time, there was little Landeis could do but close the meeting without so much as a formal adjournment.

Landeis felt the tactic amounted to a dirty trick. He had not originated the proposal for a dues increase issue, nor had he particularly supported it. The opposition had made no attempt to work with him in defeating it. Attempts to call for a special RA fell through because of questions of legality raised by the opposition.

What this end to the 1970 Representative Assembly illustrates is the growing activism of delegates. Between 1965 and 1970, largely establishment delegations gave way to younger, more militant delegates more inclined to the activist tactics of the 1960s. It helped set the stage for far greater changes that were to mark the 1970s!

Prior to the 1970s and the advent of what would be known as the UniServ Program, two forces competed for power in the structure of WEA. The Urban Associations, exemplified by Seattle's and Tacoma's push for Professional Negotiations legislation, represented one force. The WEA structure itself, with Joe Chandler and later Cecil Hannan and Bob Addington at the top, represented the other force.

By the late 1960s those in the "urban" camp grew in number to include several smaller Urbans and large suburban locals. Spokane, Seattle and Tacoma were the first to have offices and executive secretaries or directors of their own, and had the organization and financial resources to compete with the WEA. They were joined by Highline, Bellevue, Edmonds and Vancouver with their executive secretaries and offices. They were among the first to follow Seattle's lead to gain authentic collective bargaining rights.

As Representative Assemblies became more spirited gatherings each spring, the Urbans came with a more progressive agenda of their own. This created a growing tension with the more conservative WEA Executive Secretary, the WEA Board still dominated by administrators and the smaller local associations that were still content to follow WEA's lead.

The contest between WEA and the Urbans would come to a head with adoption of the UniServ Program by NEA in 1970. WEA wanted regional service offices headed by WEA employees answerable to the Executive Secretary. The Urbans wanted locally autonomous offices with directors hired by and answerable to local associations.

1965 WEA Staff

When Cecil Hannan became Executive Secretary in 1965, he inherited a staff and structure from Joe Chandler that reflected his personality and management style. With Hannan on board, the WEA commissioned the Seattle firm, Booz Allen Hamilton, to examine the WEA from top to bottom. The firm charted the existing staff structure. It was a virtually flat structure in which Hannan directly supervised all seven directors, an office manager and the Records and Accounting Supervisor. (See Appendix 2.)

The seven program directors were:

- Special Services, Vern Archer
- Governmental Relations, Wally Johnson

- Publications, Al Gerritz
- Professional Services, Ray Broadhead
- Field Services, Don Murray
- Public Relations, Dave Broderick
- Research, Stayner Brighton

The office manager was Irene Branch, and the Records and Accounting Supervisor was Margaret Ballard.

On the plus side, according to the report, the structure stimulated individual initiative, had professional depth and permitted a high level of communication. But the report criticized the WEA staff structure in six key areas.

The management span of the Executive Secretary was excessive. Operational functions were fragmented. Communications among related and interdependent activities was inadequate. Planning was hindered by the lack of a formal budget and control mechanism. Administrative services were inefficiently utilized. And there was a significant lack of continuing contact between Association members and staff members.

The report recommended a reorganization plan that included combining several related functions with each major area managed by a assistant executive director. The report and subsequent reorganization were just one more indicator that the WEA of Joe Chandler had changed significantly.

The power of the Executive Secretary would begin to diminish after Hannan abruptly left to go to work for NEA in late 1966. There was no obvious successor as Hannan had been following Chandler. The search boiled down to three finalists: WEA staff members Stayner Brighton and Ray Broadhead and a research person out of the California Teachers Association named Bob Addington. According to Bea Carlberg, by then secretary to the Executive Secretary, the board interviewed all three finalists. Unfortunately, Brighton and Broadhead became embroiled in a flap over some recently mailed WEA published materials that had offended some of the administrator members of the board. Both candidates were questioned pointedly as to how they would have handled the situation.

Addington, who had nothing to do with the flap, looked very good by comparison and the board hired him. Addington was a large person with a round face and a balding head who lacked the charisma or speaking ability of his predecessors. He was a competent enough administrator who was well liked by the growing staff of the organization. But as member militancy grew in the Association and a newer breed of Presidents vied for power, his perceived lack of leadership would lead to his forced resignation in 1973.

Local Executive Directors

By the mid-1960s the state's larger local associations established offices and to hired ongoing professional staff in order to provide more effective services and more contact with local members. Many saw the local staff person as a professional negotiator. This shift was one more sign of the growing militancy in the larger locals.

Spokane in 1956 was the first local association in the nation to hire a full-time Executive Secretary, or Executive Director as the title came to be changed in the late 1960s. John Christenson held that post until the mid-1970s.

By the mid-1960s the movement caught on in Washington as members passed local dues increases to fund an office, an Executive Director and an office secretary. Seattle and Tacoma were followed by Bellevue, Highline, Edmonds, Vancouver and later Kent, Renton and Federal Way.

Most of these locals also became involved in the National Council of Urban Education Associations (NCUEA), which by the late 1960s had become a real and growing power in the NEA.

One of the goals of the NCUEA was to get the NEA, along with the states, to fund a national network of staff for local associations. Such a program would also help fund local executive directors for the Urbans. Perhaps for political reasons, it would also fund staff for groupings of smaller local associations.

At a November 1969 NCUEA meeting in Washington, DC, NEA Executive Director Sam Lambert laid out NEA's plan for what he called the UniServ Program. It was to be funded in equal parts by the NEA, the state associations and the local associations, and a UniServ unit would be based on groupings of 1,200 members. The priority for funding was for states with bargaining laws or which were actively seeking bargaining laws.

In Washington the WEA also saw the need for increased staff to assist local associations. The WEA favored a program that kept the employment and direction of such staff within the WEA. Regional offices were set up first in Spokane and Olympia. The Tri-Cities was next, and Yakima had high hopes of landing a regional office but never did.

The NEA adopted the UniServ Program at its San Francisco convention in July 1970 and set the stage for the biggest change and expansion of the Washington Education Association in its history.

CHAPTER TWO

The UniServ Revolution

By 1970 a new breed of classroom teachers was vying for control of the leadership of WEA and its local associations. Most of these new leaders sought a stronger voice for classroom teachers in decisions vital to education and to their own welfare.

They were more than ready for the assistance the new NEA program called UniServ promised. Between 1965 and 2000 UniServ would prove to be the single most defining event in WEA's history. The NEA created a whole new organizational structure that, it envisioned, would jump-start teacher collective bargaining in locals across the nation and would put the NEA and its locals in a position to stop, if not reverse, the gains made in the early 1960s by the American Federation of Teachers.

The term "UniServ" was concocted from "unified service." It was a creature of the NEA as well as state and local associations, and it was created to provide trained professional staff assistance for locals and groups of locals totaling about 1,200 members each. It was to be funded jointly by all three levels of the Association. The Chinook Council's first UniServ Representative, John Chase, recalled the genius in the program. "The conceptual idea of having a person who served only the membership was a most brilliant idea." Nationwide, the NEA added 1,000 new staff in two years. "Classroom teachers," said Chase, "were going to be represented!"

He recalled with some amusement that the UniServ Program had two hurdles to overcome. "We had a name that no one knew what it meant and couldn't spell, and a triangular logo that reminded everyone of the Camp Fire Girls! We also got phone calls asking for UNICEF!"

UniServ created a revolution and greater teacher vitality inside the Association and in the greater education community that would endure into the next century. Without UniServ, subsequent scenarios simply would not have occurred.

The formation and growth of the UniServ Program in Washington, more than in most other states, lacked the formal structure and control that WEA historically exercised over its staff and services. Its loose structure, independence and, in the eyes of many traditionalists, its apparent chaos would ensure that the program would become the engine that drove WEA headlong into the future.

Washington's UniServ "Plan"

The NEA adopted the UniServ Program at its 1970 Representative Assembly in San Francisco. Anticipating passage, the leaders of ten Washington urban associations met in a room in the St. Francis Hotel during the convention and staged their coup for immediate UniServ funding from WEA. They were not willing to wait until WEA could bring the rest of the state into the program. The "Urbans" also insisted that UniServ in Washington would be a strictly local program independent of WEA control.

The existing urban associations received NEA UniServ funding plus $3,000 each from the WEA in the very first year of the program. WEA had to borrow the money to start the program right away in September. In addition, WEA pushed ahead with its plan for regional offices in Seattle (the Puget Sound office), in Olympia and in the Tri-Cities. Spokane already had a regional office for Eastern Washington. Outgoing WEA President Ken Landeis went to the Tri-Cities office. His colleague in Yakima, Doug Suhm, went to Puget Sound and Vancouver's Jack Byers went to Olympia. These regional staff were employed and managed by WEA.

In the very early years of the UniServ Program, there was a strong perceived difference between urban locals and what were to be UniServ Councils. Though the Urbans were anxious to get UniServ funding, they viewed themselves as more advanced than the smaller locals just entering the program. Many of the larger Urbans had offices of their own, executive directors and support staff. Organizationally, they were quite sophisticated with infrastructures that allowed them to be powerful in their districts and within the WEA. They had strong relationships in their communities and had access to local news media. They had much higher local dues and a larger funding base than their rural counterparts.

No multi-local UniServ Councils were set up in Washington in 1970. While other states like Oregon implemented a state-controlled UniServ Program in 1970, WEA, having gone the route of regional offices, had not planned for independent UniServ Councils. Through the leadership of Don Johnson and with the help of other WEA staff, however, the WEA worked that first year to convince a large number of local associations across the state to band together to apply for UniServ funding the following year.

During the 1970-1971 year, larger suburban locals like North Shore, Lake Washington, Kent and others were feeling left out by the UniServ

Program and felt a little irritated with the Urbans. These locals wanted on board and they wanted the money that went with it. Smaller locals wanted to participate, and farsighted leaders set about to form councils.

Those who formed Washington's first UniServ Councils saw three major purposes for the program: creation of power equalization between locals and their school district managements; providing onsite staff assistance for local leaders and members; and developing member and leadership skills through training and organizing.

The UniServ Program that evolved in Washington was neither orderly nor neat. Its unsystematic and rather chaotic evolution would help ensure, however, that it would dramatically alter the face of and the balance of power within the WEA forever.

To get into the program, locals had to organize councils into "conglomerates" of approximately 1,200 members each. Putting together a council was not easy. Membership in Washington's UniServ Program was strictly voluntary at first. Recruitment was time consuming, difficult and often hit-and-miss. WEA had no established council boundaries. Boundaries evolved according to which locals wanted to join a particular council. In addition, councils had to form governing bodies capable of establishing offices, setting up an additional dues structure and creating governing documents. These governing bodies hired and managed their UniServ Representatives.

By the end of 1970-1971 conglomerate councils were formed with North Shore and Lake Washington, in Southwest Washington (later named Chinook), in the Puget Sound area (housed initially in the WEA Headquarters), in WEA Board District X (the Yakima Valley), in Eastern Washington (based in Spokane), in Lower Columbia (including what is now Riverside) and in Southeast Washington (based in the Tri-Cities).Added to the program in 1972 were Fourth Corner (based in Bellingham), North Central Washington (based in Wenatchee), Olympic (based in Silverdale near Bremerton) and Pilchuck (based in Everett).

These eleven multi-local councils formed in 1971 and 1972 became UniServ's "freshman class." Out of this class came the leaders of the UniServ revolution in Washington.

Originally, funding for the program was to be one-third from NEA, one-third from the state association and one-third from the participating locals. All of that was to be secured by a three-way contractual agreement between the parties. In fact, the NEA and WEA portions fell short, and the locals picked up the largest part of the tab.

NEA made UniServ a priority for states that were bargaining or were seeking bargaining rights. Washington, of course, with its Professional Negotiations Act, had a ready-made role for its new UniServ Representatives. Many members had the misconception that UniServ Representatives were simply hired negotiators. In fact, their role was much broader.

While the formation of the new councils and the hiring of staff were local functions in Washington, Don Johnson coordinated the program from WEA, wrote the initial three-way or "tri-partite" contracts as they were called, and assisted councils in the whole process. The councils' supervisory role was new to most local leaders. UniServ Councils had the local control they valued as well as the stress of maintaining the employment relationship with UniServ Representatives (Reps), who were high powered and resistant to being told what to do and how to do it.

In contrast to the Urbans, the new UniServ Councils were made up of many smaller local associations. That dictated a different delivery of staff services to those locals.

When UniServ was firmly established in Washington, the regional offices would be phased out. Staff hired in the regional offices were given the option of moving into the UniServ Program or remaining WEA employees. Jack Beyers stayed on with WEA as a Director of Negotiations in the Olympia office. He continued to work with locals and assisted the UniServ staff in that region. For the next few years WEA maintained a regional office in the Tri-Cities. Joe Dupris, a teacher from the South Central School District, was hired to replace Landeis, who became the UniServ Representative in the Tri-Cities. Several WEA staff were stationed in the Spokane office. Dick Iverson had a primary role there in coordinating bargaining for Eastern Washington. These WEA regional staff played a major role in helping UniServ staff in the initial stages of the program. Jim Raines, Dale Troxel and other WEA staff also provided onsite assistance and training to the UniServ staff.

Washington's UniServ "plan" was not exactly a tightly conceived plan, but it worked far beyond the wildest imaginations of WEA members at that time.

The Nature of the Job

UniServ was a new creature to the Association. The work of the UniServ Representative grew out of necessity and out of a sense of mission. "Whatever was written down on paper at first was usually not what we did," said John Chase. "We developed a philosophy based on where we were going."

These conglomerate UniServ Councils were organizations with no established models to follow. Certain basics, though, had to be put into place just to survive.

Once various locals decided to create a UniServ Council, they had to write and adopt bylaws setting forth how they would operate, what officers would govern the council, how the locals would be represented on the council, what the dues structure would be and, in general, what the program would be.

The next tasks of the council governance were to develop a job description for the UniServ Representative, post and advertise the UniServ position, create an interview team, determine interview questions, identify a candidate selection process, review resumes, set up interviews and select their first UniServ Representative. It was a daunting task.

Don Johnson, Jim Raines, Wes Ruff, Jack Beyers and Dale Troxel from WEA were instrumental in providing insight into which candidates should be interviewed. They identified candidates who they thought would be successful. Most of those people ended up being hired. Johnson, in particular, recruited three promising young staff out of Oregon.

In their one year on the Oregon UniServ staff, John Gullion and Steve Kink had gained reputations for challenging the status quo in the Oregon Education Association (OEA) establishment and for championing teacher rights and collective bargaining. Johnson wanted them in Washington. His third recruit came out of Portland. He was a 24-year-old NEA intern named John Chase who had been the Student NEA President in 1968 and had but a year of teaching experience in Colorado.

After they interviewed in several councils, Kink ended up in Lower Columbia, Gullion took the Puget Sound position and Chase went to Southwest Washington.

Another group of UniServ staff were homegrown. All were veterans of the Professional Negotiations wars of the late 1960s. Some had entered through political leadership and some were sponsored and well trained in negotiations by Wes Ruff.

Past WEA President Ken Landeis was hired in Southeast in 1971. His successor at the WEA helm, Jackie Hutcheon, was hired by Pilchuck in 1972. As WEA President, Landeis had championed a new collective bargaining law whereas Hutcheon, out of Bellevue, felt the PN law was more suited to education.

In 1971 Roger Cantaloube opened the Eastern Washington UniServ office. Cantaloube had taught in Omak and Eastmont. Cantaloube was a bull of a man who used few words to forcefully make his point. He became a local negotiator and was recruited by Wes Ruff to be a Professional Negotiations (PN) consultant. In Omak, where he first started teaching, he wanted a pay increase and was asked by his association to negotiate for them. "I got a hold of Wally Johnson at WEA," recalled Cantaloube. "We found the money for a raise in the District budget. Instead of a raise, the District used the money to buy school buses." He brought with him to UniServ a tough demeanor that added one more ingredient to the diverse mix of the new UniServ staff.

Doug Suhm brought his year of experience in the Puget Sound Regional Office back to Yakima where, along with Council President Mike Smithhisler and other activists in the Yakima Valley, he got the District X (named after the coterminous WEA Board District) UniServ Council started.

Mike Schoeppach, from Grandview, and Marysville's John Ward had been stalwarts on the WEA PN Commission and had been recruited by Ruff as PN consultants to help locals with negotiations. In 1972 Schoeppach went to Fourth Corner, based in Bellingham, and Ward went to Wenatchee to serve North Central Washington.

The ranks of the so-called urban associations were also changing. Anticipating the UniServ Program beginning in September, Clover Park, a growing 800-member local in Pierce County, hired George Blood in July 1971. Seattle hired its outgoing President, Warren Henderson, as its first Assistant Executive Director. Kent hired its immediate past President, Cory Olson. In 1972 Edmonds' Executive Director Stan Jeffers went to work for WEA. Edmonds hired its past President John Cahill to replace Jeffers. Cahill had chaired the WEA PN Commission and had served a year on the executive board of the National Council of Urban Education Associations. Highline's Jim Ennis left for the Overseas Education Association, and was replaced by Bill Hainer out of Issaquah.

This freshman class consisted of hard-driving activists and competitive teacher advocates. They brought a variety of approaches to the job and learned from each other's background and experience. One thing they had in common was their initial NEA training that emphasized organizing as the core tool. It heavily relied on the teachings of Saul Alinsky, a nationally known radical community organizer.

In an era before the word "diversity" was coined or the concept given any serious consideration, this freshman class had, with the exception of Jackie Hutcheon, no women and no people of color in its ranks. And in the culture of the early 1970s their absence was barely noticed. It was a flaw that was slow to be recognized and slow to be corrected and one that would create its own backlash in the 1980s.

There was a distinct stylistic difference between UniServ staff and WEA and Urban staff. Although suits and ties were assumed to be the preferred form of professional dress, many of the new UniServ staff dressed for different purposes. John Cahill, Edmonds President in 1971, remembers the first time he met Steve Kink. "Several of the new UniServ staff were in our office getting office management training from Stan Jeffers. Kink was dressed in a red, white and blue Stars-and-Stripes outfit with bell-bottoms, a US flag sweatshirt and red tennis shoes!"

John Chase, who would organize the state's first K–12 teacher strike in 1972, was primarily an organizer with a strong family labor background. He admitted he had no experience at bargaining, particularly with Washington's peculiar PN Act. Steve Kink, too, emphasized organizing and the same teacher rights issues he had championed in Oregon. He brought something else to the mix. He grew up in politics. His uncle, Dick J. Kink, was a state representative. He knew how to organize political campaigns.

Landeis, Ward and Schoeppach were seasoned table bargainers. Landeis had developed a popular prototype collective bargaining agreement. The Urbans had one too, but his became more widely distributed. He copied it, bound it up and shared it readily with his eager colleagues. Though they were urban executive directors, Stan Jeffers and John Christenson eagerly helped and trained new UniServ staff to set up and manage an office. John

Cahill brought communications skills to the mix. His experience with using newsletters, flyers and speeches to organize Edmonds' teachers went into the bag of tricks of UniServ staff.

This group of UniServ staff had several other traits in common. Though very verbal, they believed that actions and accomplishments spoke louder than words. They also believed that plagiarism of good ideas was the expected norm. They felt they were constrained by few, if any, "rules." Roger Cantaloube often said, "There are no rules!" Being "professional," particularly as that term historically had been used by school administrators to keep teachers in their place, was not a part of their makeup. Mixed with a strong dose of the profane, their introduction to the negotiations table shocked school boards and superintendents and caught them off guard. Many UniServ Representatives felt their jobs were to get school management to overreact to them and then to use those overreactions as issues to further organize teachers.

They were thoroughly committed to the cause of empowering teachers. Chase called it "leveling the playing field." They were also committed to the cause of individual teacher employment rights and felt it was their role to advocate for teachers rather than judge them. "It was not our job to judge our members, it was our job to make sure they were all treated equally," said Chase.

He said to his council leaders, "No teacher stands alone. Teachers should not have to teach afraid." Administrators, at that time, wielded great authority, largely unwritten, over teachers. Some administrators told teachers they could not go to local taverns or be seen buying beer in town. An accusation about something a teacher said in class from a parent or influential person in the community might lead a principal to discipline that teacher without the benefit of any due process. Teacher dress and grooming codes were common. Seldom were the rules written down in policy. The rules were what the principal or superintendent said they were.

"It was a cause," Cahill said. He wanted to see the teaching profession stand up on its own two feet and assert itself. He saw UniServ and a strong association as the vehicles.

Olympic UniServ Council President Ron Gillespie put it bluntly. "UniServ gave us gonads! We wanted someone onsite to help locals organize and kick some butt when needed. Bremerton, heavily influenced by administrators, wanted someone they could control and not be so confrontational. The kick-butt crew won and we hired Kink." Gillespie remembers Kink always teaching them some valuable bargaining lessons: " 'No' is an unacceptable answer" and "We never lose, we sometimes just postpone victory."

In that cause UniServ staff felt they were on a mission, and most were willing to work sixty to seventy hours a week and take risks — personal and Association — to get there. Some felt their jobs went even further — to make radical change.

A few UniServ Representatives were really aware of the revolution they were creating. "We did not simply continue the changes of the sixties," explained Chase. "We created a trampoline effect off of what Ruff had accomplished. We were impatient with people who wanted to move slowly. We went around people who were in the way. Washington hired ten to twelve like-minded people who were bright and unbelievably courageous." Chase pushed the envelope harder than most. "I pissed a lot of people off. We made it big as fast as we could. We had the freedom to do what we wanted in Washington."

What was it like being a new UniServ Representative in the early 1970s?

After being hired, most of these new UniServ representatives were faced with major logistical decisions related to the Council. First, they had to negotiate an employment contract with the Council. The reality was that they were UniServ Council employees, not WEA employees. Their contracts were personal service contracts and varied in compensation and working conditions. The contracts contained job responsibilities, salary, length of contract, evaluation, due process and dismissal rights and fringe benefits such as car allowances, travel expenses, health insurance, moving expenses, vacations and holidays.

Most of the first councils had adopted a tentative operating budget. The revenues for the budget were established using local association funds earmarked for UniServ, WEA funds and NEA funds. The budgets generally contained line items for the UniServ Representative and secretary salaries and fringe benefits, office and office-related expenses, travel expenses, materials and supplies, various insurance programs, training and meetings. The greatest portion related to staff costs.

Once UniServ Representatives were hired, the process of inventing councils did not end. The mundane but time-consuming task of setting up offices had to be done. Office space, if not previously rented by the council, had to be found and furnished. That meant more work that UniServ representatives had little experience in handling. Leases had to be signed. Office furniture and equipment, including desks, chairs, meeting tables, file cabinets, mimeograph machines, typewriters and calculators, had to be purchased or leased. It didn't end there. Other needs included supplies and materials and telephones. Most UniServ Representatives leased staff cars, which required negotiating a car lease with a local dealer.

WEA insisted that councils and locals incorporate to shield them from personal liability. Much of that work fell on the new UniServ staff.

Hiring an office secretary was usually a part of the UniServ Representative's job description. The secretary was generally responsible for taking incoming phone calls, maintaining office and equipment leases, maintaining office equipment, keeping supplies on hand, producing printed materials, tracking and reporting budget expenditures and the catchall "other duties as assigned!" The UniServ secretary's job assumed even more importance. This person played a key role in maintaining good relationships with the council members and leadership. The office secretary's job was usually a prescription for stress and overwork.

All of these initial start-up responsibilities had to be done simultaneous with responding to member and local leader needs. Every local in the council wanted to meet and size up this new person with a strange title. The demand for attendance at local meetings was intense. Wild rumors about the person usually preceded the visits.

Once the logistics of setting up a council were accomplished, the program of the council could begin. Program areas varied from council to council, but generally they included training, collective bargaining, grievance processing, levy campaigns, communications and organizing.

Of all the program activities, organizing was the most vital to the success of the council. It began with visiting locals and explaining the UniServ Program and what it had to offer. This was instrumental in giving the UniServ Rep the ability to set the tone and attitude for how the program would work and how locals would have to change. It was also an opportunity for members to share their issues and frustrations over their working conditions and treatment by their administrators.

UniServ Reps had a can-do attitude. Their messages were about pride in oneself and pride in their local association. Members and their leaders were told they had rights and collectively they could exert power that could make their working lives better. It was about standing up and speaking out against unfair treatment by autocratic administrators and school boards. It was having someone on your side advocating for each member. UniServ provided hope for a better future. To them, there was no conflict between teachers asserting their rights and their professional obligations to their students. They believed that assertive teachers were better teachers and better role models for their students.

Organizing also meant that UniServ staff had to bolster local associations, many of which had little or no organization or program. The infrastructure within the local association was often nonexistent. Many locals were not properly affiliated with the WEA and NEA. Many had to create new bylaws or amend old ones.

All of this infrastructure work was crucial to exerting effective power within their school districts and within WEA itself.

In most Councils, it was a goal to recruit new locals and to increase membership, if for no other reason than to build strong council budgets and to have a greater program impact in the council region. During this time membership was voluntary and many had not joined. "I spent many hours hustling membership into the Council," recalled Roger Cantaloube. Time spent recruiting locals was a delicate issue because that meant time away from locals that were already paying dues. It meant a lot of nights on the road meeting with locals and selling them on joining the UniServ Program.

Steve Kink recalled that his travel area in the Olympic UniServ Council extended from the Tacoma Narrows Bridge to Forks on the other side of the

Olympic Peninsula and from Mary M. Knight School District on the south of the Peninsula to Port Townsend on the north.

John Chase took a different approach. Despite having a total budget of just $25,000 with a cash balance of only $300 at the end of his first year, he had a core of larger locals from Olympia to Grays Harbor. "We worked hard," he recalled, "building strong locals. I didn't spend as much time hustling locals. I took the attitude that the small locals would want what the larger locals had. They would not want to be tail draggers. Locals were recruited by their own peers in neighboring districts."

When Mike Schoeppach started work in Fourth Corner in 1972, the council had 1,150 members. By 1975 it had increased to about 2,200, and the council was able to hire Ron Scarvie as its second UniServ Representative.

John Ward, in North Central Washington, had many more square miles and few teachers. The travel time was enormous. UniServ staff began talking about "windshield time." Ward's territory went from Moses Lake to Oroville near the Canadian border — over 10,000 square miles. Oroville was a three-hour drive from his office in Wenatchee. His Council President had a Piper Cub that they once flew out of Lake Chelan to recruit a local up north.

"I talked to them about bargaining, policing contracts and political action," said Ward. "Their eyes got pretty big on this. Most of them had been born in this town and had husbands who worked in the mills and orchards. They had friends on the school board. Even so, they joined the council as a 'professional obligation,' but then they went MIA [missing in action]. I would call them every once in a while. They would say things were just fine."

Recruiting and the lack of any WEA-imposed council boundaries led to some interesting situations. Ward recalled that North Central Washington was recruiting to the east while Eastern Washington was recruiting to the west. "We ended up competing over Nespelem and Grand Coulee. We gave them to Eastern Washington because, by then, they had two UniServ staff."

Sometimes councils ended up overlapping a neighboring council. Centralia to the north ended up joining Lower Columbia, while Chehalis to the south joined Chinook.

A few years later WEA not only established council boundaries, but also passed what was called "mandation," which required all locals to be in the UniServ Program.

A major part of the organizing program was to identify new leaders — leaders who would build strong and active locals, carry the council program to their members and make an impact inside the WEA. During the early 1970s, UniServ Reps identified a wealth of young teacher leaders. As UniServ Reps went to various local meetings, they were quick to notice members who exhibited leadership qualities. They would encourage them to get involved, invite them to various meetings and training sessions, and meet with them individually to talk about their issues. This initial effort paid off when many of these members soon became leaders in their locals, in UniServ Councils and later in the WEA and NEA. Many, like Sheryl Stevens from Central Kitsap and Dick Johnson from Evergreen, became UniServ and WEA staff.

A natural outgrowth of organizing was identifying active members who understood power, had the drive and were able to persuade their fellow members to take action. UniServ staff not only identified these people but made sure they got the training and mentoring to help them succeed in moving the program forward. UniServ staff encouraged them to run for office in their locals and in WEA.

Local association "Building Representatives," who were union representatives in each school, were key figures in developing strong locals. Traditionally, many Building Representatives ended up in the job because they missed a building meeting, and their colleagues "elected" them to avoid having to do the job themselves. However, after the UniServ Rep raised the level of importance of the job, those positions were often sought after and contested. Most UniServ Reps elevated the jobs through training, meetings and creating Building Representative manuals or handbooks. "BRs" soon became the first line of expertise in an exciting expansion of Association power.

To those UniServ Reps who had a long-term vision, organizing was about helping members to help themselves. Initially, it meant that UniServ staff would do much of the work to illustrate that it could be done and, more importantly, how local leaders could do it themselves. It was a take on Saul Alinsky's Iron Rule: "Never do for people what they can do for themselves." Alinsky was the well-known community organizer from Chicago who headed up the Industrial Areas Foundation. Unfortunately, not all UniServ Reps made the transition to letting the members do their own work. This often inhibited members and locals from developing their full potential and established UniServ staff in the role of caretaker.

Training was another must-do job for the UniServ staff. Training sessions usually were held in the UniServ offices. The UniServ Rep and the Secretary would develop all of the training materials onsite. Many of these ideas were liberally shared among the UniServ staff statewide.

Teachers were comfortable with the idea of training. It was used to promote the cause, to encourage and support leadership activities, to create a "can-do" attitude, to review strategies and to deliver much-needed Association skills.

The trainings were many and varied. Topics included how to be a Building Representative, contract language, bargaining teams, chief bargainer duties, coordinated bargaining, rights and responsibilities of grievance representation, grievance representative functions, arbitrations, local president duties, local association structures, communications and political organizing. Typically, a UniServ Council held training sessions a couple of times a month.

It was not unusual to bring other UniServ Reps and NEA and WEA staff into a council to help conduct the training. Often they brought with them special expertise that gave council members a broader view of the Association and what it had to offer members.

These training sessions not only provided needed skills and promoted the cause, but also developed peer respect and competition. Local leaders could learn from each other. They swapped stories of successes and failures. They compared their favorite villains in their school administrations. They learned together and soon took pride in their own accomplishments. They also created the attitude that they were all in this cause together and often would help each other through the sharing of skills and expertise. Above all, it was a lot of fun. This shared experience was a major factor in the development of statewide support for locals and members who went on strike.

Bargaining was the "glue" of the council's program. Few locals had collective bargaining contracts. Though locals had five or six years of experience with Professional Negotiations under the 1965 act, that law was proving itself ineffective. At a staff meeting in Olympia dealing with bargaining, UniServ Representatives decided that they would regard the PN Act as a collective bargaining law and move to bargain contracts. "I showed up to that meeting late," recalled Clover Park's George Blood. "Don Johnson had brought in John Dunlap from NEA. He was a great spokesman for collective bargaining. He was like an evangelist. Don Johnson took me aside and asked me where I stood on bargaining and strikes. Our role was to make this happen, not just respond to what the members were asking."

Chase observed that locals could not bargain without power. "It was not merely a process. It was an opportunity to organize for power." He believes that teachers in Washington would not have real collective bargaining if it had not been for the UniServ Program.

The shift in attitude and strategy from professional negotiations to collective bargaining was a shift from persuasion to the use of power. Collective bargaining was the instrument that created equal power between teachers and school boards and administrations. For the vast number of locals, this meant taking on their own administrations. It meant confrontation. It meant conflict! Because bargaining was such a key program for the success of UniServ, much time and energy were spent on it.

UniServ Reps would help local Presidents identify those members who had the instincts and personality to represent their members at the bargaining table. UniServ staff would meet with bargaining teams and chief bargainers. Training was crucial in establishing new strategies. Bargaining manuals were developed by UniServ staff to provide common approaches and a common language.

Local bargaining teams were schooled in how to identify member issues, how to turn issues into good contract language, how to write "master" (distinguished from teachers' individual service contracts) contracts, how to develop bargaining strategies, how to use effective verbal skills in bargaining, how to set bargaining team responsibilities and how to use coordinated bargaining.

The UniServ role in bargaining varied from council to council. In most, the UniServ Rep served as the local bargaining team spokesperson. This was true especially for the local's first contract. This provided onsite expertise for the bargaining team and gave them insight into how it could be done. The atmosphere at the table can best be described as confrontational and hostile.

Most district administrations resisted giving up any power and resented even having to go through the bargaining process. The UniServ Rep's job was to equalize the power through a bargaining contract that members could use to assert their rights. The inherent conflict played out in many ways, and the language used at the table often was crude and colorful! Districts felt threatened and were caught off balance and forced to operate in a world not of their choosing.

Most UniServ Reps selected so-called "lighthouse" locals in their council. A "lighthouse" was a local that appeared best organized and ready to bargain a good contract, thereby setting a precedent for the other locals in the council. In many places the first contract was attained after a strike or strike buildup.

The notion of organizing for power led to the first strikes in the state. "When you create power," said Chase, "and the other side says 'no,' you had to use your power! We did not want to resolve conflict. We had to have the confrontation. It was not as much about economics as it was about dignity. Bargaining was very threatening to management. It set up rules they had to follow. To take the strike out of our arsenal meant we would not have been a union."

Within the first year and a half of UniServ in Washington, it was clear that the staff would have to acquire another skill. They would have to learn how to organize strikes. There was limited experience at WEA to provide this expertise. NEA had experienced staff that provided assistance in urban strikes. However, most of Washington's early strikes came from small locals, like Aberdeen and Evergreen, in conglomerate UniServ Councils. Washington's UniServ and WEA staff organized these locals. UniServ staff soon developed the expertise to serve in all strike organizing roles.

Another aspect of UniServ work was the protection of individual member rights. UniServ staff would go to bat for members treated unfairly by school administrations. Very soon they developed a direct pipeline to WEA network attorneys like Mitch Cogdill in Everett, Gary Sexton in Bremerton, Bill Powell in Spokane, Parks Weaver in Olympia, Bob Van Siclen in Auburn and others. This network of attorneys specialized in representing teachers with respect to their employment issues and dealing with restraining orders, injunctions, arrests and the like. The lawyers, like the UniServ staff, communicated with each other and shared strategies as they went about setting legal precedents for association members and leaders. Because of them, members not only felt their rights were being protected, but also saw how unfairly they were being treated. It fed into the need for locals to organize for power and to build strong organizations able to stand up to unfair administrative power and intimidation.

WEA Network attorneys — drawn to the same cause as were teachers and the UniServ Reps — were also trailblazers.

Grievance administration was a major UniServ Council program for protecting member rights. Initially, most UniServ staff had to deal with unfair treatment of members by district administrators. The UniServ staff relied on their creativity, persuasion, threats, bluster and a broad, if not fanciful, interpretation of policy, law and the Constitution to protect member rights. They had to deal with many issues like probations, firings, transfers, harassment, involuntary transfers, assignments, Reductions In Force (RIF) and incorrect placements on the salary schedule. In most cases they did this in the absence of formal grievance procedures. Eventually, grievance procedures were created through the bargaining process.

The UniServ Rep would help local Presidents identify members who had the personality to represent members at the building level in the grievance process. UniServ staff developed grievance representation manuals and provided training in advocacy and representation. Because the local association was designated as the legal bargaining representative for all certificated staff, local leaders needed to be trained in their duty of "fair representation." This was accomplished through grievance training covering all technical aspects and the process of grievance adjudication.

When the freshman class of UniServ Representatives began their work in Washington, they ran smack into one of the worst economic downturns in the state's history. It coincided with the end of the post–World War II baby boom and was a time of sharply declining school enrollments in many districts. Boeing laid off about half of its workforce, and a famous billboard in Seattle read, "Would the last person leaving Seattle please turn off the lights."

Education felt the impact of the economy in more school levy failures. In those days levies could account for up to 40 percent of a district's budget. When levies failed, teachers were laid off.

UniServ staff addressed levy failures in three ways. First, they challenged the district to prove beyond a shadow of doubt that the district had no money to retain teachers. In some cases districts had stashed huge cash reserves and could be forced to retain teachers. Second, UniServ staff would provide laid-off teachers with a network attorney who would represent them. In some cases class action suits were filed. Third, UniServ soon recognized the need to help pass local levies.

Some UniServ staff began political action programs in cooperation with local districts to pass levies. The Olympic UniServ Council was the first to run a coordinated levy campaign with four districts in Kitsap County. All four passed, and local legislators took note and soon sought out teacher support in their campaigns.

These local levy campaigns coupled with the first major teacher rally in Olympia in 1975 led to WEA's statewide political action program. Over a two-day period during the legislative session some 10,000 parents and WEA members, many of whom had been laid off because of levy failures, rallied in front of the Capitol. They wanted more money for their school districts, and they opposed a plan by Senate Majority Leader August Mardesich of Everett to decrease benefits under the Teachers Retirement System. Nervous Capitol police had never seen a gathering this large. Their worst fears seemed realized when the throng filled the rotunda to hear Governor Dan Evans and a few friendly legislators speak to them. Quick negotiations with WEA President Blair Patrick got the teachers back outside.

Another program that required attention and staff time was communications — both within the Association and the community and with the local news media. The foundation of a council's communications program was a mimeographed newsletter reporting council activities, accolades to successful locals and leaders, grievance reports and other advocacy articles. Newsletters were exchanged among the council offices and some articles got wider circulation. Most UniServ Reps also created separate bargaining newsletters to tout successes at the bargaining table. When John Cahill left Edmonds in 1974 to become WEA's first Communications Field Representative, he was assigned to help councils and locals improve their skills in communicating with their members and with the local news media.

UniServ Council offices became centers for communication, partly because council staff and leaders could not rely on WEA and partly because council newsletters became a necessary organizing tool.

"After the 1972 Aberdeen strike," recalled John Chase, "we realized we had to publish our own stuff." The WEA *Action* headline above the story about the first K–12 teacher strike in the state read, "Court Orders Aberdeen Teachers Back to Work." Chase and his colleagues who had organized and worked the strike were livid. At the next UniServ staff meeting in September 1972, they attacked Executive Director Bob Addington for the headline written by his staff Director of Publications, Barbara Krohn. Chase slammed a copy of the newspaper down on the meeting table and railed at Addington for WEA's lack of advocacy. "Why don't you have the balls to fire her?" he yelled.

This dispute highlighted the difference between the old and the new WEA. Barbara Krohn was a holdover from the Joe Chandler days and adhered to his philosophy of keeping both teachers and administrators happy under one roof. She found the very idea of teachers going on strike appalling.

The UniServ offices needed their own advocacy publications. They controlled the message. It worked. "We looked for leader locals and gave them a lot of ink," said Kink. It created a healthy peer competition among local leaders. They vied to be the next lighthouses or they set out to become the standard bearer.

John Ward and most others relied on simple mimeograph machines to crank out newsletters. John Chase, never one to be second best in any competition, bought an offset printing press in 1974.

Local publications forced WEA to reform its own publications. In 1974 Barbara Krohn, realizing that the Aberdeen strike was not a horrific aberration, resigned. WEA combined its Publications and Public Relations Departments into a single Communications Division and put Bill Davidson in charge. And a 1971 Representative Assembly directive introduced by Edmonds President John Cahill to make WEA publications "member advocate publications" was finally and fully implemented.

Some UniServ staff developed great working relationships with local reporters who sought them out as sources for education stories. This was in contrast with most school districts, which preferred to keep the media at arm's length. Relationships with reporters usually resulted in pro-Association articles during a bargaining crisis, strike, legislative campaign or school levy.

What UniServ Representatives wanted to do most, were those things that gave teachers power, namely organizing, bargaining, defending teacher rights and identifying new leaders.

Chase saw his program goals as bargaining contracts, empowering teachers ("No teacher stands alone") and building an employee organization — not an employee/administrator organization. He saw himself as an organizer, trainer and motivator. He noted that many of his colleagues saw themselves in "provider (caretaker) roles."

"We argued and screamed about it, and we learned from each other," he recalled. "I walked with some very smart people. We had a lot of freedom to do what we wanted."

John Ward recalled setting up an accountability chart on the corkboard on the wall of his office meeting room. Listed down the left side were the names of each local. Across the top were categories like "constitution and bylaws" and "incorporation," but also, and more important, were bargaining goals like "salary," "benefits," and others as they were added. "Whenever we had a council meeting, the members had to sit across the table from it and look at it." That was the start of his coordinated bargaining program.

Ward said that his office typed locals' contracts using carbon paper, hoping not to make any mistakes.

Work in levy campaigns was not the only political action with roots in the early UniServ Program. It had been customary for urban executive directors to come to Olympia periodically at Chief Lobbyist Dave Broderick's request. Now UniServ Representatives followed in their footsteps and began building their own relationships with local legislators.

UniServ Representatives would organize member letter-writing campaigns to help in the lobbying effort. They also became promoters of PULSE (WEA's political action committee, Political Unity of Leaders in State Education). But involvement in political campaigns to any extent was still a few years in the future.

Mutual Support

Though the original UniServ Representatives were very competitive with one another, if one of them needed help, they would put down what they were doing and respond immediately, without question.

That was the group's ethic.

That mutual support nurtured the program. More got done where it needed to be done first. And in the process they returned to their home offices with new skills, new tricks, new insights into what it took to organize teachers and a few new outrageous war stories. If a particular strategy did not work, so be it. It was part of the learning and just another war story that became a part of the collective wisdom that was handed down. In those stories, facts often were incidental to the larger truth.

In many ways UniServ work was a lonely job, and the need to get together to unwind and share ideas and experiences was great. "We were really isolated on the east side," recalled John Ward. "Doug Suhm would call me from Yakima, and we would meet in between for lunch." Certain restaurants or "watering holes" became almost legendary as places where UniServ and WEA staff would gather informally, share stories and plot new exploits. In Spokane it was the Pine Shed or the Chapter 11. In Olympia it was the Falls Terrace or Shakey's Pizza. In Silverdale, they met at the Sand Piper. In Mukilteo it was Taylor's Landing. And in Seattle it was the 13 Coins or the University Towers.

One of the contractual requirements of the UniServ Program was a provision that allowed the NEA or the state affiliate to use a UniServ Representative's services elsewhere in the country for up to twenty days a year. It became known as the Shared Staffing program. It might mean working a bargaining representation election in Hawaii or San Francisco or a strike buildup in Billings, Montana. The Washington UniServ staff was highly sought after by the NEA for these assignments. The skills gained and the insights into what things were like in local associations outside the state proved invaluable back home. And though local council leaders would often complain about their staff person being gone, they appreciated the fact that they could get the same help when they needed it.

The early teacher strikes in the state proved the value of shared staffing. Assistant Executive Director for Field Services Don Johnson would arrange from his end at WEA to staff a local strike team, but local staff could and often did request shared staff. Reputation, skills and compatibility dictated who was requested. Johnson supported that process.

FOUR STORIES

Most of the early UniServ Representatives brought with them a background and a personal story that explained their passion and drive for the work. And it was the combination of their talents, drive and dedication that made them a force for change in the WEA. These are just four of their stories.

Steve Kink

Steve Kink grew up in Bellingham. Organization, power and politics were not new to him. His father, Mitch Kink, was a teacher and represented Skagit and Whatcom counties on the WEA Board. His uncle, Dick J. Kink, was a Washington state legislator.

As a commercial fisherman in Puget Sound and Alaska waters with his father and uncle in the summers, he was familiar with labor disputes. When the fish buyers wouldn't offer them a high enough price, they went on strike until they got an agreement.

Kink began teaching junior high school history in Florence on the Oregon coast in 1966. He was one of several new teachers hired that year. In addition to teaching, he coached basketball and was advisor for the yearbook. His beginning salary was $5,400. These new teachers shared a certain sense of rebellion against authority. When the superintendent met with them at the beginning of the year, he told them that they were not to go into a certain tavern in the town, not because he didn't want them drinking in the town, but because, he said, the owner would not support school levies.

That was all Kink and his new colleagues needed. After the meeting some of them went down to the tavern, bought a few beers and struck up a conversation with the owner. They told him who they were and that they were new teachers in town. They raised the issue of his support for school levies. The tavern owner said that this was the first time anyone from the schools had ever talked to him. From then on the owner became a strong supporter of the schools.

Kink joined the Association that year but was not active. He did learn one valuable lesson about the value of membership. He recalled having a great Building Representative who took pride in having 100 percent membership. However, there was one new PE teacher who was a holdout. The BR remained persistent. Finally, she did join. Soon thereafter, one of her students got hurt on the playground. Fortunately for her, the NEA million-dollar liability insurance covered her. Kink saw her become a staunch advocate for the Association overnight!

One year, Kink gave the mayor's son, who had never received a grade lower than A, a B in his history class. The mayor's wife stormed into his room after school and demanded that he change the grade. He refused. She then went to the principal, who came to his room and asked him if he would consider changing the grade. Again he refused. She then went to the Superintendent and he came to Kink's room and asked him to change the grade, saying that if Kink did not, then he would. "Sure you can do that, but if you do it, academic freedom would be the first thing on the bargaining table," Kink said. The next day the mayor came to Kink's room and told him that there would be no further problem with the grade. His son had told him that he deserved the B.

In 1969, Kink was elected Association Vice President and was sent that year to the Oregon Education Association Representative Assembly. The state association was proposing a dues increase that his local opposed. Though he felt the increase was justified because he thought his part of the state needed more financial help, he helped defeat it. He then made a speech on the floor explaining his vote and said that he in good conscience could support a lower increase. It passed. The state President thanked him and appointed him to the Professional Negotiations Commission. Kink used his position to begin informal coordinated bargaining in Lane County.

In 1970 the state President, Hal Swafford, asked Kink to apply for one of the state's nine new UniServ positions. He chose Lane County, his home territory. It stretched from the Cascade Mountains to the Pacific Ocean. "I felt I could do more for public education in that role," said Kink. It was a huge risk for me. My dad said, "Don't do it." My mom said, "Do it!"

With his summer commercial fishing job now out the window, his $10,000 starting salary represented a $6,000 cut in pay. He was the lowest paid of Oregon's new UniServ staff because, at 27, he was the youngest. He was unhappy about that, but he felt that, given the risk, the challenge and the opportunity for personal growth, it was worth it.

As a representative sample of NEA's new UniServ Representatives, he was featured in an article in the NEA newspaper and was pictured there along with NEA President Helen Bain.

Four of Oregon's new UniServ Representatives were the "ring leaders" on the staff. Besides Kink, they included John Gullion from Multnomah County, Larry Phillips and Marilyn Johnson, who would go on to have a long career with the NEA. They were under the supervision of Oregon Executive Secretary Cecil Posey. Posey had been at his post since 1949.

"They put me out front and supported me," recalled Kink. "One day Cecil Posey asked us to his house and offered us a drink. There were nine of us and all he had was one six-pack. He had no clue."

Staff meetings with Posey mostly were about how the UniServ staff were exceeding their budgets all the time — too much spent on long-distance phone calls to each other, etc. Finally, at one meeting they were fighting about budgets and Posey was talking about how "his" budget was limited, and John Gullion told him in a rather loud voice, "Well, up yours!" referring to Posey's budget.

Kink wanted to get more publicity for NEA in his area. He set up a tape exchange with NEA President Helen Bain. When he was behind the wheel, he would tape a message, relay member questions and mail the tape to her. She would tape a response and send it back. "I would play the tapes at meetings," said Kink. "The members thought they were cool."

The NEA was putting the heat on Bruce Claire, Executive Secretary of Eugene, remembers Kink. "We were in the same office complex. The NEA sent in an Urban Assessment Team. They wanted to know what I thought about the Eugene Education Association. That's where I met WEA's Jack Beyers, who was on the Assessment Team."

Kink tried without success to get a pay increase the next year from Posey. Shortly thereafter, he got a call from Jack Beyers asking him to apply for UniServ positions in Washington. He interviewed in Northline. "Carol Coe [a future WEA President] liked me," recalled Kink, "but Lake Washington, which had one more vote than North Shore, wanted an attorney. So they selected Gene Huguenin." He also interviewed in Kent and Puget Sound.

"Jim Raines, a good friend of Jack Beyers, helped set me up for the Lower Columbia job. He briefed me on the Larry Wiegle legal case. Wiegle recently had been fired by Longview for writing strongly opinionated letters to the local newspaper. The Longview Education Association opposed giving him legal help, but the WEA and NEA were giving him legal assistance over the local's objections. He eventually won. The Longview members of the interview team were mostly principals. They asked me this supposedly hypothetical question about what I would do in a situation just like this case. I was prepared. I said that I thought a teacher had a constitutional right to say what he wanted outside of school. I said I would support a person's constitutional rights despite any feelings about the individual. The other team members liked my answer, and I was hired."

Lower Columbia had 1,500 members and thirteen locals from Castle Rock to Washougal. Kink soon discovered that Evergreen, a 300-member local east of Vancouver, was well ahead of the other locals in its readiness to move aggressively in bargaining and organizing. It had strong leaders in people like Fred Ensman, Dick Johnson and John Zavodsky. "Terrible conditions there made that local ripe for a strike, and I told them they would need a strike," said Kink.

When he moved to Olympic UniServ the next year, he kept his commitment to return to Evergreen to help that local in its strike. But once in Olympic, he quickly identified Central Kitsap as having the committed leadership to be a lighthouse local. South Kitsap had great issues but a membership reluctant to take the ultimate step, and North Kitsap had a progressive superintendent, Bob Minitti, with whom Kink developed a great working relationship. So it was Central Kitsap that had the first Association strike and the first Association contract in the council.

John Ward

John Ward came to Marysville in 1966 to teach in the junior high school. During his previous three years in The Dalles, Oregon, Ward had not joined the Association for the simple reason that no one had asked him to join.

When he interviewed for the job, Marysville Superintendent Wally Blower asked Ward if he smoked or drank. Ward responded that he had a drink now and then. "In this district we do not drink in this town!" Blower directed.

"We went to Snohomish and Everett to have a drink," Ward recalled.

A year later Ed Brillault, who himself would go on to serve on the WEA Board and become a UniServ Representative in the Puget Sound Council, asked Ward to run for the Marysville Education Association President-elect.

Ward, knowing little about the Association, said "yes." Elections in those days were conducted in a general membership meeting. As was the custom, candidates would stand and make a few remarks on their own behalf. Ward promised that the junior high teachers would no longer have to use soupspoons to eat their lunch. It seems that teachers in that school had to use utensils left over from the student lunches and there was a shortage. This was the sort of issue that represented to teachers how they were being treated. Besides, the Junior High was the hotbed in the district, and Ward's sturdy platform carried him to victory!

During his year as President-elect, Ward served on the salary committee. He was one of ten committee members. High school math department head Dave Ibea was chair. Ward recalled that the committee met four or five times that year. They did a lot of research including making comparisons with other districts and doing various power studies. Power studies were computations of the career earning power of different salary schedules using different base salaries and a consistent hypothetical set of assumptions of how fast a teacher would progress on the schedule.

Then Ward encountered one of those experiences that radicalized him. It was typical of what happened in those days in locals across the state.

"A meeting was set up with Superintendent Blower," Ward recalled. "We all got dressed up in jackets and ties. We walked into his office. There were two rows of chairs lined up in front of the Superintendent's desk."

"I'm here to listen," said Blower. He took notes. "We had made several charts mounted on boards," said Ward. "We went through our rationale. We gave a percentage recommendation."

The committee concluded its presentation and Blower responded. "Here is what I am proposing to the board." It was a percentage much lower than that recommended by the committee. "Thanks for your work. Thanks for coming." That was all!

"What the hell was that!" Ward raved when the committee got out in the hallway. "It was survival for me, and we got treated like that. It was demeaning! Ibea said that was the way it always was."

The next year Ward was determined to build a local association that the Superintendent could not so easily ignore. He and Brillault attended a Building Representative training session in nearby Edmonds. Edmonds then was approaching 1,200 members and had a sophisticated organization and a President, Blair Patrick, who would go on to be a WEA President. "We wanted to see what an association really looked like," said Ward.

As President, Ward went back to Marysville and appointed a small committee to rewrite the bylaws. "We created a Representative Council and passed a dues increase."

"That year," Ward continued, "we made a presentation to the school board about what our members wanted in the upcoming school levy. It was a large meeting that included the Superintendent and one Association representative from each school. We had done an extensive survey of our members. They were on board! Among other things, we were asking for elementary specialists so teachers there could have planning time."

"When we finished, Blower said, 'Thank you very much, here is what the levy will be.'"

"I called Wes Ruff at WEA and asked him what we should do," said Ward.

"Ask them to bargain the levy," Ruff advised.

"I sent out a newsletter to my members with just three words on it," recalled Ward.

"We shall negotiate!"

"I appointed Ed Brillault negotiations chair," explained Ward. "Next, we went to a school board meeting and made a statement saying we wanted to negotiate the levy. Blower took us out into the hallway. I thought he was going to have a stroke! He turned purple with rage. We did not get the changes we wanted in the levy and it failed."

That was Blower's last year as superintendent.

Ward persisted in trying to get a fair deal for Marysville teachers. "In 1970 we went back to influence the amount of the levy. Milt Snyder was now superintendent. We made our pitch. We negotiated. We even called an impasse. Milt determined he would go out to each school to present what he had decided. We asked to videotape it. He put the junior high [Ward's school] last on his list."

When he finished, Ward responded: "If we had a negotiations law worth a shit, you would have just committed an unfair labor practice. You are acting just like General Motors going around our bargaining team and meeting with faculties."

"By the end," said Ward, "he was sitting and I was standing. We got it all on tape."

"We got to impasse and got no resolution there. We had to decide what to do. I was not an officer but was advising the bargaining team. We went to Rep Council to decide what to do. The levy had nothing we wanted in it. We asked Everett Attorney Mitch Cogdill to file an injunction against the levy because it was not bargained. Imagine the play we got in the *Everett Herald*. To put it mildly, it was not positive for the levy. We lost in court. The District could not believe we would do it. But what else could we do to make the board realize they could not just blow us off?"

Instead of working for passage, the Association sat on its hands during the levy election, according to Ward. "The levy got a 22 percent yes vote! You do things to make them realize they have to deal with you!"

Ward was elected to the WEA Board. He was also appointed Professional Negotiations Commission chair by WEA President Jackie Hutcheon. In that role he tried to convince the WEA Board to make local negotiations the Association's highest priority. "The WEA Board was just going through the shift to becoming an advocate organization," recalled Ward. "But it still had too much baggage in the form of principals who were tied to older programs."

Several new UniServ Councils were ready to start up in 1972. As a Professional Negotiations Consultant under the tutelage of Wes Ruff, he felt he was already doing the work and felt he would like to do it full time. He had considered applying in Pilchuck where his local, Marysville, was a member. He felt there was wisdom for him to look elsewhere. He applied and was hired in North Central, where he had grown up.

John Chase

John Chase came to Washington by a different route. Growing up in Denver, he was influenced by his uncle, who was President of the Electricians Union and his father, who was a firefighter and active in his union. He recalled that his uncle was kicked out of his union because, as President, he doled out jobs to all of his members on an equal basis regardless of whether or not they had been born in the United States.

Chase went door to door with his father helping to press the firefighters' case for pay increases that were at the time subject to a vote of the people.

When he went to college, he discovered he could get out of a really bad education class if he would do some work for the Student NEA chapter on his campus. He got hooked and soon was elected President and became the first student member to speak on the floor of the Colorado Education Association Representative Assembly. Chase recalled that in the mid-1960s the issues there centered on classroom teachers vs. administrators. Teachers, as in Washington at the time, believed they should have a larger voice in their association.

He went on to be elected Student NEA President and became one of the national movers to amend the United States Constitution to provide for the 18-year-old vote.

Though not a delegate, he attended the 1968 Democratic National Convention in Chicago and got a firsthand lesson in how those in power can abuse their power. He and a couple of his friends were walking along a street near the convention one night. Everyone was being cautious because of clashes between Chicago police and demonstrators. A group of police spotted them, and Chase remembers hearing one of them yell, "Get 'em."

Chase and his friends ran. They fled down an alley and hid in the shadows. The police chased them and sent their only African-American colleague down the alley to see if they were there. The officer came down the alley right to where they were and yelled back, "They're not here!"

He taught school for one year, got into clashes with the school administration and felt that teaching really wasn't for him. At age 23 he became the youngest-ever NEA staff intern and was assigned to Portland. His mentor was an NEA regional staff person, George Green. Chase was heavily influenced by NEA staff people like Ed Robran and John Dunlap, both revered field organizers.

Portland was a hotbed of competition between the NEA and the American Federation of Teachers (AFT) for exclusive bargaining rights. Since losing many of the major cities of the country to the AFT in the early 1960s, the NEA was determined to stem the tide. The NEA vigorously pursued bargaining rights for teachers and poured resources into those campaigns.

It was in Portland during a bargaining election that John Chase met Steve Kink. Both knew the other by the aggressive reputations they were gaining.

When Washington opened up its first UniServ positions in 1971, Chase applied. He interviewed in Kent, Renton and Southwest Washington. He accepted the Southwest Washington position. Key leaders in that new council wanted to unionize and that is what Chase knew best. "There were people in the state who knew bargaining much better than I did," said Chase, "but this job allowed me to use the skills I was developing — mainly organizing." Chase saw himself as an organizer, trainer and motivator.

"Actually, the other side organized for us," observed Chase. He set out immediately to change the balance of power between teachers and school managements. "It was about power equalization. You could take some from the other side, and you could develop your own. To hell with rationale, organize!"

Chase was impatient and had little tolerance for people who wanted to go slow. He became a catalyst among his UniServ colleagues and with WEA staff for an aggressive organizing approach using the union model. "We did what the industrial unions did during the 1930s."

Chased summed up the revolution that UniServ created in the WEA. "UniServ turned the Association upside down. What services WEA had to provide locals changed dramatically. There were some powerful fiefdoms in the Association. When members got a taste of victory with their managers, they turned on the WEA."

Mike Schoeppach

Mike Schoeppach was a homegrown member of UniServ's freshman class. He started teaching high school social studies and English in Grandview. He was motivated to get into teaching by some great high school teachers of his own.

He recalled that he was one of about 100 teachers in Grandview. "I was always shooting my mouth off about being treated fairly," said Schoeppach. This was particularly true when he found out he had to go all the way to Prosser to have a beer. The superintendent prohibited teachers from drinking in Grandview.

In his second year there the President talked him into running for Vice President. He did and he won. He went to WEA's summer leadership training program, at that time called the VIP Conference. There he met Dale Troxel and Wes Ruff. "I was impressed," recalled Schoeppach. "They were funny, personable and they were telling people that they could stand up for their rights."

Schoeppach got on his bargaining team and came up against a school board member who told his team, "As long as I'm on the board, no teacher will ever make $10,000."

"As soon as we achieved that salary," recalled Schoeppach, "he resigned!"

Schoeppach also has the distinction of negotiating "asparagus time." This was a late start in the daily schedule during the spring to allow the high school students to harvest the crop.

Schoeppach was appointed to the WEA Professional Negotiations Commission, the staff advisor of which was Wes Ruff. Along with Jim Raines, they selected teacher members for impasse committees. "I was on the impasse committee in 1972 in Aberdeen prior to their first strike," recalled Schoeppach. "I helped manipulate the impasse report so that it was bad. I knew full well that it would move those teachers to hold the first strike in the state. WEA consultant Jim Raines and Superintendent of Public Instruction contact Lew Griffith knew what I was doing."

In 1972 Schoeppach applied for some UniServ positions and got the one in Fourth Corner. Besides heavily recruiting new locals to join the council, he spent a lot of his time bargaining, dealing with grievances, training and providing legal assistance. He recalled putting 65,000 miles a year on his car. "I loved it!"

He remembers one legal case in which he got WEA Network Attorney Mitch Cogdill to represent a 65-year-old woman teacher the district was forcing to retire. The WEA did not want to take the case. "The case went all the way to the state Supreme Court and she won."

⟨━◆━⟩

While the UniServ Program was a creation of the NEA, in Washington it was a local program and each aspect of it had to be created at the council level. This gave it independence and a vitality many state-based programs lacked.

UniServ made a huge impact on every element of the Association and on those who were the pathfinders. To Roger Cantaloube it was the most exciting thing he did in his life: "The right time, the right place and the right people."

Don Murray thought the UniServ Program was a way to keep the states from running away from the NEA.

Kent's Cory Olson believed it was easier being an advocate from a UniServ position than the local President because you were not tied to the district. Mary O'Brien said, "UniServ was the backbone of the organization."

"UniServ took idealists and activists to a world larger than the classroom," said Everett's Mike Wartelle.

"UniServ pushed the WEA to do things," said Aberdeen bargainer and President Sharon Amos.

"Without UniServ, small locals would die — it equalized the playing field," said Leona Dater. She was hired by the Eastern Washington UniServ Council in 1980.

The UniServ Rep and the UniServ Secretary teamed up with their council leadership and worked from a single office to deliver services to locals and teachers within a geographic region. They were accountable to those members and informally to one another, not to the WEA. They were committed to a cause and would do whatever it took in time and energy to succeed in that cause. Peer competition and mutual support provided additional motivation. It was common for UniServ Reps to work sixty to seventy hours a week. The long hours, time away from home and the changes in lifestyle took a toll on their home lives and marriages.

The UniServ revolution in Washington brought representation to WEA's smaller associations both at the bargaining table and within the governance of WEA. Within WEA the balance of power and the focus of activity and services radically shifted to the locals. It encouraged a whole new group of local leaders to emerge and take control of the Association.

There was also a change in style. Quiet, professional persuasion gave way to a strategic use of power. That approach was used in bargaining and later in the political arena. By the mid-1970s WEA would take on the task of bringing a collective bargaining contract to every local in the state.

Left: Joe Chandler, WEA Executive Secretary 1940–1964

Below: 1971 NEA Leadership and Staff workshop, San Diego. Washington UniServ staff are seated: far left, Nat Gross of Renton; next Jim Kanthak of Vancouver; fifth from left (seated), George Blood of Clover Park; fourth from right (seated), John Gullion of Puget Sound; eighth from left (standing), Jim Wright of Edmonds; far right (standing), Steve Kink of Lower Columbia.

Aberdeen Education Association bargaining team
(left to right) Sharon Amos, Harry Cartham and
Mike Poitras in May 1972 during the first K–12
teacher strike in the state

Striking Evergreen teacher, May 1973

Dick Johnson (right) and Association President Fred Ensman (left) hold their last news conference before going to jail during the 1973 Evergreen Strike.

Don Murray: WEA Eastern Washington Field Rep and later Training Director and Research Director

Wes Ruff: Seattle Teachers Association founder and President and WEA Bargaining Director

Jim Raines, Vancouver President and Executive Director, WEA Bargaining Director and Organizing Team Leader

Dale Troxel, Vancouver bargainer, WEA PR&R Director and UniServ Program Director

Ken Landeis, WEA President 1969–1970, and Southeast Washington UniServ Rep

WEA lobbyist Bob Fisher (right) talks with State Representative Dick King of Everett.

Mead teachers Carolyn Kuehn (left) and Bonnie Sabiston silkscreen picket signs at 1 a.m. during their 1974 strike, the first in Eastern Washington.

Jack Beyers, WEA Field Services Director stationed in WEA's Olympia office

Striking Federal Way teachers try to block scab cars from crossing their picket line at Thomas Jefferson High School on September 10, 1974.

WEA strike organizer Joe Dupris addresses striking Federal Way teachers in 1974.

Carol Coe addresses the WEA Representative Assembly in 1975.

Steve Kink (seated) and rookie UniServ Rep Ron Scarvie review daily activities during the 1974 Olympic College strike.

Puget Sound UniServ Rep John Gullion addresses teachers from his council during the 1975 March on Olympia.

State Superintendent of Public Instruction Buster Brouillet addresses some 10,000 teachers during the 1975 march on Olympia. Flanked behind him are (left to right) WEA Chief Lobbyist Dave Broderick, Executive Director Wendell Verduin and, to the far right, Bill Hainer.

Teachers flood the Capitol Rotunda during the 1975 March on Olympia, making Capitol police very nervous.

During the 1975 West Valley (Yakima) teacher strike, UniServ Rep Doug Suhm holds a news conference.

*In 1976 the Chinook UniServ Council organized phone banks to help elect
local candidates.*

*Left: WEA Communications Field Rep John Cahill and Eastern Washington
UniServ Rep Roger Cantaloube during the 1975 Central Valley strike*

Right: Chinook UniServ Council phone bank coordinator Leslie Kanzler

In 1977 striking Omak teachers march past their
school administration building.

Left: WEA President Jim Aucutt and Eastern
Washington UniServ Rep Roger Cantaloube during
the 1975 Central Valley strike

Right: WEA Network Attorney Bill Powell worked
many teacher strikes in Eastern Washington. Here he
is addressing striking Central Valley teachers.

Chinook UniServ Rep John Chase and WEA Staff Dale Troxel "negotiate" with Aberdeen police officers during the local's second strike in 1977.

It was a snowy and muddy day when Leavenworth teachers began their strike on March 7, 1978.

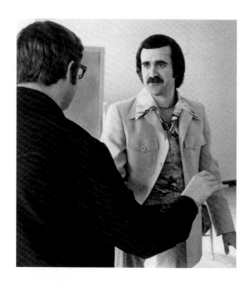

WEA Political Action Director Steve Kink, 1978

Chinook UniServ Rep Bob Graf and the Aberdeen bargaining team negotiate with their District administrators in 1978.

UniServ Rep John Morrill addresses a rally of striking Everett teachers in 1978.

Top left: In 1978 Larry Vognild defeated Senate majority leader August Mardesich.

Top right: WEA worked to keep anti–teacher strike Initiative 363 from getting enough signatures to make it on the ballot. In 1980 WEA almost succeeded in getting its campaign finance initiative, 401, on the ballot.

Bottom right: WEA General Counsel Judith Lonnquist argues a case before the state Supreme Court, ca. 1980.

Top left: Eastern Washington UniServ Rep Leona Dater

Top right: Armand Tiberio worked on the anti-I-363 campaign.

Brochures that were part of WEA's organizing campaign for the 1980 Democratic precinct caucuses.

Left to right, State Labor Council President Joe Davis, Gil Gregory, Carol Coe, Representative Tom Foley and Senator Henry Jackson line the stage behind President Jimmy Carter as he makes his final campaign speech the night before the 1980 election.

Communications Field Rep John Cahill talks with KOMO-TV reporter Connie Thompson, ca. 1979.

CHAPTER THREE

Strikes, Levies and Internal Struggles

The early 1970s was a time of turmoil and change within the Washington Education Association. Existing power and leadership were being challenged in ways that reflected upheavals in the larger culture of the time. Just as opposition to the Vietnam War spilled onto the streets of America and a host of movements were changing old cultural assumptions across the country, so too were new forces within the Association vying for control over its nature.

The urban locals, notably Seattle, which had led the Professional Negotiations revolution of the late 1960s, felt their grip on power within the organization challenged by the smaller locals that were organizing under the UniServ banner. The WEA Board and a new breed of younger, more aggressive local and UniServ Council Presidents sought to reassert their power to chart the future of WEA. All claimed to best represent the will of the membership.

Competition for the resources of the WEA was strong. The need for far greater financial resources to fund a stronger leadership, an aggressive collective bargaining campaign and an expanded legislative program ran headlong into declining revenues. Declining school enrollments meant fewer members to pay for these programs. Dues needed to be raised, and forces within the Association fought over the proposed use of these monies.

The decline in student enrollment hit the urban locals particularly hard. Seattle, which had over 99,000 students in 1969, lost more than half of its students by 1975. Edmonds, one of the fastest-growing suburban districts in the nation during the 1960s, closed several schools a year after 1970. The "Boeing Bust" of the early 1970s compounded all of this. Fewer dollars from the state caused school districts to increase local school levies, which in turn led to increased school levy failures. The competition for financial resources extended to other school districts throughout the state as well. This competition played out between the local associations and school district administrations across the bargaining table.

An expanded WEA staff organized and used collective bargaining to demand increased salaries and retirement benefits. Equally important was the demand by local association leaders to be treated as equals at the bargaining table. These same leaders also vied for a greater voice in the programs, strategies and direction of the WEA.

Within the WEA structure, aggressive younger Presidents and board members were challenging the vestiges of the Executive Secretary's power to run the Association as Joe Chandler had. The other major struggle within the association was over which negotiations law would best benefit the membership. Was it to be the older Professional Negotiations Act of 1965 or a completely new collective bargaining law?

The forces advocating for a new law prevailed with the adoption in 1975 of a collective bargaining statute patterned closely after the National Labor Relations Act. With few changes this Act remains in existence today.

Collective Bargaining

By about 1970 school boards and administrations finally realized that the 1965 Professional Negotiations Act did not really require them to bargain with local associations in any real sense of the word. They became savvier at the bargaining table and stopped making most of the stupid mistakes that had caused many of them to capitulate in earlier years. They found they could give little at the table, and they were no longer intimidated by the impasse procedure of the PN Act.

This stonewalling collided with increased teacher demands for improved salaries and benefits, employment rights and a greater professional voice in educational decision-making. Teachers realized that agreements reached at the table over district policies sometimes had a short shelf life. As soon as an agreement proved inconvenient or did not suit the district, the school board simply could dissolve it through routine board action.

This increased teacher militancy across the state and brought on demands for both a stronger bargaining law and true collective bargaining contracts like those obtained in Tacoma in 1968 and in Seattle in 1969. These were not patient people willing to go slow under the limitations of the Professional Negotiations Act.

With the help of UniServ Representatives, locals put more comprehensive packages of proposals on the bargaining table and attempted to parlay them into viable collective bargaining contracts. Many locals, such as Edmonds, developed full-blown master contract proposals. There, the school board in 1972 flatly rejected the idea of any contractual agreement with the Edmonds Education Association, thus paving the way for a strike there in the spring of 1973.

Teachers were demanding to be equal partners at the bargaining table. It had as much to do with professional dignity as it did with substance. All of the early strikes had issues of dignity at the heart of the disputes. Most school districts resented having to bargain in the first place. They continually asserted their power in a variety of ways. Some would refuse to bargain certain issues. Others would only put "understandings" into school policies. Some superintendents were brash enough to tell UniServ staff and local leaders that they would never agree to a contract. These were exactly the kinds of statements that unwittingly helped radicalize teachers into a stronger commitment to achieve equality in the process.

The issues brought to the bargaining table are still familiar today: salaries, benefits, class size, planning time, Reductions In Force (RIF), leaves, evaluations and others. Most associations titled their contract proposals "Master Agreements" because that term was less offensive to school administrations. However, they were collective bargaining contracts when the language included strong recognition clauses, grievance procedures ending in binding arbitration and a set duration. With those in place, all it needed were the signatures of both parties.

To strengthen their power to bargain, UniServ Reps began to toy with various forms of coordinated bargaining. The geographic proximity of the locals within the council allowed them to agree to introduce common issues with "boilerplate" language at all tables in a region and then to hold off making concessions or drop proposals until lighthouse locals could gain agreements. This was easy in concept but very difficult to organize. Most locals were uncomfortable, at first, using their power to bargain. Holding out until neighboring locals could achieve agreements meant confrontation with their districts. That was difficult for most locals. Also, most locals were reluctant to bargain past the end of the school year. Peer pressure pressed reluctant locals into coordinated bargaining.

In 1973 the Chinook UniServ Council and the Olympic UniServ Council experimented with inter-council coordinated bargaining. According to Olympic's Steve Kink, local leaders and bargainers from the two councils would meet in Shelton and agree on common issues, strategies and timetables. Often, strong locals like North Thurston in the Chinook council and Central Kitsap in the Olympic council exerted peer pressure on locals that were reluctant to hold out for the agreed-upon goals.

Staff members were extremely competitive to get the best contracts with the best language. However, everyone tended to brag about what they had bargained, and a system to really assess and compare them was needed. Joann Kink Mertens suggested that they all bring their contracts to a staff meeting and the UniServ staff could assess each other's contracts. It was put up or shut up. Based on the assessments, according to Mertens, "Ken Landeis [in Southeast Washington] had the best contracts and Vancouver's was a joke."

Many of the trendsetters in the conglomerate UniServ Councils were not the council's largest locals. Aberdeen, Central Kitsap, Evergreen, Federal Way and Mead were not the largest, but they were ones that established contractual precedence among their neighboring locals. As a rule, less institutionalized small and medium-sized locals were easier to organize.

Though school management had grown more sophisticated, it responded defensively and harshly to any perceived loss of power. With the ideological support of the Washington State School Directors' Association (WSSDA), local school boards and administrations fought and lobbied against teacher collective bargaining and strongly resisted any proposals that limited their power. This arrogance of power managed to insult teacher bargainers, who became more willing and more adept at communicating these insults and refusals-to-bargain with their memberships. Management arrogance and subsequent teacher organizing around it became the foundation of teacher power.

Though teachers grew more aggressive at the bargaining table, they made but little headway in achieving power equalization with school boards and signed few real master contracts. Teacher frustration with the pace of bargaining progress took two, sometimes competing forms. First, they came to feel that the PN Act simply had no real teeth in it and that a true collective bargaining law, despite its "union" overtones, would force school boards to bargain. Second, many concluded that the particular law was not as important as developing and using real teacher power. That meant going on strike!

Battle Over Bargaining Laws

Dissatisfaction with the Professional Negotiations Act grew beginning in the late 1960s, particularly with the so-called impasse procedure. At first, some suggested improving that provision, even to the point of giving impasse committees the power to impose settlements. But that part of the law was not its only perceived weakness. The lack of any requirement for a contract was becoming a real obstacle.

During his term as WEA President in 1969-1970, Ken Landeis traveled the state calling for a new law. In addition, Jim Raines, hired as a negotiations director in 1970, lobbied hard within the Association for a new law. In workshop after workshop he used the growing futility of the impasses as a platform to convince locals that a change was needed. When UniServ was established, the UniServ staff quickly realized that the impasse procedure was futile and was stacked against the local association. Even those who believed in a pure power approach to bargaining became advocates for a new collective bargaining statute.

Getting agreement within the WEA to seek a new law in the Legislature was not all that simple. Strong elements within WEA fought hard to retain the PN Act. Wes Ruff, who had led efforts to get the PN Act in the first place and who shaped implementation of the law from his position on the WEA staff, led efforts to retain it. Ruff had an abiding faith that teachers could creatively use the Act to organize and pressure boards into agreeing to contracts. He believed teachers could organize and appeal to their communities to bring about meaningful negotiations. He believed in the power of professional persuasion. Seattle, which had gained a contract under the Act, supported Ruff. Seattle moved to keep the status quo and would use its clout in the Legislature to prevent any change in the law. Bellevue too supported keeping the PN Act.

The biggest argument for keeping the PN Act was its perceived unlimited scope of negotiations. The so-called laundry list of negotiable topics ending with the phrase "but not limited to" was held up as something that should not be given up at any cost. It was argued that "wages, hours and working conditions," the phrase used in traditional collective bargaining laws, was too narrow for professional educators. The fear of this loss plus the union tone of a collective bargaining law made WEA members at first reluctant to seek a new law.

At times the dispute within the Association was bitter. To many people it was a battle between Wes Ruff and Jim Raines, each attempting to gather as many allies as possible to his cause. The dispute came to a head at a staff retreat on Hood Canal in 1973. Raines' position, with the support of most UniServ Reps, prevailed.

Other WEA staff like Don Johnson and Jack Beyers came on board in support of a new law. But the key person supporting a new law was WEA Chief Lobbyist Dave Broderick. With the WEA Board's nod of approval, Broderick introduced a teacher collective bargaining law in the 1974 Legislature. But too many amendments were attached, including anti-strike language, and Broderick had it killed near the end of the session.

WEA geared up again for a new law in 1975. This time NEA Chief Legal Counsel Bob Chanin, a lawyer out of Michigan with strong labor law expertise, was brought out to work with the WEA and the Legislature to write an effective law. Meanwhile Broderick worked behind the scenes to line up legislative support for the new law. By then, the state had experienced its first teacher strikes, and legislators were convinced that the Professional Negotiations Act was ineffective and new legislation was needed to regulate the process. Debate within WEA raged as Seattle and some urban allies actively lobbied against the WEA's position and a new law. This attempt by what emerged as the Coalition of Urban Educators (CUE) to control the education legislative agenda failed as Broderick and his staff quietly guided it through both houses of the Legislature. This position of Seattle and other CUE members set the tone for other power struggles inside the WEA, which led to a changing of the power structure within the Association.

The Legislature did strip out language explicitly allowing "concerted action," which in common labor language meant strikes. Broderick did stop attempts by some legislators to explicitly bar teacher strikes. At one point, in orchestrated fashion, the Senate proposed language allowing strikes, only to see that voted down. Next, the Senate proposed an amendment to bar strikes. That, too, was voted down. The resulting "legislative intent" remained neutral on the right to strike, as it is today.

Governor Dan Evans, a Republican who had signed the 1965 Professional Negotiations Act, also signed the new law, which was officially titled the Educational Employment Relations Act. He used his item veto to eliminate a board to regulate the new law. He did so explaining that he would propose a similar board to administer all of the state's public employee bargaining laws when the Legislature convened in January 1976. He kept to his word, and the Legislature quickly passed legislation creating the Public Employment Relations Commission, or PERC, to write regulations, administer the law and provide mediators and fact finding for those in bargaining disputes.

The new law was patterned very closely after the National Labor Relations Act. It defined the bargaining units so as to allow teacher-only associations to be recognized bargaining agents. It defined the scope of bargaining as wages, hours, and terms and conditions of employment. It required good faith negotiations and, once and for all, required a contract as the final product of negotiations. One of its strongest features was a ban on unfair labor practices with the power for PERC to enforce it.

The new bargaining law took effect on January 1, 1976. Locals worked through the remainder of 1975 getting ready to bargain under it. Passage put an end to one of the biggest internal disputes within the WEA during the early 1970s. Now the WEA moved forward in a unified and concerted manner to bargain strong collective bargaining contracts in every district in the state. Bill Hainer recalled that in 1974 WEA had only twenty-nine contracts and five binding arbitration clauses. Within three years almost every local had them.

Continuing Contract Law Attacked

The same Legislature that had passed the bargaining bill in 1975 attacked the Continuing Contract Law in 1976. WSSDA, which had tried to block the bargaining bill, managed to gain the ear of the Legislature with concerns about the Continuing Contract Law.

The law at that time was perhaps the strongest teacher "tenure law" in the country. Wes Ruff said that the NEA discounted it because it was not called a tenure law. "It was, in fact, a stronger due process law than any state tenure law," insisted Ruff.

The law provided that from the day a teacher started teaching, he or she came under the act. There was no provisional period of one to three years. To fire or non-renew a teacher, the school board had to show that a teacher's performance was unsatisfactory. It had to have credible and objective proof. The board's decision, which was almost always against the teacher in question, was subject to review in superior court. And before 1975 the teacher had the benefit of an entirely new evidentiary hearing in superior court. It was also subject to appeal to higher courts.

This was too much for school boards and administrations that were still doing a bad job of teacher evaluation and were losing more and more cases to WEA network attorneys. They cried foul. "It's impossible to fire bad teachers," they told legislators.

In 1976 legislation was introduced in the House and Senate to cripple the Continuing Contract Law. Some saw it as a trade-off for collective bargaining. That was never clear. SB 3002, designed to completely eliminate teacher appeal rights to the courts, was introduced. A milder bill, HB 1364, was introduced in the House. At one point WEA was able to get the House to amend HB 1364 to its liking. It passed and went to the Senate, where a more determined body successfully amended SB 3002 and all of its objectionable features onto HB 1364, so that HB 1364, as amended, now became the vehicle for gutting the Continuing Contract Law.

Senators August Mardesich and Herbert Donohue were joined by an equally ardent Senator Joe Stortini, who was also a Tacoma teacher and coach. The recast HB 1364 passed the Senate 28-17 and went back to the House for concurrence. There, Representative Al Bauer, who was a Vancouver teacher, championed its passage. It passed the House 50-42.

What HB 1364 did was eliminate any appeal of a dismissal or non-renewal of a contract to the courts. Now, the superintendent was responsible for bringing to the school board a showing of probable cause. The board, whose decision was final, would then hold a hearing. The board, at its sole option, could ask a hearing officer to conduct the hearing, but that possibility was never taken seriously. The new law also provided for a one-year provisional period during which new teachers could be dismissed without cause.

The WEA felt that legislators it considered friends, particularly Joe Stortini and Al Bauer, had stabbed it in the back. WEA President Jim Aucutt said so in his speech to the 1976 Representative Assembly.

The WEA regrouped and came back in 1977 determined to regain rights lost in the repeal of the Continuing Contract Law. It was successful. Under the new law teachers were entitled to a hearing before a neutral hearing examiner whose decision was subject to appeal to superior court. Now, however, the appeal had to be based on the record of the hearing, not de novo as before 1976. The one-year provisional period for new teachers remained. The Continuing Contract Law, though weakened, was restored to one of the best teacher due process laws in the country.

First Strikes

True power equalization was not to become a reality until local associations proved they were capable of going on strike. Many had talked about it, but few teachers or staff really knew how to organize a strike. Most Association members assumed that one of the state's largest locals would strike first, but for a number of reasons, it was a few middle-sized to smaller locals that would go first and prove to others that it was possible.

Some of these districts had the most compelling reasons for going on strike. Also, these locals typically had less institutionalized infrastructures, which made it easier to create the necessary organizing structures for conducting a strike. These districts generally had younger teachers who were more willing to challenge unjust authority. But most of all, pulling off the first strikes was an organizing challenge understood by few people. It was a formidable barrier — a little like running the first four-minute mile.

John Chase had the organizing genius to organize the state's first strikes. He believed in the labor movement and understood how necessary strikes were to equalizing power between district managements and teachers. The first strikes occurred in the spring, not in the fall when the new school year was to begin. The reason was simple. It had nothing to do with the expiration of a contract because at that time there were no real contracts in these districts. It had everything to do with the best time to organize. Teachers then usually bargained in the spring of the year. They were still in school, not away for the summer. Chase put it simply: "The time to strike was when the teachers were ready to strike!"

The year was 1972. The first attempt to organize a strike took place in Shelton in April. The conditions were right. The district had a pompous, dictatorial superintendent named Louis Grinnell who was an ideal strike target. But taking that first strike proved more difficult than expected. The Shelton Education Association had set a high 75 percent threshold for voting to go on strike, and when the votes were counted, they did not reach that mark. In typical UniServ fashion John Gullion hung a rubber chicken above the door to the strike vote room. Though disappointed, Chase regrouped and determined to do a more thorough job of organizing in his next attempt.

Aberdeen

Aberdeen was the first K–12 local in the state to go on strike. It had strong leaders in people like Mike Poitras, Sharon Amos and Harry Cartham. It had good issues: salary, class size, health insurance and planning time. In addition, Superintendent Robert Woodruff had floated a plan to have many of the teachers replaced by teachers aides who would be supervised by a few teachers. That put the ultimate wild card into the mix — dignity! What the Aberdeen Superintendent, and others, failed to recognize was that professional dignity trumped everything else as an organizing lightning rod.

Chase and the Aberdeen leadership spent a great deal of time in the schools talking to teachers about what was happening in bargaining. Chase learned from Shelton and applied those lessons to organizing Aberdeen. By their very nature, teachers were reluctant to resort to strikes. More time and more communication were necessary to get the teachers to internalize the issues and to take that first leap into the unknown.

The organizing paid off. Aberdeen teachers went on strike May 11, 1972. They did what no other K–12 teachers in the state had ever done. They overcame their fear of the unknown. Overnight, teacher strikes went from being a hypothetical to being a concrete reality. They broke the four-minute-mile barrier! It was an event that was to shake the educational community of the state.

Chase was the organizer. Jim Raines worked with the bargaining team and doubled up to make sure the strike got major play in the state's news media. While Seattle television covered the strike, Raines took a few of the most articulate leaders to a news conference at the Seattle-Tacoma Airport. Steve Kink helped with organizing strategies and teamed with Dale Troxel to work the picket lines, keeping the morale high.

The strike held solid until the District went to the Grays Harbor Superior Court in Montesano to obtain an injunction ordering the teachers back to work.

Chase knew that he did not have the will or the votes to remain on strike in the face of an injunction. The teachers met and voted to remain defiant but return to work.

Because Aberdeen had exhausted the impasse procedure and because the strike was such a blow to the education establishment, Governor Evans created a "Blue Ribbon Committee" of the State Superintendent of Public Instruction, board members and educators to resolve the situation. Aberdeen teachers were in a newfound position of power. The committee found for the teachers on most issues. By all measures this "first" was a major success. Chase knew how important it was for this first strike to be viewed as a success. Equalizing power at bargaining tables across the state depended on it.

Evergreen Raises the Bar

In 1973 Evergreen was a growing suburban school district just east of Vancouver. Then it had only 300 teachers, most of them young with less than five years' experience. It was a district ripe for a strike. And arguably, the two-week strike that occurred May 14 to 25 would be the most important one in WEA history.

Superintendent Ray Patrick, near retirement, treated the teachers in the worst way and said everything in a manner that incited them to action. The teachers were young and radical. Most of them had a story about how badly they had been treated. Conditions in the district were poor even by 1973 standards. The teachers wanted to bargain a contract and were committed to the issues on the table. And the Evergreen Education Association had a wealth of good leaders, people like Dick Johnson, John Zavodsky and Fred Ensman in the leadership and people like Virginia Oliver and Steve Paulson on the bargaining team. Most of these Evergreen people went on to other leadership roles in UniServ and WEA.

Evergreen was the next step up from Aberdeen. As Lower Columbia's first UniServ Rep, Steve Kink knew a year before the strike that this local was ready. John Chase, again, was tapped to be the organizer. Jim Raines was brought in early to help with bargaining. A Covington Junior High German teacher, Dick Johnson, was chosen to be the Action Committee chair (organizer).

Dick Johnson was a past President and had taken every WEA training course offered. Jim Raines had impressed upon him the futility of the PN Act and the need for real collective bargaining. Bob Bell at WEA taught him school district budget analysis, a role he had played in Evergreen in the years prior to 1973. Johnson came from a labor family and believed in collective bargaining contracts. "A contract is a set of work rules agreed by both parties," said Johnson. "It simply made sense."

Johnson had an abiding faith that if you told the members the truth about what was going on in bargaining, they would make the right choices. "Once we told the members about the advantages of a contract, it made sense to them," he said. He recalled that they would record bargaining sessions and play the recordings for the members. "Patrick would say stupid things. During the bargaining of holidays, he said, 'Jews are just like other Christians' and when we laid that before the members in our *Table Reports*, they saw the reasons to strike. They made all of the decisions. They had real choices."

As staff organizer, John Chase built on what he had learned in Shelton and Aberdeen. "We knew a year ahead," said Chase, "that this would be the next strike. They wanted to bargain. We knew we had to have bigger and better strikes, and we knew we had to organize better because we had to break injunctions."

During the year leading to the strike, Chase and Kink, now in the Olympic Council, made many trips to the District. Chase's careful strategy was to take the members a step at a time. "They had to perform at a given level before we moved them to the next," explained Chase. "They never underperformed. They always exceeded everything we asked them to do. When we had a candlelight march in the rain, we asked for two from each building. Over eighty showed up. We did member surveys, and we had newsletters."

According to Chase, the administration and the board did everything right to provoke a strike. "At the table we got a 'no' every time, and we kept communicating that to the members. Management did not release the pressure by agreeing to anything. All of the issues were real."

The school board was not very smart and also said and did things that provoked the strike. "The school board," Johnson said, "were a bunch of rock throwers."

By this time most of the administrators had left the Association. "Most of them," said Chase, "were not well trained, and they screwed up most of the relations in the buildings."

Johnson credits the leadership for the role it played in organizing the strike. "President Fred Ensman and Vice President John Zavodsky were honest people, and we had a fine group of Building Representatives who did a great job of reporting to the members and getting their feedback. At organizing meetings I did more listening than talking to them."

"At one point," recalled Johnson, "Chase asked me if my members would strike. I said yes."

In the Evergreen School District there was a constant escalation toward the strike. What Chase saw in the members was a strong commitment to the issues and a belief that what they did could make a difference.

"Everything there in the District was wrong," he said. "I don't think the administration ever made a right move. Everything they did, we used against them. This was a perfect storm!"

Chase recalled that by March all the leaders, including the organizing team and Building Reps, knew that a strike vote meant they would have to break an injunction, and that could mean they might go to jail.

Yet, with all of that in mind, when the secret ballot vote was taken on Mother's Day, it was overwhelmingly in favor of striking. By the second day the District was completely closed down. "Maybe eleven stayed home, but no one worked," said Chase. "I was really surprised at the number of people we had on the picket lines."

Chase had a full strike team in place. He was the organizer. Raines bargained. Roger Cantaloube, the new UniServ Rep Dick Anderson and Dale Troxel managed the picket lines. Steve Kink handled communications, including the daily newsletter to the members and news media relations. Attorney Tom Lodge was ready for the expected injunction.

Very early in the strike, the District went to Clark County Superior Court and obtained an injunction from Judge Guthrie J. Langsdorf, who was to play a very important role in the ultimate success of the strike, unwittingly.

No vote to break the injunction was ever taken. Instead, Chase simply had leaders go to the picket lines to relay the message that the strike was still on.

The next day the Evergreen Education Association held a news conference to announce its plans to continue the strike until a contract was reached. Ensman and Johnson were the two spokespersons.

When the District sought enforcement of the court order, Judge Langsdorf ordered Ensman and Johnson to appear because they were the ones he'd read about in the newspaper. He ordered them to direct the teachers to return to work. In respectful language they declined, and Langsdorf ordered them to jail — separate jails.

Johnson recalled how the judge separated them. "He flipped a coin, and I was sent to the county jail with the murderers and the child molesters."

The strike continued. The next day John Zavodsky was appointed "Temporary Interim President." A day later he was called into court and he too was directed to order the teachers back to jail. He declined and was sent to jail.

Johnson and Ensman would serve forty-five days each and Zavodsky forty-three days for contempt of court. They could have served much less time. Every few days they were brought before Judge Langsdorf and given an opportunity to comply with his order. They declined.

Johnson recalled those appearances before Langsdorf. "He wanted us to order the teachers back to work and admit we were wrong. My answer was that I could tell them to go back to work, but I doubted very much they would do it."

Langsdorf made sure that conditions in jail were as punitive as he could make them. "We were allowed no newspapers," recalled Johnson. "Unlike other prisoners, we were allowed only ten minutes a week for visitation. The cell had very limited visibility out the window. I could not see more than sixty feet in any direction. We were not allowed any out-of-cell time, even to wash cars, which was customary for other prisoners. We slept on steel bunks with no cushion. The cell toilet was a combined toilet and washbasin with no privacy, and we had to go in front of everyone else. I tried to shave, but the blade I had been given had gone through the jail hierarchy! We paced our cage. I saw people fight over a cigarette butt."

The average contempt stay in jail was seven days. Johnson, Ensman and Zavodsky were sentenced to ninety days.

As it turned out, Johnson did not have to fear for his safety. "The biggest, worst killer was the 'gang leader.' He asked me if I was one of those teachers. He was surprised. 'They put you in here with us killers?' People in jail blamed two people for their plight, their judge and their lawyer. They left me alone."

With three leaders in jail, no real bargaining going on and the prospects of the judge picking off the leadership one person at a time looming high, John Chase, his organizing team and key leaders were determined to come up with a strategy to stop the judge and get serious talks going.

They calculated that Langsdorf would be more reluctant to jail a woman teacher, especially an older one. Gray-haired Betty Collwell fit the bill. She was willing to be appointed "Temporary Interim President." She held a news conference the next day with Kink at her side. The Portland news media was now treating this strike as a top story with all the drama of a soap opera.

The next day Collwell got an order to appear before Judge Langsdorf.

Steve Kink felt that it was necessary to expose the board. They were having a "free skate" and needed some heat placed on them. He drafted a speech for Collwell to deliver at a public school board meeting.

That night Collwell and a few selected members attended the school board meeting and demanded to be heard. The board had no intention of letting her speak, but according to Chase, the large audience of supportive parents "went nuts."

"Let her talk!" they yelled.

The board relented, and she delivered a powerful speech. She concluded her speech with "I've never broken the law or had so much as a traffic ticket, but tomorrow I'm going to jail, all because of you!" Then she turned and left the room.

The effect of her speech was underscored when one of the board members, under growing stress, broke down and cried.

By this time strike organizers knew that the court had photos of picketers and picket captains, identified by their principals. Chase figured they were next.

Chase ran the idea by the strike team of simply surrendering everyone. They all agreed and a general membership meeting was called for at Clark College that night.

"Tomorrow, the court will order all of you back to work and begin to jail us one by one," Chase told the teachers at the meeting.

Collwell spoke, as did some other members. Lodge said that as an officer of the court he could not tell them what to do.

Chase spoke next and gave the recommendation of the organizing team. "We will all surrender."

"What will that mean?" a member asked.

"We'll all go down there and offer to go to jail," he explained.

Next, there was a moment of silence, and the organizers expected questions reflecting some reluctance to go with the strategy. Instead, the first question breaking the silence was, "What can we take with us to jail?" For the members, it was not a matter of whether or not they would go to jail but how would they do it.

Lodge said they could take a toothbrush, a book and underwear.

Other questions about the logistics were answered. At the end of the meeting one of the younger women was emphatic about one more issue. "I'm ready to go," she said, "but you're going to have to find some way for us to get our birth control pills in there, because if we are in there for any time, you know what will happen!"

After the meeting Kink told an awestruck news media what the teachers were going to do.

The next morning, all of the striking teachers gathered at a park near the courthouse. Each carried a little bag filled with their toothbrush, a book and underwear. The reporters, according to Kink, "ate up the story."

Led by Collwell, they marched in single file to the courthouse, filled the small courtroom, and the overflow filled the hallways of two floors.

Lodge explained to a rattled Judge Langsdorf that the teachers were all here to surrender. Referring to Collwell, Langsdorf declared he was not going to put a woman in jail.

"You can put them all in jail," Lodge answered.

At that point Langsdorf called Lodge into his chambers and added, "Bring that NEA lawyer with you." He was referring to Chase, whom he mistook for an attorney.

In chambers, Langsdorf began to rant. "I've had it," he told Lodge. "I don't want you representing them anymore. They're breaking the law. And I don't want to put any NEA attorney in jail."

"We wouldn't want that either," said John Chase, dressed in a suit and carrying his own toothbrush.

"He's not barred in Washington," Lodge said dismissively, not wanting to disabuse the judge of his mistaken notion of Chase's role.

Next, Judge Langsdorf turned the discussion to what he was going to do with all the teachers packed into the courthouse. "I'm going to put them all in jail!" he stormed. He sent his bailiff out to make arrangements.

Moments later the bailiff returned with news that there were only eleven cells available.

Chase spoke up, a move that on later reflection he figured he should not have done. "You have two junior highs with cafeterias that are not being used. You could jail them there."

At first Langsdorf bought the idea. "OK!" he said. Then he had a second thought. "How would it look in the press — 'Teachers jailed in their own schools!' "

The strategy of offering to surrender all teachers worked. Stymied at putting more teachers in jail, Langsdorf called the board members in and told them that he would put them in jail if they did not bargain in good faith.

A federal mediator was called in from Seattle, and the State Superintendent of Public Instruction's Lew Griffith was also on hand. Authentic negotiations got underway for the first time and continued until a contract settlement was reached after two weeks on strike.

Superintendent Ray Patrick retired at the end of the year. The well-respected Wes Apker from the Office of the State Superintendent replaced him.

The teachers returned to work for the last few weeks of the school year, but an attempt to get the District to make up the lost ten days was foiled by Langsdorf, who creatively ruled that the strike was an "insurrection!"

The strike was over. The result was a negotiated collective bargaining contract, the first ever achieved by a teacher strike in Washington.

Langsdorf was not done with Ensman, Johnson and Zavodsky, however. He was still demanding an apology and a statement admitting they were wrong. They would not agree. The judge let them out of jail long enough to finish out the school year and then put them back in jail. "Langsdorf would let out rapists on work release but not our guys," said Paulson.

The judge had been well aware that Evergreen teachers had demonstrated at the jail, and so as to avoid a demonstration of several thousand teachers, he again let them out of jail in early July during the NEA convention, which just happened to be across the Columbia River in Portland that year.

After the convention the stalemate continued. The teachers would not agree to his conditions and Langsdorf would not back down. There was no move to appeal their contempt citations either. Strike strategists did not want a higher court setting a precedent by declaring teacher strikes in Washington to be illegal. The three remained in jail until mid-August, at which time

Superintendent Apker pleaded with Langsdorf for their release and an agreement was reached to have Ensman, Johnson and Zavodsky sign a weak letter that the judge accepted.

During their time in jail Evergreen teachers showed they had not forgotten their leaders. They got together and painted Ensman's home that summer.

Johnson said that after his forty-five days in jail he was amazed he could see farther than sixty feet. When he returned to school in September, his students were naturally curious about his experience. "I told them they could ask any questions they wanted that day, but after that, no more. Other than that there were no reactions from either parents or kids."

For those who believe in the adage "what goes around comes around," a footnote about Judge Langsdorf is of interest. The Clark County Court was concerned about his lack of restraint and shortly after the strike, revoked his privilege to choose cases. Nine months later, according to Dick Johnson, the Vancouver *Columbian* ran a feature with names and addresses of owners of downtown Vancouver property. Langsdorf owned two properties. While he was at his retirement party, his house was gutted. There is no evidence it was tied to the strike in any way.

Steve Paulson may have summed up the strike best: "It was a great feeling being in that situation. It was power creation."

The strike was a huge success and made all future teacher strikes in Washington a practical reality, but there were a couple of sour notes.

First, during the strike WEA Executive Director Robert Addington, who by this time had announced his retirement, called the strike team and tried to disassociate WEA from any responsibility, declaring that the organizers should abandon the strike. "He was opposed to teacher strikes," recalled Carol Coe. He was concerned about WEA's liability. They stood up to Addington and said if he followed through, he would have to answer to 300 dues-paying teachers.

WEA President Ken Bumgarner later said he was unaware of Addington's posture or his call to the strike team. "I didn't know he had called down there," said Bumgarner. "I'd been down there myself pledging WEA's complete support!"

But the most discordant note came from neighboring Vancouver, where local President Gary Holmberg and UniServ Rep Jim Kanthak opposed the strike. During the strike in Evergreen, Kink had gone to the Vancouver Education Association seeking their support to run the daily picket line newsletter. They declined. As a result, Kink went over the Columbia River to the Portland Association of Teachers, which was more than willing to give whatever support it could.

After the strike, on June 14, 1973, Holmberg wrote a sharply worded letter to Bumgarner and President-elect Gene Fink condemning the strike as the "Evergreen Disaster." He called for an "investigation and evaluation study by objective parties." He implied that there was support for his request from other urban associations and raised the specter of urban opposition to WEA support for strikes. "I have talked the concept [of an investigation] over with elected leaders of other urban associations of the state and have been assured that my proposal is a sound one and one you can expect them to support..."

Holmberg went on to condemn the Evergreen strike team. "We had grave doubts that a strike in Evergreen in the spring of 1973 would bring anything more than misery especially if carried out under the direction of the particular state and UniServ staff members that had been named and assigned by WEA to the strike organizing." Holmberg called it a "no win strike."

"The study," he wrote, "should be for in-house distribution — not a public spanking of the individuals responsible for bad judgments, etc. by calling for and carrying the strike out..."

Holmberg sent copies of his letter to CUE and Senator Al Bauer. Bumgarner preserved the letter but took no action to initiate any investigation. He clearly favored the strike and understood its significance. After all, his own local, Edmonds, went on strike later in May 1973.

Other Early Strikes

The spring of 1973 saw two more teacher strikes. The first was at Elma, and it lasted from May 15 to 22. The issue there was Reductions In Force (RIF). Organizers including John Gullion, Mike Schoeppach and Stan Jeffers were dubious about the probable success of a strike. They urged the leadership to set a high strike vote threshold of 75 percent. The first vote was just shy of the 75 percent mark. They met the next day, took a standing vote and to the person reached 75 percent.

While the strike was a success on other issues, it failed to get the school board to back down on its plans to RIF several teachers.

Elma was the first district to employ strikebreakers, or "scabs," to break the strike. It did not seek an injunction. Gullion was jailed briefly when he and several teachers locked arms and tried to block buses from leaving the bus garage.

Within a year an unhappy Elma went independent as the Elma Teachers Organization. They did not reaffiliate with WEA until 1991.

Edmonds, on May 25, was the first large local to go on strike. The issue was a collective bargaining agreement, which the school board adamantly declared it would never negotiate.

Edmonds had more than 1,300 members by 1973, and organizing a strike of that size was an enormous undertaking. Organizing began the previous September when the board formally rejected the bargaining of any contractual agreement. For them negotiations were to be limited by their narrow interpretation of the Professional Negotiations Act.

Organizing was a step-by-step process. In December six members picketed in sub-freezing weather in front of a school board meeting. Later that month ten members picketed on the street in front of the administration center. In January a similar demonstration included 125 members. By April more than 600 teachers had signed a full-page ad in the Edmonds *Enterprise*.

In May the leadership, exercising caution, did not recommend a strike to its Representative Council, but presented a list of other options. Building Representative Blair Patrick, who had just been elected WEA President-elect, stood and made a motion that the leadership bring back a strike plan of action to the next meeting. It passed overwhelmingly, as did the plan itself two weeks later.

The strike vote was taken at the Lynn Twin Theatre. Although the number of yes votes had been carefully calculated, the number of administrators, still a part of the bargaining unit, who showed up to vote no had not been anticipated. Edmonds voted by 54 percent to go on strike the next day.

The District immediately went to Snohomish Superior Court and obtained an injunction. The leadership, under President Robert Brown, did not back down. It waited out the three-day Memorial Day weekend and called a general meeting to be held at the Seattle Center on Monday night.

Brown stood before the assembled teachers with news media present and delivered a forthright speech calling for a continuation of the strike. "By my making this recommendation, I am already in violation of the judge's order," he thundered. He was ready to follow his Evergreen colleagues to jail.

A request for UniServ Rep John Cahill to read the entire injunction was made, and he delivered a spirited reading of the court order.

An unexpected motion to require a 60 percent vote passed, and the motion to continue on strike was put to the members. When the votes were counted, only 40 percent voted to continue. The announcement included only the result, not the vote totals. The news media reported that while a majority favored continuing the strike, the Edmonds Education Association did not get the required 60 percent.

Edmonds returned to work, but the EEA did not act defeated and did not give up its quest for a contract, which it achieved by 1976.

Because there was no amnesty or back-to-work agreement ending the strike, the District retaliated against Blair Patrick, a high school vice principal, for his participation in the strike. He was stripped of his administrative position, becoming the only WEA member ever to be penalized for going on strike. His demotion was upheld in superior court.

Since that time locals on strike have, in almost all cases, negotiated strong amnesty clauses as a condition of ending a strike.

The last of the spring strikes, all successes, would take place in 1974.

The first strike in Eastern Washington took place in Mead just north of Spokane. Roger Cantaloube, a veteran of Aberdeen and Evergreen, was the lead organizer with his new partner, Roger Gray. "I met with Ken Landeis and we agreed that we would not make any more progress until one of our [Eastern Washington] locals went on strike," said Cantaloube. The Mead Education Association sought a contract and ran into a district that tried to prevent any UniServ staff from even coming to the bargaining table.

The strike was carefully organized, with the District making many of the same mistakes as had Evergreen management. The strike vote was 134 to 33. But in what was to prove to be a trend in later strikes, the vote to break the injunction days later was 152 to 22. Clearly, the example of Ensman, Johnson and Zavodsky was an inspiration. A few members, jailed briefly, were let out when the order was appealed to the Spokane County Superior Court and later to the Washington State Supreme Court.

Although a bad ruling by the Supreme Court posed a risk, it was one that attorney Bill Powell was willing to take.

As high courts sometimes do, this one dodged the issue of the legality of teacher strikes altogether. The court overturned the injunction on the narrow grounds that the District had failed to follow the state Open Meetings Law in authorizing court action to end the strike. The Open Meetings Law required public bodies, like school boards, to make all decisions in meetings open to the public. According to Powell, the Open Meetings issue was barely mentioned in his arguments before the court. To this day the WEA has not taken the issue to the high court again.

The strike lasted from April 26 to May 5, 1974, and achieved the Mead Education Association's first collective bargaining agreement. The issue of UniServ being able to go to the bargaining table was also settled once and for all.

One-day strikes took place on May 15, 1974, in Goldendale and in Central Kitsap. The bargaining following the Central Kitsap Education Association's intentional one-day strike achieved that local's first collective bargaining agreement, becoming the "lighthouse" precedent for the Olympic UniServ Council.

The last spring strike was in Kelso on May 30–31, 1974. Wes Ruff, who had organized Goldendale, headed the organizing in Kelso. Teachers there were successful on issues of salary, class size and teacher aide time. Again, ederal mediation proved very helpful.

The First Fall Strikes

By the fall of 1974 UniServ and local leaders were confident enough of their basic organizing skills to attempt fall strikes. This move would also tie strikes to a normal contract cycle beginning each September 1.

A trio of successful strikes led off the year.

The 900-member Federal Way Education Association went first on August 29, 1974, followed by Tacoma on September 3 and Mukilteo on September 5. All three involved contracts, and all three had issues of salary and class size, among others.

All involved District attempts to obtain injunctions, but this time judges, not wanting to repeat the excesses of Judge Langsdorf, acted with restraint in enforcing their orders.

Federal Way was particularly important, as had been Evergreen, in paving the way for future strike successes. The Federal Way School District decided it would try to break the strike by hiring scabs at a super rate of $42 per day, a rate exceeding the going substitute rate in 1974.

The lead organizer was Joe Dupris out of the WEA Kennewick office. Led by zone coordinator Roger Cantaloube, Dupris's team decided to challenge the scabs and attempt to turn around as many as they could with heavy picketing tactics. Though some teachers were reluctant to yell at scabs and attempt to block them, teachers at Kilo Junior High and Thomas Jefferson High School, in particular, were more than eager to challenge the scabs.

After more than a week on strike, Ken Landeis, the Southeast Washington UniServ Rep and former WEA President, was brought in to run the anti-scab campaign. Federal Way had a huge number of younger teachers ready for fun and adventure. Landeis organized a tail-a-scab campaign patterned after successful tactics Cantaloube had devised at Kilo Junior High and Jefferson High School. Teachers would follow the scabs home and try to convince them not to return to school the next day. The campaign disrupted the District's attempt to recruit scabs, and it demonstrated that teachers would not stand passively by while strikebreakers took their jobs. In addition, there was considerable bitterness directed toward regular teachers who worked during the strike. This challenge and the resulting hard feelings caused Districts in the future to question the ultimate value of employing scabs.

As in Mead, Federal Way had a high strike vote, 89.45 percent, and when it came time to break the injunction the vote rose to 93 percent. The judge was more even-handed than Langsdorf had been. He delayed the start of school for a week and then continued to monitor the situation until the strike ended. He never issued penalties.

Tacoma was the product of a yearlong organizing drive headed up by NEA organizer Bill Cullinane. The District was divided into five high school strike zones with an organizer in each zone. Attorney Parks Weaver foiled District attempts to get an injunction by citing judicial error. And District attempts to hire scabs at $42 per day late in the strike failed. Most of them either were or had been in Federal Way and were unavailable. Tacoma used two federal mediators to reach agreement. A pair of community college strikes rounded out the 1974 season.

Green River Community College, which was represented by the American Federation of Teachers but had a coalition bargaining team, struck briefly in late September. And Olympic College in Bremerton had a strike lasting a couple of weeks in October.

Earlier that year, the WEA had hired UniServ Representative Armand Tiberio specifically to work with Community Colleges. He joined Kink's Olympic College strike team as the bargainer along with John Cahill, Jack

Beyers, John Chase and Ron Scarvie, who had just been hired in Fourth Corner. On the final night of the strike, with tensions running high, one of the striking instructors came to Kink with an ominous message. "There are bombs planted somewhere on the campus!"

"Find those damn things now!" Kink ordered. Three crude Molotov cocktails set for lighting were discovered. One was found outside the President's office where the bargaining was taking place. Kink pulled Beyers and Tiberio out of the bargaining session to tell them of the news. Tiberio's mouth dropped and stayed open for several minutes and Beyers simply said, "If this were known to the other side, it would not have a positive outcome in the bargaining process."

Kink's reply: "Really!"

These two strikes were to demonstrate that strikes were just as viable in community colleges as they were in the K–12 system.

As a result of the early strikes, the WEA, with the urging of Don Johnson and others, came to accept strikes as a normal part of teacher collective bargaining. Staffing and funding strike operations, in practice, became the highest priority of the Association. A healthy budget line item for strikes was established.

In addition, colleague support for striking locals grew. The spectacle of Vancouver's criticism of the Evergreen strike was not to be repeated. Neighboring locals embraced striking locals, walked their picket lines and sent them financial support, food and the like. Locals soon saw that a strike in a nearby local gave them added power at their own bargaining table.

Bob Pickles, President of Enumclaw in 1973, tells the story of his superintendent discovering a bundle of EEA picket signs visible in his car following Bob's trip to Elma to support striking teachers there. Pickles thought quickly. "Oh, this is the year of strikes for locals starting with the letter E, and we're next!" Quick to buy into WSSDA stories of WEA conspiracies to create strikes, he reached a quick settlement with his teachers.

These early strikes gave impetus for the Legislature to pass a teacher collective bargaining act in 1975.

Levy Failures

During the early 1970s levy failures accelerated not only in number but in the dollar impact on school districts. As the Legislature ratcheted back its share of school funding each year, districts increased the amount they asked voters to approve at the polls.

By the mid-1970s levies in the large Puget Sound area districts had grown to 40 percent or more of district budgets. Upward pressure at bargaining tables was also a factor.

The State Constitution and laws governing special levies made passage more difficult. Levies were good for only a year at a time. That meant districts had to go to the voters every year just to maintain funding levels. Unlike other states, Washington school districts could not go to the voters just for increases, they had to pass the whole levy each year.

That's not all. Passage required a 60 percent super-majority. And turnout in the election had to be 40 percent or more of the voter turnout in the last general election. In those days general elections were held in even-numbered years only. If a district failed the first time, it had but one more chance to pass it that year.

Add to this the state's economic turndown of the early 1970s and scenario began to spell disaster for more and more school districts.

At first, WEA reacted to the levy failures and the subsequent Reductions in Force (RIF) by urging locals to resist any and all cuts, rather than bargaining how and to whom the layoffs would be done. Under the leadership of Wes Ruff, WEA drew up a policy paper on resisting both cuts and the bargaining of RIF provisions. At first there was some success in forcing districts to utilize cash reserves, which in some cases amounted to huge pots of money.

But soon that strategy ran into a brick wall. Locals ran out of reserves and began laying off teachers in greater and greater numbers. The WEA policy stopped making sense.

Without bargained RIF provisions, the numbers of those RIFed were not controlled. Who stayed and who was let go was left up to the whims of the districts. Favorites were kept and perceived troublemakers were ousted. And once let go, there was no guaranteed right of return when levies began passing.

Again, the UniServ Councils took the lead in negotiating RIF provisions in contracts. Roger Cantaloube in Eastern Washington, Kink in Olympic and John Chase in Chinook were the first. Chase got hold of a flight attendants' contract, analyzed its layoff provisions and fashioned RIF language for his locals. This was widely shared with his UniServ colleagues.

The first lesson learned from other districts was to negotiate RIF language well ahead of any levy failure. "In a RIF everyone has a dog in the hunt," warned Chase.

RIF provisions ranged in quality from weak to strong. The best ones bargained straight seniority, some even with super-seniority for the local association President. Some had to settle for categories or RIF pools of teachers by grade level or subject matter.

The best ones had economic triggers so as to prevent districts from RIFing for frivolous or insufficient reasons.

Another basic provision was recall rights, generally in the order of reverse seniority or last-RIFed-first-rehired. In the Olympia area Chase was able to bargain inter-district cooperation, which meant that Olympia, North Thurston and Tumwater agreed to hire RIFed teachers from the other districts before hiring on the outside.

RIF policies, especially those bargained well before a RIF and those that had the simplest and most straightforward seniority provisions, were perceived by members to be the fairest. These RIF provisions also had the effect of reining in districts that were tempted to overuse RIFs to "clean house." Chase argued that this was good solid union behavior. "If you made it [RIF] hard on the districts, they were less likely to RIF."

Another dilemma faced local associations. Locals were often bargaining salary increases at the same time they were fighting RIFs. The question: do you bargain salary increases at the expense of teachers, or do you forgo salary increases to save teacher jobs? Some locals went one way and some the other.

Locals strongly into the UniServ Program took the hard line and continued to bargain salary increases in the face of RIFs. Chase, Kink, Cantaloube and others argued that in the long run locals would lose if they took it upon themselves to "buy teacher jobs" by forgoing raises. They observed that districts were reluctant to make up the lost raises when levies began to pass again.

In 1975 Seattle experienced a levy failure and the Association was faced with the same tough decision other locals had faced. The District laid off some 1,000 teachers, according to then Assistant Executive Secretary Warren Henderson. "Dallas Shockley, Seattle's Executive Secretary, personally reached an agreement with the Seattle superintendent to roll back the 8 percent salary increase our team had bargained and use those dollars to hire back laid-off teachers," said Henderson. "This angered many of our members, including members of STA's combined bargaining team." To make matters even worse, when laid-off members were rehired, many of them criticized the Seattle Teachers Association for giving up the salary increase. "This was a low point for STA," said Henderson. There was a verbal promise that the district would make up the salary loss if the levy passed the next year. In 1976 Seattle passed its levy and found itself in its first strike because the district did not want to honor that promise.

John Chase recalled, "We had yelling matches in staff meetings. On both sides, it was about what we believed."

Two More Attempts at Tax Reform

In 1972 and 1974 the State Legislature, at the urging of WEA and other groups, attempted two more times to pass tax reform as a means of providing adequate funding for schools.

The 1972 attempt was a remake of the 1969 effort with a constitutional amendment providing for personal and corporate income taxes and a companion statute setting specific rates. It attempted to correct some of the perceived flaws in the 1969 measure.

But it met the same fate at the polls.

Sandwiched in between the two attempts at tax reform was Governor Evans' feeble attempt to balance the state budget by using teachers' retirement funds. "The WEA sued him and won a Supreme Court decision 9-0," recounted WEA lobbyist Perry Keithley. This led to another attempt to raise revenue.

In 1974 the attempt took a different twist. The Legislature proposed a corporate income tax, or corporate franchise tax as it was termed. The idea was that this would be more palatable to the voters. Known as HB 314, it too did not even get close to 50 percent of the vote. The state's largest businesses mounted a $500,000 media campaign to defeat HB 314.

No Legislature since then has attempted to pass an income tax, and to this day Washington schools have been under one funding crunch after another.

Levy Campaigns

The roots of the WEA political action program that emerged in the 1976 electoral campaigns can be found in the levy campaigns of the early 1970s. The need to preserve teacher jobs could not rest on RIF provisions alone. Better campaigns were needed to pass levies.

Out of necessity local associations and UniServ Councils got involved. As it turned out, organizing for a levy campaign, or for any political campaign, was just an extension of the organizing local associations had found to be successful in bargaining contracts.

Levy campaigns were typically short of three ingredients for success: money, volunteers and know-how. Associations could generate all three. Some of this work had been a part of levy campaigns for years, but when UniServ became involved, the teachers took over in a big way and began dictating more of the campaign strategy.

Campaigns required volunteers to do doorbelling, addressing and posting mailings, putting up yard signs and phoning voters. Young teachers with energy and the prospect of being RIFed first if the levy failed were a pool of ready volunteers. UniServ also realized that a little beer and pizza made the job a lot more fun.

Because UniServ often crossed district boundaries, it could be a catalyst for getting neighboring districts to combine their resources and act in concert to pass their levies. In 1974 most of the districts in Kitsap County lost their first levies. Steve Kink saw an opportunity to use his political campaign skills not only to pass those levies but to extend the power and influence of the locals in the Olympic Council.

He was able to get all of the districts to coordinate their campaigns, to set their next levy elections on the same day and to go with the same theme, signs, literature and advertising campaigns. He mobilized the teachers in the locals to do all of the volunteer work. One could travel the entire county and see the same yard signs promoting the levies. The impact was tremendous and the coordinated campaign worked. All of the levies passed.

Local political hopefuls, seeing the effect of these levy campaigns, sought out UniServ to work in their campaigns for the school board and the Legislature.

Internal Disputes

Though the WEA in the early 1970s still retained the organizational structure it had when Joe Chandler dominated the Association, new and often competing forces would change the structure and the culture by the middle of the decade. Administrators, who had tried to maintain the WEA as a professional organization, had lost most of their numbers and their influence on the board. Newer board members had been local Presidents and bargainers who clashed with superintendents and school boards.

To many of the new breed of members on the WEA Board, Executive Director Bob Addington represented an older and more conservative attitude toward the proper role of the Association. "He was of the old school," explained Ken Bumgarner, who was President in 1972–1973. Newer board members and many in power in local associations increasingly began to criticize him.

Some of his critics wanted Addington to take a bolder approach to problems, while others felt he had lost control of a staff that were too free to act and shape the direction and the policy of the organization.

Though the two had an amicable relationship, Bumgarner's "craft union" mentality and sense of advocacy were often at odds with Addington's vision of a more "professional" organization. In 1972 the WEA had taken Governor Dan Evans to court over his attempt to use teacher retirement funds to balance the state budget. Addington, like everyone else, saw this as a great victory. In the 1973 legislative session Bumgarner favored going for a 2 percent retirement formula. The retirement system then had a 1 percent formula.

Bob Addington opposed the move. "It's fiscally irresponsible," he argued to Bumgarner. "If we have an opportunity to double every teacher's retirement, we should go for the benefits," argued Bumgarner. He prevailed and the WEA achieved what would come to be known as Plan 1 of the Teachers Retirement System.

There was another rub. It started, according to Bumgarner, in 1968 when Ester Wilfong became the first release-time President. "Suddenly, he became the Association spokesperson, not the Executive Director. When Hannan was the Exec, the board and the President were just ceremonial."

That rub was also present when Bumgarner became President. "Addington felt the board should give him direction, not the President," said Bumgarner.

Bumgarner saw Addington's problems beginning with his differences with Wes Ruff. "Bob and Wes could not get it together," recalled Bumgarner. "Wes started organizing. A 'Wes' cult on the board emerged. The group thought Wes should be advanced in the organization. That faction thought Addington had to go. It got to be a board-Addington thing, not a Ruff thing. It moved fast."

Jim Aucutt, who would become WEA President in 1976, said that he believed that Bumgarner encouraged anti-Addington board members to pressure Addington to resign.

"Bob called and talked to me one day," said Bumgarner. "He said he was moving in a direction of not being effective anymore and could see he was being an impediment."

"I'm losing the support of the board," Addington told Bumgarner. "I want to resign with dignity."

He gave his letter to the board the next day.

"He resigned with almost a year to go on his contract," said Bumgarner. "That gave too much time to find a successor. Shockley wanted his job. He was a finalist. Seattle felt they were snubbed. Seattle raised heat. They were in the news. That's when Seattle moved away from WEA and formed the CUE [Coalition of Urban Educators]."

The leading contender to succeed Bob Addington was Don Johnson. He had the support of the staff, and he had been instrumental in implementing the UniServ Program in the state and moving the organization to a more activist role.

But some board members, led by Issaquah's Mary Jo Eldenberg, who had led the movement on the board against Addington, opposed hiring Johnson or anyone on the inside, particularly if they were popular with the staff. The first nationwide search was unsuccessful, and it was opened up a second time.

Out of nowhere came a candidate right out of the business world with no education or Association experience. According to Bea Carlberg, Wendell Verduin had worked most recently with a governmental agency, and he ran headlong into the culture of the WEA staff for insisting on running the organization by issuing standard operating procedures, or SOPs. Verduin was seen by the WEA Board as someone who "would manage the staff into place." Right from the beginning he ran into a buzz saw of controversy.

WEASO Strike

In 1973 the WEA staff union, the Washington Education Association Staff Organization (WEASO), was negotiating with the board for a new contract. WEASO demanded a salary increase as well as a 2 percent retirement formula, just like the one WEA had achieved for teachers in the Legislature.

WEASO was still smarting from a move earlier in the year, when the WEA Board had challenged the inclusion of the Assistant Executive Directors in the WEASO bargaining unit. They originally had been included in the mid-1960s, just as school administrators had been included in bargaining units under the PN Act. In the unit clarification hearing before the NLRB, Don Johnson, Dave Broderick, Ray Broadhead and others were stripped out of the unit.

The contract negotiations were contentious from the very start. The WEA was short of money, and board negotiators, led by Jim Aucutt, had been given zero parameters by Bumgarner and the board. That meant no movement on salary and retirement.

Talks remained stalemated throughout the spring and summer. WEASO geared up for a strike but kept its plans close to the vest. Whenever Aucutt reported to the board, he was asked when there would be a settlement. "The question isn't when will there be a settlement. The question is when will there be a strike," Aucutt told the board.

To make matters worse, new Executive Director Wendell Verduin was thrust into the talks completely unprepared for what he would face. The board had made his role that of an observer. The staff team saw his role otherwise. Jack Beyers and Jim Raines yelled at him repeatedly to use his position to help forge a settlement. They didn't like the idea of an outsider in his position to begin with. Now they came to dislike him personally. These negotiations mimicked what was now going on at teacher negotiation tables all across the state.

As the conflict grew, teacher leaders across the state divided their loyalties between the staff and the board.

Wes Ruff, a key strategist in the WEASO organizing, said there was another unspoken underlying cause to the strike buildup. "We wanted to show teachers they could go on strike too," he explained years later.

Though their contract expired on September 1, it was not until midday October 3 that WEASO sprung the strike. It lasted for seventeen days. WEASO had a strike headquarters a few blocks up the hill from the WEA building in an apartment on Cherry Street in Seattle.

WEASO picketed the Association of Classroom Teachers (ACT) Fall Conference in Spokane, forcing the NEA President to cross their picket line to participate in the conference.

At the strike's midpoint, the state UniServ staff went on a two-day sympathy strike, adding to the pressure on the board. This action was more difficult than it seemed. The UniServ staff had personal service contracts with their individual councils. Supporting the WEASO strike meant that they were, in essence, violating their own contracts. Kink recalled the council meeting in Olympic when he told the council he was participating in the sympathy strike. "I told them why I was doing it," recalled Kink, "and that they had options ranging from doing nothing to firing me. 'This is something you need to decide without me, and you can get me down at the tavern when you are done.' I later found out that the principals from Bremerton who were on the council wanted to fire me. A battle broke out between Bremerton and the rest of the council over what to do. They ended up docking me a day's pay, and then later in the year gave me an extra day's pay at the holidays. They were great to work for!"

With the help of a federal mediator a two-year agreement, including salary increases and a 2 percent retirement formula, was reached.

In a fitting conclusion to the strike, the chief bargainers for both sides, Aucutt and Raines, both recall being sent around the state together to sell coordinated bargaining to the UniServ Councils. It was a demonstration of a growing consensus around the common cause of bargaining for teachers across the state. It was a cause that would bring competing forces together in the 1970s.

As for Wendell Verduin, his relations with the staff remained rocky until his resignation in 1977.

Three Forces

After UniServ gained a strong foothold within the WEA in the early 1970s, three forces vied for power — the WEA Board, the urban associations and UniServ.

The first was the WEA Board. Though it had changed and seen many new faces since Joe Chandler's days, it still tended to hold on to the past and supported programs like TEPS (Teacher Ethics and Professional Standards) and separate departments for administrators that had ever-dwindling constituencies. Its power was in the governance of the organization and in its control of the budget. It viewed with some suspicion a UniServ Program that, to some, seemed out of control. WEA Presidents, who themselves now came from a very activist stock, rightly felt they and the board best represented the aspirations of the members. They were not anti-UniServ. They just thought its role was to work for the governance of WEA.

The main agenda of the urban associations was to operate independent of the WEA. After all, it was Seattle, with support from other Urbans, that had challenged WEA in the mid-1960s to secure passage of the PN Act. The Urbans represented the pulse of their own memberships. Some of them, notably Seattle, Tacoma and Bellevue, had made great progress in bargaining under that law. All three had contracts with their districts. John Chase recalled that the Urbans had established relationships with their school boards and had media centers that gave them a voice. They did not want to see what they had achieved eroded by WEA or by the new UniServ Program.

The Urbans had used their power to assure NEA and WEA UniServ funding for their locals. After all, what became the NEA UniServ Program had been strongly lobbied for within the NEA structure by the National Council of Urban Education Associations (NCUEA). They had also used their power in the 1970s to ensure that UniServ would be a strictly locally controlled program, not a series of regional offices controlled by the WEA.

In early 1973 Seattle's Dallas Shockley led the formation of the Coalition of Urban Educators, or CUE as it was known. Urban solidarity was not new within WEA. Their Executive Directors and Presidents had been holding regular meetings since the late 1960s. In fact, those meetings had the blessings of WEA, and Jim Raines had been appointed to be the WEA staff contact. CUE was a more formal and independent attempt to hold the Urbans together in order to protect their place within the WEA structure.

George Blood (his local, Clover Park, was a CUE member) recalled how Shockley set up a separate lobbying office in Olympia. "He hired his daughter to run the office," said Blood. Seattle and Bellevue and other CUE members were concerned that WEA would seek to replace the PN Act with a collective bargaining statute. CUE had a reputation for working contrary to many of WEA's positions.

CUE understood that money was power. "CUE sent me to a meeting in Fresno," explained Blood. "It was about dues transmittal. Rather than send our dues directly to WEA and back to the locals, we collected the dues locally and sent the state dues to WEA ourselves. This created a thirty-day float to the advantage of the locals." Blood recalled that Seattle, Vancouver, Tacoma and Clover Park collected dues locally. There was always the implied threat that if WEA got too far out of line, the Urbans could delay or withhold the transmittal of dues.

CUE was also suspicious of these new UniServ Representatives and their brash behavior. "At one meeting," recalled Blood, "when a few of us were being selected to go to a meeting in New Orleans that had something to do with UniServ policy, Shockley encouraged me to go. His reason was that he did not want Steve Kink representing us!"

CUE's influence lasted but a few short years. "The Urbans' days in the sun had passed," said Blood.

UniServ was the upstart on the block. "This group of hotdogs were bright and articulate," said Blood. "They were demanding to be heard and demanded their share of the goodies."

By forming strong councils, UniServ combined the forces of many smaller units, and for the first time they experienced a taste for power not only within their districts, but also within the WEA.

The councils developed a new layer of leadership they felt was on the leading edge of change, and they felt they better represented teachers than did the WEA. Besides, they had a network of hired UniServ staff across the state that was more than willing to help them take over the world! The council leadership was as brash as their UniServ Representatives.

UniServ understood power formation. They knew that if they combined forces across the state, they could control WEA. They had the numbers.

The 1973 RA: UniServ Power Emerges

By the time of the 1973 WEA Representative Assembly, held at what is now the West Water Inn in Olympia, UniServ came prepared to take on an issue strongly backed by the Urbans.

Though he cannot recall the specific issue today, Bumgarner remembers that it was over whether or not WEA was going to listen to the Urbans enough.

"It was over whether the Urbans or UniServ was going to be in control. When the issue was on the floor, they saw there were too many rural votes. They went to the microphone and requested a caucus and that I meet with them. We hammered out a compromise and brought it back to the floor."

However, when it came time to vote, representatives from the new UniServ Councils would not agree. They carried the day. They even pulled support from Edmonds, the home local of Bumgarner. "At the time the UniServ position on the issue seemed to make more sense for Edmonds," recalled John Cahill, who as a local Executive Director was eligible then to be a delegate.

According to Blood, that Representative Assembly ended the "glow of 'we [Urbans] can do what we want.' "

Edmonds' support of the UniServ position highlighted a split within the urban coalition. Edmonds and other large suburban locals were meeting stiff resistance to bargaining contracts, or "master contracts" as they were called then. Their school boards and administrations were more conservative than their city counterparts. Following the urban path was not producing results. UniServ's organizing and power approach seemed much more promising. As urban locals hired new staff, these people came more from the mold of those in the UniServ ranks. Within a few years the distinctions between Urbans and UniServ faded away.

John Chase recalled that UniServ supported the WEA program much more than did the larger Urbans. But UniServ would soon be a real force behind making WEA a teacher-only organization, giving more financial support to the UniServ Councils and for passage of a true collective bargaining statute.

The 1975 Representative Assembly in Spokane

The next battleground pitted UniServ against the WEA Board and Wendell Verduin, and it took place at the Representative Assembly in Spokane. When it was over, UniServ's future place in the Association was ensured.

WEA was badly in need of more revenue, and the board, under the leadership of Blair Patrick, put together a dues increase proposal and took it to the delegates.

In the eyes of the UniServ Councils and its local leadership, the dues increase did nothing to help fund them. They needed new funds as much as did the WEA.

The proposal had been circulated in the Association long before the Representative Assembly, giving UniServ a long time to organize, and organizing is what UniServ did best. They wanted a significant part of the dues increase, and if they did not get it, they were prepared to reject the entire increase.

Each time the measure was brought to the floor, local leaders from the councils stated that they could not support it unless UniServ got a part of it.

Each time, the vote fell short of the two-thirds needed for passage. UniServ solidarity remained firm.

To his credit, WEA President Blair Patrick remained calm and let the will of the delegates prevail. "The 500-pound gorilla in the room can do as it wants," he said referring to the delegates. But behind the scenes it became a battle of wills, the board on one side and the UniServ Council delegates on the other.

Renton board member Dick Nichols exhibited his frustration and that of the board when he went to the floor microphone to accuse the UniServ Reps of controlling the will of the RA. "The UniServ Reps behind the ropes [the area where non-delegates viewed the proceedings] are calling all the shots," he said. "The delegates have to jump through their hoops before anything can happen."

From that time, on the 1975 RA has been called the "Hula Hoop Assembly."

Finally, after three attempts to pass the dues increase, Verduin was dispatched to see what he could work out with the opposition. The UniServ Councils had set up a leadership committee, and no deal would be accepted until it passed the committee. However, Verduin went looking for Chase and Kink. He found them in the bar and said, "What do you bastards want?"

At first they told him that the deal had to be made with the committee. But Verduin insisted they were in control, so they talked about what ifs. The bottom line is Verduin wanted a deal, and a split of the dues increase was worked out between the committee and the board. The measure then passed with a healthy vote. Kink recalled that Verduin and the board underestimated the UniServ governance leaders. "They were in control of the issue before they even got to the RA," said Kink. "Yes, we had advised them on how to deal with the issue, but the final decision always rested with them."

The power of UniServ within the WEA had now been settled once and for all. But another measure passed indicating that UniServ was also changing. Without too much controversy, the delegates passed the State Option UniServ Program (SOUP), in which a council could opt to have its UniServ Rep be employed by the WEA. While the council still would direct its program, WEA would handle much of the business end of the operation. Those councils no longer would have to negotiate contracts and salaries with their Reps and office staff. By now, however, the independent nature of UniServ was well established, and WEA, which at the inception of the program wanted control of the staff, now permitted the State Option UniServ Program councils (SOUPs) to operate as independently as the Local Option, or LOUP councils.

Administrators Out

By 1975 most school administrators, of their own volition, had left the WEA. They could read the collective bargaining handwriting on the wall. Most school administrators viewed themselves as management, and in matters of negotiations their superintendents required them to sit on the management side of the table. Not fully appreciating the realities of labor-management relations, many teachers felt betrayed that their administrators had chosen to sit on the opposite side of the table.

However, it would take several years before WEA Representative Assembly delegates would take formal action to make the WEA an employee-only organization. The Professional Negotiations Act, which was not replaced until January 1, 1976, still required bargaining units to include administrators. And there remained many teachers, particularly elementary teachers, who retained hopes that inclusion still could work. Many teachers kept strong ties to their principals.

When Central Kitsap, angered at the presence of principals across the bargaining table, voted them out of the Central Kitsap Education Association, elementary teacher and strong union supporter Sheryl Graham (Stevens) had the same reaction as many of her colleagues. "We liked our principal," she recalled. "We tried to keep them in."

The new bargaining law included a little-known provision allowing principals very limited bargaining rights, which could be exercised in separate or inclusive organizations.

Another impediment to outright ouster was a small number of locals, notably Bremerton and Longview, which retained active principal constituencies. They raised the argument at Representative Assemblies that they should have the option to include principals.

The Olympia Scene Changes

By 1975 WEA's lobbying operation and the nature of the Legislature began to change.

In 1970 the state's first Open Meetings Law was passed by initiative, and for the first time the legislative process was much more open to public scrutiny. Candidates had to disclose their financial affairs, lobbyists had to file periodic reports including all expenditures related to influencing legislation, and political action committees, like PULSE (Political Unity of Leaders in State Education), had to disclose all contributions to candidates. Previously, WEA had kept such contributions secret, even to its own members.

Pressures were mounting within the WEA for members to play a more direct and active role in legislative campaigns and lobbying. Chief Lobbyist Dave Broderick, a master of the older politics and a very successful lobbyist, resisted these changes. His success depended on being able to control all aspects of the operation. He was adept at building strong personal ties to key legislative leaders. He decided who got the goodies and what monies were spent to lobby which legislators.

Broderick and his staff were instrumental in getting income tax provisions on the ballot in 1972 and 1974. In 1973 he secured passage of the 2 percent retirement formula for teachers. And by the 1975 legislative session, he had lined up the necessary support to pass the landmark Educational Employment Relations Act, better known simply as the teacher collective bargaining act.

Broderick was able to fend off the destructive amendments that had scuttled the bill a year earlier.

But problems were emerging. Teacher RIFs had skyrocketed. Legislators were beginning to attack the Continuing Contract Law, and forces led by Senate Majority Leader August Mardesich were coming after the 2 percent retirement formula, which proved to have a huge price tag for the state.

In 1975 WEA members rose up and decided to mount a march on the capitol, the first in the Association's history. WEA President Blair Patrick, who had led an attempt in the Special RA of 1968 to have just such a demonstration in Olympia, was more than ready to lead this one.

The movement spread across the state. When 10,000 teachers, almost a third of the membership, took a day or two off school and descended on Olympia carrying signs demanding money to relieve RIFs and opposing changes to the retirement system, legislative leaders and Dave Broderick were more than a little nervous. Broderick was trying to keep Mardesich happy. He became upset when a cartoon printed up by John Cahill, now in WEA's Communications Division, was distributed to the marchers. The cartoon had Mardesich saying to a dismayed RIFed teacher, "I'll give you back your jobs if you give me your pensions!"

Capitol police were especially nervous when the marchers went inside the Capitol Rotunda while the House and Senate were in session. They convinced Patrick to take the teachers back outside.

The march succeeded in getting another $60 million for schools, but the Legislature passed Plan II of the Teachers Retirement System. It saved money by requiring teachers hired after October 1, 1977, to work until age 65 and averaging their benefits over their highest consecutive five years rather than over their highest two years as in Plan I.

In 1978 WEA would get even with Mardesich, and Broderick's lobbying style would become history.

By the mid-1970s the WEA had implemented the UniServ Program and demonstrated its power at the bargaining table. The ability to strike, if necessary, had been well established by initial strikes that were well organized, bold and successful. With the passage of a true collective bargaining law for teachers in 1975, the framework was there to bargain good contracts across the state.

School financing still remained a major hurdle, as did other challenges to WEA power in the Legislature. Members were poised to become a part of the lobbying program in Olympia, and it would be fortified by one of the most robust political action programs in the nation. And WEA's legal program would also see a major expansion into new areas.

CHAPTER FOUR

Peak of Power

B y 1976 the Washington Education Association had achieved passage of one of the strongest teacher collective bargaining laws in the country. WEA had one of the most aggressive UniServ programs in the NEA family. Competition for power within the Association largely had stabilized. The legal program was about to come under new leadership and expand its role in the Association. And WEA was about to become, at least for a short few years, from 1976 to 1980, the premier political power in the state.

It was a wild five years. Anything seemed possible.

Governance Strengthened

In the mid-1970s, the governance structure of the WEA essentially was the same as it had been in the days of Joe Chandler. Presidents served one year as "President-elect" before serving a single year as President. The tradition of rotating the presidency between the east side and the west side of the state remained. In many ways the role was still rather ceremonial, leaving the Executive Director with the real power to administer the Association.

A series of activist Presidents, such as Ken Landeis, Ken Bumgarner, Blair Patrick and Jim Aucutt, expanded the role of the President and set the stage for restructuring the governance of the organization and making the WEA President a much stronger figure within the Association. WEA President Gene Fink changed the status quo when he became the first person to serve two terms. Fink, a Mead music teacher, was elected in 1970, and during his term as President in 1971–1972 he ran again and was elected over the CUE candidate from Bellevue, Maury Hauser. He served as President-elect again, this time under Bumgarner. In 1973–1974 he served his second term as President.

This unprecedented event served rather well to demonstrate how antiquated the president-elect system had become and how much better a multi-year presidency could be. When Carol Coe, who had been President of the Association of Classroom Teachers (ACT) in 1973–1974, ran in 1975, she did so with the idea of restructuring the governance of the Association. Coe was a petite blond with sharp features and an air of determination about her. While most people were not aware of her intent, she exacted support for her plan from Jim Aucutt. "When I was President," recalled Aucutt, "we had lunch one day to talk about her role. I wanted her support. She agreed provided I would not run against her for the first two-year presidency. She also got me to agree that I would not oppose her on the board for one year after she became President."

Coe wanted to consolidate WEA governance. "We were very badly split," recalled Coe. "It was big vs. little and East vs. West. The board was split too. We had locals that wanted to secede from WEA."

Carol Coe mastered the art of internal politics in WEA perhaps better than any previous WEA President. "I never took an issue to the WEA Board until I had counted my votes," Coe said. The emergence of UniServ in 1970 paved the way for a new group of very active and very strong local Association Presidents. Many had been identified, recruited and mentored by UniServ Representatives. "Previous WEA Presidents," explained Coe, "saw the WEA Board as their constituency — their power base. I saw the local Presidents as my power base."

There also was some competition with UniServ for the loyalties of this new power base. At one point Coe as President found she was getting little support from the Chinook UniServ Council. Before long John Chase discovered that none of his members were getting appointed to WEA committees and commissions. "They complained to me," recalled Chase. "So I went to Coe and asked her why. She told me that every time she said up, I said down. And every time she said down, I said up. I agreed to back off, and she started appointing my members. I was very impressed with her toughness. I gained a lot of respect for her."

Though Coe had some disputes with UniServ, she avoided open conflict. "I was committed to never take on staff publicly," she said. "It would have appeared we were not united."

Coe spent much of her time calling local Association Presidents and visiting locals all over the state. "I put 40,000 miles on my car the first year just visiting locals, and I tried to call at least one President every day," said Coe.

Coe gathered support for reforming the governance structure of the WEA. Her plan was to have a President elected for two-year terms with a two-term limit. She proposed to eliminate the President-elect and substitute that position with a Vice President. She also saw, like most Association leaders by this time, how obsolete and costly the departments were.

The annual Representative Assembly of the Association of Classroom Teachers (ACT) had become no more than a dry run for the WEA Representative Assembly. The other departments had all but ceased to exist. Coe therefore proposed to do away with the department structure. "I felt we had adequately integrated instructional issues within the WEA," said Coe.

"It was also one of Verduin's ideas. He wanted to save money. Our budget was very stressed."

Even though there was considerable support for eliminating the Association of Classroom Teachers, Coe encountered stiff opposition. "ACT loyalists did not want to give in to the other side of the organization represented by bargaining," she said.

Coe disliked controversy. "I tried to resolve it," she said. So she compromised. In place of the ACT, she proposed to have a second Vice President in charge of instruction.

Coe got the necessary constitutional amendments through the WEA RA. She was so successful and so popular that she went on to become the first two-year President and the first to hold that office for a second term. Coe, in all, served for five years and transformed that office into one of power and strength.

It was significant for the WEA, with a membership composed of two-thirds women, that Coe would be the one to create the strong WEA presidency and be the most dominant President of the past century. From her terms on, gender would never be raised as an issue in WEA politics.

Coe also was responsible to a large degree for the strong role WEA would play in the politics of the state. Coe would go on to serve as President from 1977 to 1981.

Aucutt Leads the Charge

By 1975, there was a strong consensus among governance leaders and staff that WEA needed to energize the members and put the state's power brokers on notice that the WEA was a force to be reckoned with.

With less than a month to go before the 1976 WEA Representative Assembly, the decision was made to have President Jim Aucutt deliver a speech. "In fact," said Aucutt, "it was the first time any WEA President had ever delivered such a speech."

Verduin, Aucutt, Kink, Chase and Cahill met and, using a newsprint easel pad, laid out the major themes of the speech. It was to attack three forces — political, corporate and school management — for their intransigence in dealing with the crises facing education.

"I was given an armload of newsprint and the task of drafting the speech," recalled Cahill. "When I was done with the first draft, it was well over twenty pages long."

The other members of the team supported its length. Throughout the process it underwent minor changes, but Aucutt spent hours, some with Coe's help, rehearsing the speech. As a part of his preparation he used a piece of new technology — videotape. "I remember looking at the tape and thinking how flat it seemed," recalled Cahill. "I had a mental image of how it should sound, and I wasn't sure he could pull it off. We had gone all out and invited the news media to cover it."

At the Representative Assembly, when the moment came for the President's speech, Aucutt came alive. Cahill's doubts disappeared. Aucutt's delivery was forceful and dramatic. Delegates interrupted him with several standing ovations. Clearly, Aucutt struck a responsive chord.

In his speech, an abbreviated version of which was reprinted in the next issue of WEA *Action*, he made reference early to legislative repeal of Continuing Contract rights. "We face a hostile Legislature that held funding for our schools hostage so they could destroy our due process rights. Then they shot the hostage," he said.

He added to his list of targets the Washington State School Directors' Association (WSSDA). "We face a state school directors' association, armed with public money and a bevy of second-rate attorneys, ready to throttle teachers anywhere, anytime they can. We face resistance to teacher collective bargaining unequaled heretofore," he said in reference to the struggle to gain a bargaining bill.

"We face an over-RIFing of teachers more akin to a purge than a cutback," he went on. "We face a surging decline in educational opportunities in this state unequaled since the 1930s."

Aucutt's remarks did not leave the state's business community unscathed. "Since 1968, the WEA has been the only consistent advocate of school funding, while big business in Washington has perpetuated the present, disastrous school finance structure. After spending more than $500,000 in a statewide media campaign to defeat Initiative 314 and after lying to the public with a promise to support tax reform if 314 were defeated, their support for tax reform amounted to pouring in another $100,000 to maintain the status quo of special levies, which we know don't work."

He took on the WSSDA for spending great sums of public money to lobby — free from any requirements of the Public Disclosure law at that time. He went after school boards on teacher evaluation. "School boards have failed to evaluate teachers as required by statute, and certainly management evaluation has been virtually nonexistent. Instead of better evaluation, WSSDA won from the Legislature the right to fire teachers without having to build the kind of case a good evaluation system might require. After all, they only have to prove it to themselves now!"

He continued his criticism of the Legislature. "By any measurement of public opinion, politics — especially legislative politics — in our state is dirty business," he said. "What frightens all of us is that those turkeys are conducting the state's business and running rampant over your professional future and mine."

Governor Evans, when asked by a reporter to comment on Aucutt's reference to "turkeys," commented, "At least he didn't call us chickens!"

Aucutt saved some of his rhetoric for three legislators largely responsible for passage of House Bill 1364, repealing crucial Continuing Contract rights. "We had our traditional enemies such as the distinguished senator from

Dayton. I'm disturbed with Senator Donohue. He hates us and we are not too fond of him either. That's an enemy we can understand.

"It's the other kind — the self-proclaimed teacher spokespersons — who go to the House and the Senate to tell the world what teachers really want — like 1364.

"I'm referring to Senator Joe Stortini and Representative Albert Bauer. Some teacher spokespersons! Some teachers! They are so ashamed of their own profession that they had to join and lead the forces against it. We don't need teacher apologists in the Legislature, and we don't need them in the classroom either."

In his fiery speech, Aucutt went on to lay out the need for vigorous collective bargaining and political action programs and told the delegates it would not be easy or comfortable. It was a ringing call to action.

"We have a choice," he said. "We can conciliate and win some immediate, temporary victories at a tremendous cost, or we can forgo temporary gains and build for the real gains to be had when we are strong."

He posed another rhetorical choice. "We can let our hard-won collective bargaining rights fall into disuse and thereby gain favor with our school boards, administrators and building principals, or we can risk uncomfortable conflict with those who would treat us with paternalism."

In the end, he prophetically warned the delegates to be prepared for future organizational criticism. "Let's not be misled," he said. "The course your leadership is suggesting for this organization is a difficult and often discouraging one. If you think we're taking heat in the kitchen now, just wait until we're further down the road to organizational strength. We will be criticized by every pillar of society that doesn't want us to rock the boat. We will be stepping on a lot of 'sacred' interests that are contrary to education's interest.

"I believe we must continue to take the difficult, the uncomfortable and unpleasant course to organizational strength. I would rather walk on the hard road than crawl on the easy road."

UniServ Faces Changes

With the short-lived exception of the time Jackie Hutcheon was the Pilchuck UniServ Rep, UniServ was an all-male club in its early years. The imbalance was more a product of the culture at that time rather than anything deliberate. With each council independently doing its own hiring, no one had the authority, or for that matter the inclination, to step in and correct it. Whatever the reason, the status quo was unacceptable.

As UniServ Councils began to expand to two-person offices, even members of this all-male club recognized that women needed to be brought into the system. In 1975 the Olympic UniServ Council was ready to add a second UniServ Representative. Steve Kink and his council deliberately used this opportunity to hire a woman.

He went to the NEA Convention, where he and his council leadership used the NEA hiring hall, called the "meat market," to interview several candidates. The one who stood out was Marline Rennels, recently President of the Illinois chapter of the National Organization for Women (NOW). She also had been a classroom teacher and active in her local, Elgin, which had had recent strikes. She seemed a perfect match for the job and for the aggressive culture of Washington UniServ.

Rennels brought into UniServ work a background and a compelling story. As a teacher for eleven years, she began in Elgin, Illinois. "I liked the kids but hated the system," recalled Rennels. By 1968 she moved to Birmingham, Michigan. In Elgin she had been no more than an alternate Building Representative in the Elgin Education Association, but upon arriving at her first day of school in Birmingham she met a picket line. The teachers were on strike. "I'd never seen a strike of professionals," said Rennels. "The next day I joined the picket line. The district fired all of us who were on probation [like provisional status in Washington]. The teachers all stuck it out for two weeks, and I kept my job."

After Rennels' quick initiation about what an Association could be, she returned to Elgin in 1970. Dick Kroll, who would replace Shockley in Seattle in 1976, was Elgin's Executive Director. By this time Elgin had launched the first of four strikes in the early 1970s. "I saw they had some guts," recalled Rennels. "The women there became very vocal during the strike."

The same year Rennels convened a chapter of the National Organization for Women in Elgin and began to speak out on issues of sexism. That led her to involvement with the Alinsky Institute in Chicago. "I met Ed Chambers, who was about nine feet tall!" said Rennels. Chambers was Saul Alinsky's number two person in the Industrial Areas Foundation and would take over leadership when Alinsky died in 1973. She took the institute's two-week organizing seminar. "These were intensive fifteen-hour days," said Rennels. "I loved it. I discovered you can do what you want to do and get other people to do it too. It was the best education of my life."

"The Illinois Education Association invited me to give a speech at its RA on sexism," said Rennels. "I still didn't have any positional power, but I was vocal." That's when the local Association began to show some interest in Rennels. "Elgin was scared to death I was going to say how sexist the local was," said Rennels. "The EEA asked me to meet with its executive board to tell them how sexist the local Association was. They just wanted me to stay in line. They asked me to run to be a delegate to the Illinois Education Association RA. I got more votes than anyone else. That made me a two-year delegate. I met a lot of really neat people like Terry and Neil Bergeson."

Elgin asked Rennels to be on the bargaining team, and then went on its second strike.

The next summer was a fateful one for Rennels. The RA was in Los Angeles. Before she left, she took the LSAT and submitted applications to several law schools. She also took a leave of absence from teaching. At the RA she was doing "go-fer work" for Roberta Hickman, who was running for NEA President.

"I'd never had a nail-them-to the-wall interview and decided to go through the NEA hiring hall [for UniServ jobs]," said Rennels. Hickman encouraged her. "I had an interview first with Chip Tassoni, of the NEA staff, who asked me how serious I was about interviewing. I said I wasn't qualified."

"I have a friend in Washington state who is looking for a woman as a second staff person," Tassoni told her. "You want to talk to him?"

"Sure," said Rennels.

She first talked with Kink in a bar. "He was a banty rooster," recalled Rennels. "He talked to me about what Washington was like. He told me I needed to let him know how serious I was." At this point Rennels, who had done the interview, was still not certain, but she went ahead. "I had my Illinois supporters check out Steve Kink. They said he had a good reputation."

"The next day," said Rennels, "Kink said he had checked me out. He said I wasn't bad. I said I had him checked, too!"

"What did they say?" asked Kink.

"Not bad," said Rennels.

"I still need to know if you are serious," said Kink.

"I said yes," Rennels recounted. This was a big step because she still had all those law school applications. She also had a husband who was a sculptor in Illinois. She called Fred and talked it over. They agreed he would stay another year in Illinois. He eventually got a job with the University of Puget Sound.

She went to Washington in August to finish the interview with the Olympic council board. "I really did not know anything, but I was gutsy," said Rennels. She was hired and began work in September.

In January Kink left the Olympic UniServ Council to become the WEA Director of Political Action. "I was all alone for two and a half months," said Rennels, whose mentor was now gone. "I got my baptism under fire. I was sent to work on a strike in Pocatello, Idaho. Bill Cullinane from the NEA was the organizer. They asked me to sit down and type. I said I couldn't type, so they had me work the picket lines."

Breaking into Washington UniServ's all-male club was not all that easy. John Chase and others tested her mettle. "He was real mean," said Rennels. She stood up well to this harassment, but the friction was slow to dissipate. The culture was difficult to change.

"I came back from Pocatello and remember going to my first staff meeting," said Rennels. "I was the only woman in the group. I felt I didn't belong there, but they were nice to me. Later it got technical. I felt, by things said and not said and the intonations, that they really did not want me there. It was so vivid in my mind after leaving the meeting that I put my tape of 'I Am Woman' in my car's tape deck."

"You can bend but never break me," sang Helen Reddy.

"I barely knew what to do," recalled Rennels. "I called Dale Troxel a lot. We had seven locals that had not yet joined the council. Kink had said I had to get those people or I'd be out of a job next year! We needed the money. I got all seven of them to join. Port Townsend was the largest."

After a few months Armand Tiberio, who had been a UniServ Rep for higher education, came to Olympic UniServ. "I was so excited someone of Armand's skills was coming to replace Kink," said Rennels.

But the culture still was not friendly to women. "When Armand, Beyers and I had [joint council] meetings, they gave me little part in them," recalled Rennels. "When it was my turn on the stage, they would leave. I had come into an all-men's club!"

The new bargaining bill took effect in January 1976. "I had not done some of the things Armand expected," said Rennels. "He took charge. He was so focused and so damned intense. I really respected him."

One day some leaders from Bainbridge Island came into the office. "I started to talk to them," said Rennels. "Armand just usurped me. I felt discounted. Shortly afterward, we were having martinis at the Sandpiper. I said that we needed to talk! I went through everything. It was heartfelt. From that day on it was a 180! He treated me like an equal and a partner. We worked together for another three years. I learned so much from him. When he shared his knowledge, he shared his power. We had the same workaholic tendencies."

The barrier had been broken, and other women followed. In 1978 Eastern Washington hired Leona Dater, who came to the state via Colorado, Indiana and Nevada. At about the same time Linda Peretti was hired by Northline. Nancy Murphy came to Seattle in 1980.

Even though the barriers were broken by the late 1970s, a big imbalance in the ranks still remained. It would, in part, influence a backlash in the 1980s. Staff meetings still were male dominated. "They were incredible," recalled Dater. "The testosterone level was high and internal fights were common. The male/female issue was hard to overcome. It was not a problem with members, but more with other staff and especially the school district administrators. I would come over to the west side because there was a support system with more women being hired."

Verduin Fires Broderick

By the end of 1975 the old lobbying style practiced very successfully by Dave Broderick and others of his time collided with demands for a new style that was less controlled by one person, more open to public scrutiny, less "wine and dine" all night and more open to member participation in both lobbying and political action. Broderick also did not want to give up control over whom the Association would endorse at election time. "When I was chair of PULSE," recalled Carol Coe, "I questioned his budget. That was unheard of because he had appointed the PULSE Board!"

Broderick had opposed wide-open political involvement in legislative campaigns and members having a big role in lobbying. He also did not want to give up using the WEA credit card to show legislators a good time. At the same time President-elect Coe and Executive Director Wendell Verduin wanted change. "It will not be easy to change him," Aucutt warned Verduin.

The standoff continued for some time. Broderick, who had successfully won the 2 percent retirement formula and the collective bargaining law, enjoyed great power within the WEA. He would not be moved easily.

Broderick would play a role in his own undoing. In preparation for the 1976 legislative session, Broderick hosted, by some accounts, a rather lavish retreat for legislative leaders in the San Juan Islands. When accounts of the "party" leaked out, this became the final straw for Verduin.

According to Carol Coe, Verduin had told Broderick not to hold the event. "He just thumbed his nose at us," said Coe. "I supported his firing."

Verduin told Aucutt he wanted to fire Broderick and get a handle on the money being spent. In late December, he fired Broderick. According to Aucutt, Broderick wanted six months' severance. "I approved it," he said.

The announcement was not made until the first week of January. Assistant Executive Director for Communications Bill Davidson was hurriedly called back to the state from a meeting of the NEA Public Relations Council to handle the news media just days prior to the start of the session. It was an awkward moment. WEA gave no real reasons for Broderick's hasty departure, and the media was not satisfied with WEA's explanation.

Verduin needed a new chief lobbyist, and fast! He called in Don Johnson, who was enjoying great success as Assistant Executive Director for Field Services and who was also a personal friend of Broderick. That made for an awkward situation for Johnson. Verduin said he wanted Johnson to be the chief lobbyist. "I didn't want the job," said Johnson. Verduin, in a style that was eventually to be his own downfall, told Johnson that if he did not accept the Olympia job, he would fire him.

The transfer of Johnson to Olympia left a big hole to be filled in Field Services. That division of WEA was poised to organize to bargain contracts in every district across the state. Bill Hainer, who had been hired by Verduin in 1974 to fill the newly created position of Assistant Executive Director for Collective Bargaining, was moved into Johnson's position.

Judith Lonnquist Becomes First General Counsel

By 1976 the load of legal work had increased and UniServ Representatives had created new demands on this service. According to Bill Hainer, retained legal counsel George Mack was at odds with the UniServ staff and was not effectively managing the network attorney program he had created. WEA also anticipated a great deal of legal work with the new Public Employment Relations Commission over challenges to the new bargaining law and over many anticipated scope-of-bargaining cases. These cases were crucial to setting the right kind of precedents. Neither Mack nor many of the network attorneys had any background in labor law.

Bill Hainer favored WEA having an in-house legal counsel with a strong labor law background. So did Verduin. They knew that the new bargaining law would mean increased litigation. He had just met Judith Lonnquist, who had moved to Seattle following ten years as legal counsel for the Chicago Teachers Union. He persuaded Verduin to interview her. Verduin was also from Chicago and the two, though very different in style, clicked. She also had a connection to Marline Rennels, whom she had known as the President of the Illinois chapter of NOW. She recalled that when she was introduced to the WEA Board, Tacoma board member Terry Bergeson liked her. The board agreed. In November 1975 Verduin hired her, and she set out to make the new WEA Legal Division an active and aggressive part of WEA.

Lonnquist quickly stepped in and began to make changes, not all of which were viewed favorably by everyone. According to Lonnquist, she had three immediate goals. First, she had to decide which of the network attorneys to keep and which to dump. In her opinion, there were some bad lawyers in the program. Second, she was determined to take control of the process for determining which members got legal assistance from a network attorney. And third, she wanted to bring some labor attorneys into the program. In the process she upset many of the attorneys and the UniServ staff. "I was blunt and it pissed them off," recalled Lonnquist.

She immediately pared down the network, retaining specialists in various areas of litigation. "The large network had been diluted," explained Lonnquist. "With a smaller network, I was able to give each of them plenty of work." According to her, many of the UniServ staff did not like losing their easy access to an attorney.

Lonnquist's blunt personality and legal style quickly got her a luncheon invitation from network attorneys Mitch Cogdill, Bob Van Siclen and Ken Gross, who explained to her that "we practice law here differently. We remain friends with opposing counsels!" She kept all three on the network, but assigned Gross to work higher education cases.

But Lonnquist quickly gained the respect of her early detractors. She visited both the attorneys and all of the UniServ Reps and began to build a team.

Lonnquist took control of all cases going to the Public Employment Relations Commission (PERC). She required local associations and UniServ Councils to go through her to get to PERC. That way she could pick the best cases to set the kind of precedents that would enhance WEA successes under the new law. She worked hard to get the law interpreted as much like the National Labor Relations Act as possible.

According to Lonnquist, her first best case was the Edmonds "Calendar Case." The Edmonds School Board was still smarting from its loss a few years earlier on whether or not the school calendar was a mandatory subject of negotiations under the old PN Act. When John Cahill was Edmonds President in 1971, the board refused to negotiate the school calendar. The Edmonds Education Association challenged the board in the Snohomish County Superior Court. The judge, a former Edmonds School District legal counsel, ironically ruled in favor of the EEA. The board was determined to regain lost ground and felt the new law gave them a good chance.

Lonnquist skillfully laid out her case before the new PERC, even calling Cahill to testify on the earlier case. She won and set a precedent that exceeded what most other state associations had achieved under their bargaining laws. It was a major victory that paved the way for more favorable decisions that gave Washington teachers a scope of bargaining that was arguably as broad as they had exercised under the 1965 Professional Negotiations Act. Other PERC cases followed. Lonnquist won on class size and officer release time.

Lonnquist worked the early Title IX cases as well. Title IX required equity for girls in school sports at all levels. The most important case was at Washington State University. Although WSU was not a WEA affiliate, the case had ramifications for all K–12 girls' sports and women coaches. Lonnquist and a few other attorneys were up against twenty-eight attorneys in the King County Superior Court. They lost at that level only to prevail in the state Supreme Court. "By the time we won," she recalled, "bargaining had pretty much taken care of the problem." Her persistence on the issue of women coaches' salary equity made locals sit up and bargain the issue.

The first time the Legislature tried to enact teacher salary limitations through language inserted in the state budget, she took the case to the state Supreme Court and prevailed. She established that the Legislature could not enact substantive legislation via the state budget.

Although the WEA did not participate in either the Northshore school funding case, which was the first attempt by school districts to assure equity in school funding, or in Doran I, the first successful case to assure adequate funding for Basic Education, Lonnquist got WEA to participate in the second Doran case. She was able to get Doran to agree that special education, among other programs, was a part of Basic Education.

Lonnquist's legacy included establishing a strong contract arbitration program. She had all cases go through WEA for funding, and she assisted in selecting the best arbitrators for each particular contract issue. This practice strengthened locals' ability to win in the early days of the new bargaining law.

She left WEA in 1984, having achieved her goal of getting the bargaining act interpreted as the WEA had sought. She had a very pro-union bias. "When WEA got rid of administrators, it became a union!" said Lonnquist.

Judith Lonnquist went on to private practice in Seattle.

Collective Bargaining

Even before the final passage of the new teacher collective bargaining act, the WEA moved quickly to gain collective bargaining agreements in every district across the state.

Rather than using a foot-in-the-door approach to bargaining contracts, WEA decided early on to introduce a full-blown prototype contract at every table. It was designed with the most favorable language possible on every issue.

WEA also decided to give maximum organizational support to bargaining. That meant money, staff and coordination. The state was divided into five regions with a WEA staff person placed in a support role in each region. Dick Iverson, Jim Raines, Wes Ruff and Jack Beyers plus Bill Boynton, an NEA field staff person out of Michigan, each had a region.

Edmonds UniServ Rep John Cahill was hired in 1974 as a WEA Communications Field Representative. He was assigned to give communications support to contract bargaining across the state. He traveled to the regions and gave workshops on how to give effective internal and external communications support to bargaining. He knew that one person could not be everywhere. After a year-long project in Kent, testing all of the theories for effective member communications and news media relations while that local bargained its first contract, he wrote a bargaining communications manual entitled *Speaking Out* and distributed copies to locals statewide. It took an aggressive, Alinsky-like approach to communications. It treated communications as an organizing tool for bargaining, and WSSDA frequently quoted from it to show what the WEA was up to. Cahill was also assigned to give communications support in strikes.

Each of the regions set up some form of coordinated bargaining. The basic approach was to set agreed-upon bargaining goals and attempt to win those goals at each table. If a local could not attain the goals, they agreed to hold up their settlement to an agreed-upon date to allow lighthouse districts to settle first and establish good precedents in the council and region.

The system depended upon discipline and coordination. Though far from perfect in its execution, coordinated bargaining produced great results. Within just a few years the vast majority of contracts negotiated had all of the major components of a good contract and few, if any, had the clauses WSSDA sought. The major provisions included a full economic package, recognition, grievance procedures ending in binding arbitration, progressive discipline, evaluation, seniority RIF with strong recall language and strong working conditions. Many contracts also achieved class size provisions, teacher participation in curriculum and textbook adoption, student discipline and agency shop, a contract provision similar to a union shop requiring non-members to pay a fee equivalent to member dues.

Putting prototype contracts on the table turned out to be a fortunate decision. In the early stages school boards were less prepared than their local associations across the table. In later years they proved better prepared and more resistant to association proposals.

The years from 1976 to 1978 saw the greatest concentration of strikes in WEA history. In 1976 Seattle teachers, paraprofessionals and secretaries went on strike, primarily over salary. The strike lasted thirteen days in September and was the first strike under the new bargaining law. The Public Employee Relations Commission and Governor Evans played a key role in the mediation process.

A month later Everett went on strike for six days. The teachers there faced a school board willing to bargain economics but little else. In the fall of 1977 the floodgates opened. That year saw ten strikes lasting from one to twenty-three days in Sunnyside, Renton, Methow Valley, Ellensburg, Granger, Omak, Bainbridge Island, Central Valley, Aberdeen and (in March) Leavenworth.

These strikes were significant for two reasons. First, the majority were in small Eastern Washington districts like Methow Valley, Omak and Leavenworth, thus dispelling the myth that small districts could not strike successfully. Leavenworth proved to be the longest and most bitter strike, but in the end, despite weeks without pay, the thirty-three teachers there prevailed. Roger Cantaloube was the chief bargainer in the Leavenworth strike. He remembers that the real win for Leavenworth came in the second and third years of the contract with good salary increases each year.

Second, Aberdeen, veteran of the first K–12 strike in 1972, became the first to have a second strike. With harsh weather, scabs and many picket line incidents, this strike was much tougher than the first, but successful.

In 1978 the pace of strikes continued. They ranged in length from one day in Lower Snoqualmie to twenty-nine days in Tacoma's second strike. Second strikes also occurred in Seattle and Everett. In both strikes, the courts issued strong injunctions. In Everett, the District was prepared this time. It hired enough scabs to fully staff the classrooms and they were given four days' paid in-service training to prepare them. After two weeks, the District obtained an injunction and the court imposed $100-per-day fines on all teachers if they continued on strike. The court also strongly admonished the District that if it did not seek enforcement of the order, the court would sanction the District as well. The teachers returned to work but not before attorney Mitch Cogdill convinced the court to oversee the negotiations. Having to negotiate in the courthouse under the watchful eyes of the court, the judge caught the District off guard and put it in the position of having to actually deal with the issues it had flatly refused to bargain. The District found that it had lost more control over the bargaining process than it had during the strike. It was a signal to Districts that they might want to think twice before rushing to court to seek injunctions.

In Seattle, the teachers met to vote on breaking the injunction. But Seattle Teachers Association President Pete Neushwander, without explanation, omitted the last line of his carefully prepared speech, in which he was supposed to strongly recommend that his members remain on strike. His recommendation was considered crucial to getting the teachers to defy the injunction. The teachers voted to return to work, and in subsequent negotiations the teachers lost the right to grieve the content of their evaluations. That year was the last year any Association went back to work in the face of an injunction without first getting an agreement. Other strikes that year included Lake Washington, Central Kitsap (for the second time), University Place and Oak Harbor. The Tacoma strike that year set a longevity record of twenty-nine days that was to last until 1987 when Edmonds eclipsed it by a day.

By the end of the 1970s, most of the major bargaining battles had been won. Washington now ranked with states like Michigan, Pennsylvania, New Jersey and Wisconsin in the breadth and quality of teacher collective bargaining agreements. "WEA was in the top three states of the NEA family," said Bob Pickles, who had been active in Association governance in the early 1970s and later as a staff member in charge of instructional issues.

Education Seeks Resolution to School Crisis in Courts

Having failed three times to find relief to the school funding crisis with various income tax proposals put before the people, and with levy failures and RIFs at an all-time high, school districts sought relief in the courts.

Traditionally, Washington school districts had received a higher percentage of school funds from the state than the national average. In 1961 districts received 61 percent of their funds from the state, but by 1971 the percentage had dropped to 49 percent. With the Boeing recession of the early 1970s there was a rapid acceleration in the percentage of local funding. The increase came primarily from special levies that became increasingly difficult for districts to pass.

Special levies, which had been used by many districts since the 1950s, required a 60 percent favorable vote plus other onerous requirements that made it easy for tax-resistant property owners to oppose.

As we have seen, early attempts to address the school finance problem in Washington centered on tax reform that included constitutional amendments to provide for an income tax.

With the failure of tax reform at the polls, school districts next looked to the courts for relief. That idea stemmed from the school civil rights movement, which saw disparities in school finance as an equity issue just as in the early school desegregation cases.

In 1971 the California State Supreme Court issued its famous decision in *Serrano v. Priest*, which gave hope to those who supported school finance based on equity. Washington's disparity in school finance from rich to poor districts was much like California's. In *Serrano* the California high court said that the state's system of school finance based on local property taxes was unconstitutional because it did not assure an equitable educational opportunity for all children.

The first such case in Washington was brought in 1972 by the Northshore School District and other school districts. The theory put forth in the Northshore case was the same one put forth in *Serrano*. WEA did not participate but remained an interested spectator.

In December 1974 the state Supreme Court rejected Northshore's claim in a very fractured decision. Three justices rejected it outright. Three supported it, and three others concurred with the decision but suggested that Washington's system of school finance might be found unconstitutional on other grounds and with a stronger record.

This decision did not escape the attention of the Legislature, which in 1975 shifted property tax collections to the state and appointed Wallace Miller, a former state budget director, to study Washington's school finances and issue a report. He quickly prepared a September 1975 report that relied heavily on the recommendations of the 1971 School Formula Committee. The implementing legislation for HJR 47, HB 1128, was based on student-teacher ratios much like those that would be put in the Basic Education Act of 1977. This formula was the product of the School Formula Committee, created by the Superintendent of Public Instruction and the Joint Committee of the Legislature on Education. WEA lobbyist Perry Keithley was one of the formula's authors. In November 1972 the committee recommended a ratio of fifty certificated staff per 1,000 students, a ratio that was the state average at the time.

This report became the "reference book" for future school finance reform.

Nineteen seventy-five saw the highest rate of double levy failures in state history. It was particularly severe for Seattle, which lost 37.7 percent of its revenues. Governor Evans urged the Legislature to provide $100 million in relief statewide, but it provided only $65 million. Despite a veto of this watered-down measure, the Legislature refused to budge off its position.

As a result the Seattle School District and others brought another suit against the state. This time they did not rely on the equity theory advanced in the Northshore case. They argued that Article IX, Section 1 of the Washington Constitution required the State to provide an adequate level of funds, which the levy system was insufficient to do.

Article IX, Section 1 begins with the following sentence:

> It is the paramount duty of the state to make ample provision for the education of all children residing within its borders, without distinction or preference on account of race, color, caste, or sex.

In his famous 1977 decision, Thurston County Superior Court Judge Robert Doran ruled that this language had force and effect. He ordered the Legislature to define Basic Education and to fund its definition without reliance on special levies. These were to be used only for enrichment. He cited the Northshore case in saying:

> The State's constitutional mandate must be understood to embrace the educational opportunity that is needed, in the contemporary setting, to equip the children of this state for their role as citizens and as potential competitors in the labor market and the marketplace of ideas.

Doran did not require the Legislature to enact a levy lid.

While the case was under appeal, the Legislature went ahead and passed the Basic Education Act. In response to the Doran decision it defined Basic

Education and laid out a plan for the state to fund it. The timing was good, because a budget surplus allowed the Legislature to pass it without raising taxes. Despite WEA urging to the contrary, there was considerable consensus in the Legislature that it must contain a levy lid that would ensure legislative control over education costs. That was the first indication that WEA would not like all of what the Legislature would do in response to the Doran decision.

The Legislature also said that school districts could not use levy money for salary increases, the measure that Lonnquist was able to defeat in the state Supreme Court. This proved to be only a temporary win for WEA.

The Basic Education Act also adopted the fifty certificated staff (certs) per 1,000 students ratio for funding and also added many other restrictive provisions for student contact time, course offerings and the like.

In 1978 the state Supreme Court upheld Doran but extended the deadline for the Legislature to act until 1981.

By 1981, the state had gone into a recession, and the budget surplus had disappeared. The Legislature attempted to underfund the Basic Education formula in order to balance the budget. Again, Seattle and other districts, this time with the WEA as a party, took on the state in court in what became Doran II. Seattle Education Association President Reese Lindquist, on behalf of his school-age son, was WEA's plaintiff.

Doran ruled that the state had to fully fund its own formula and added special education and transportation to the requirement. The Seattle School District also tried to get Doran to require the state to provide an "urban factor." He declined to do so, requiring only those things that the Legislature already had enacted. No one appealed this case.

What Doran had done was to require the Legislature to act. He did not specifically tell them how to act to define and fund Basic Education. While full-funding advocates hailed his decisions and the Basic Education Act as victories, turning to the courts to resolve school funding issues in Washington proved to be a mixed bag. Some of the larger districts felt they were punished by the Legislature for taking them to court. Doran II was the last attempt to use the courts to solve school funding problems in Washington.

By 1988–1989 about 21 percent of school funds were local, about 73 percent were state and about 6 percent were federal.

State funding became a leveling process. While smaller, property-poor districts were brought up, larger, property-rich districts were brought down. This would have severe ramifications for bargaining in the 1980s.

Gil Gregory Replaces Verduin

From the day he walked in the door at WEA in 1973, Wendell Verduin was a controversial figure. He came from outside the organization. He was a corporate and government manager with no background in education or with unions.

He became Executive Director right at the time bargaining between the WEA Board and the Washington Education Association Staff Organization

(WEASO) was heating up to a strike. Though he was at the bargaining table, the board allowed him only to be an observer. WEASO blamed him for not taking a more decisive role in reaching a resolution.

According to Jim Aucutt, who became WEA President in 1975–1976, Verduin backed out of conflicts when he should not have. "This led to his downfall," said Aucutt. Verduin lacked the ability to be a staff leader. "He was going to manage the staff into place," said Aucutt.

According to Bill Hainer, Verduin was often in conflict with the staff. "He always had a script for staff meetings," said Hainer, "only to have the UniServ staff disregard it to deal with their issues. He did not like local strikes and conflict in general."

When WEASO returned to the bargaining table in 1975, Verduin again ran into a buzz saw. This time WEASO's chief bargainer was Communications Field Representative John Cahill. "The real mover on the WEASO team, however, was Bob Bell, who had years of experience in research," recalled Cahill.

Bell, who had risen from a chief bargainer for the North Shore Education Association to Research Director for WEA, managed to get through a three-year contract that had salary increases of 10 percent each year. That was also the year that WEA stopped covering locally employed UniServ staff in the WEA Staff Retirement Plan. This move alienated Kent UniServ Rep Cory Olson and others. "I felt pretty much alone and abandoned by the WEA," said Olson.

Soon after those negotiations, Verduin tired of confrontations with WEASO. He hired Bob Bell to be his Deputy Executive Director. Now Bell was on the management side of the table. It was not too long afterward that Bell became the one who had most of the direct face-to-face contact with the staff and WEASO. Aucutt remembers telling Verduin that he thought this was a mistake. "He wanted a buffer between him and the staff," said Aucutt. "I told him he had to become a staff leader."

In early 1977 WEA opened contract negotiations with WEASO to cut back on staff raises and to add a RIF provision to the WEASO contract. WEASO proved stubborn on both issues.

Later that year Verduin announced his plan to solve the budget problem by RIFing a number of staff and reassigning a number of others, some to other parts of the state. "I told him I'm not sure that's the best way to do it," recalled Aucutt. Longtime staff person Dale Troxel, for instance, was to be assigned to Yakima. All of this was to be effective on September 1. Yakima UniServ Rep Ken Bell was one slated to be RIFed.

Shortly after announcing his controversial plan, Verduin announced he was resigning on August 31.

According to WEASO President Cahill, WEASO felt the budget problem was more contrived than real and that the RIF was in retaliation for the role the staff played in the conflict with Verduin. WEASO had asked Research Director Don Murray to analyze the WEA budget.

Years later Hainer, Verduin's spokesperson in talks with WEASO, revealed that Verduin did have hidden funds. According to Hainer, Verduin threatened to fire any manager who revealed those funds. The funds were enough to have averted a RIF, but not enough to make the WEA budget healthy.

Bob Bell, slated to be the interim Executive Director until a new person could be found, was concerned that WEA would be split apart unless a compromise could be negotiated with WEASO before any RIFs took effect. He was in a bind, however, because Verduin refused to permit any further negotiations to take place while he was still Executive Director.

With the secret blessings of new WEA President Carol Coe, a longtime friend of Bell from their days in Northshore, Bell approached Cahill and initiated talks. Incoming WEASO President Jim Raines concurred. "Because of the secret nature of the talks," said Cahill, "Bell and I went to his summer home on a lake north of Seattle and spent an entire day working out a deal." All of the RIFs and the transfer of staff to other parts of the state were rescinded. WEASO agreed to five days without pay, but only if those days were without work.

On September 1, 1977, Verduin was gone, and WEASO held a morning meeting at the WEA headquarters and ratified the deal. Ken Bell got a phone call from Bob Bell the night before asking him to come to that meeting. "I told him he had fired me and I did not have to do what he told me anymore," recalled Ken Bell. "Then I got a call from Cahill, who told me I might want to be there!"

Now it was time to find a new Executive Director. That job fell to Coe. According to Coe, the board wanted someone who understood field organizing and could be an effective staff leader. The NEA ran the selection process. "At first," said Coe, "Herm Coleman, Executive Director of Michigan, was considered, but we selected Gil Gregory, an Assistant Executive Director for Field Services from Pennsylvania. Gil had the field piece over Coleman, and NEA recommended him."

Gil Gregory had begun his teaching career in 1959 in New Jersey at the Oakland Military Academy, making $300 a month plus board and room. Originally, he had started training to be an Episcopal minister, but washed out because he was "too liberal" in his views. He went into education because it seemed to be the next closest thing.

He ended up teaching sixth grade in Yeadon, Pennsylvania, in 1963, where he soon got involved in "professional negotiations." "Even before the law, we had the audacity to ask our school board for a contract," said Gregory. He rose in the regional and state levels of the Pennsylvania State Education Association.

Gregory became a Field Representative in 1967. During that time Pennsylvania expanded from thirteen to thirty-three field offices, and Gregory soon became an assistant to the Assistant Executive Director for Field Services.

Gregory did not seek the WEA executive position; it sought him. WEA made the first contact. "I interviewed twice and decided to take the job," said Gregory. "I was ready for a change."

One of the changes Gregory had to get used to was Washington's UniServ Program that was part local option and part state option. He was used to the entirely state-controlled UniServ programs in Pennsylvania and New Jersey.

When he came in he saw "a lot of tug-of-wars" going on. "There was a rift between staff and governance," said Gregory. "I figured if you can't fix this, then you're going nowhere fast."

Gregory became Executive Director in December 1977. He was immediately popular with the field staff, who felt he understood their work, and they were willing to follow his lead. But according to Bill Hainer, there was another side that the staff did not readily see. "I thought he was here to get control over the WEA and UniServ staff," said Hainer. If that was his purpose, he did it through leadership and some popular staff shifts. He put Dale Troxel in charge of the UniServ Program and in 1980 elevated John Cahill to Assistant Executive Director for Communications when Bill Davidson left to go into business for himself.

He also used bargaining with WEASO to strengthen unity. "The first round of bargaining straightened things out," said Gregory. He was able to use the process to explain many issues to both the staff and the board. "It helped a lot and put things in place," he explained.

WEA Moves to Federal Way

Even before Gil Gregory came to WEA, it was apparent that the WEA headquarters building at 910 Fifth Avenue in Seattle was too small to accommodate a growing Association and staff. The small parking lot could no longer accommodate the staff, and paid parking in downtown Seattle had become expensive for the Association. The boardroom could no longer hold a growing WEA board.

The board began talking about building a larger headquarters building. But where? Little seemed to happen until Gregory came on the scene. He favored the move and got the board to commit to it. "I pushed them to a yes or no to move them ahead," said Gregory. He put Bob Bell in charge of the project, including selling the current office, finding a new location and building a new office. "He did an excellent job," said Gregory. It was a big project for the Association. According to Gregory, the design changed ten times.

Olympia was a strong contender for a headquarters. Most state associations were located in their respective state capitals because that put them where they could best lobby their legislatures. Indeed, Gregory somewhat favored that location because he came from Pennsylvania, which had its headquarters in Harrisburg.

But a move sixty miles away to Olympia loomed as expensive, considering that all of the staff that would have to be relocated. "Federal Way was as far south as I could get them to go," said Gregory. At first the WEA located a spot near Southcenter, but that deal fell apart.

A piece of land in Weyerhaeuser's new West Campus Business Park was settled on and construction began in early 1979. The only thing controversial about it was Bell's plan to make it an open-concept building with staff located in cubicles rather than in the offices to which they were accustomed.

The architecture of the new building won an award for its design and outward appearance. For the WEA, it had the room and the parking the Association needed, and it was much closer to Olympia. Gregory recalled that the state was putting in new exits from I–5. It was more accessible to members and leaders coming in from around the state.

The move to the new offices took place in November 1979, even before the construction was completed. "The skylight over the central stairwell," recalled Cahill, "was not yet in place, and when the fog rolled in, the building filled with fog. Gregory simply closed down for a day or two until we could get the skylight in and the heat turned on!"

Association Finances

Gregory inherited the tight financial situation from Verduin. "When I came in I had to sit down with Bell each month and decide which bills to pay," said Gregory. "We got a change in the dues structure and got rid of the second Vice President."

Then the economy stepped in. "All of a sudden, interest rates went up on savings," recalled Gregory. "We bet on the come. We talked to a couple of banks and put as much money into protected funds as we could. Interest rates went up to 17 percent. That helped us take the next step. We were able to purchase all new better equipment when we moved to Federal Way."

However, there was a downside to having more money. "We had to deal with the people who knew you had the money," mused Gregory. "They all wanted a piece of the action. Governance wanted more; so did UniServ."

"During my first three years," recalled Gregory, "we made a lot of progress!"

Political Action

Equaling bargaining in intensity and scope, political action was the major Association achievement of the second half of the 1970s. It was, at least for a period of years, a defining moment for WEA.

Between 1976 and 1980 the Washington Education Association exploded onto the Washington state political scene with an unprecedented effect. In nearly every community throughout the state, WEA members volunteered in organized and targeted campaign activities. They came together in unprecedented numbers and exercised their political clout in a variety of campaign activities. Their innovative political organizing activities led to historic campaign successes.

Before 1976, the political action activities of the WEA consisted of WEA lobbyists and a few PULSE members helping some WEA-endorsed candidates in their campaigns. As we have seen, Dave Broderick, WEA's chief lobbyist, tightly controlled these activities. There had been attempts to implement a statewide political action program, but they failed because those who really supported a field-based statewide program could not prevail over Broderick's insistence on maintaining total control.

WEA Executive Director Wendell Verduin and President Carol Coe, among a few others, wanted the WEA to become a powerful political force. "Political action and the member lobbying program just made sense to me," said Coe. "The NEA had that model first. We needed to have members work legislative campaigns so they would be credible to lobby legislators later on."

In late 1975, they took a major step in this direction by hiring Steve Kink, who was the Olympic UniServ Council's director. Kink brought a political background and an organizing mentality to politics. "I believed that the ultimate members' political power rested at the grassroots level," said Kink.

He had demonstrated this power on a limited basis in the Olympic Council through coordinated levy campaigns, political rallies and school board and legislative campaigns. "The purpose of a political action program was to make Association leaders a major force in the political decision-making process at all levels," said Kink.

Kink had little time to create and deliver a statewide program for the 1976 fall elections. He started in January by traveling to each UniServ Council throughout the state to seek input from staff and leaders. It became clear that the program had to contain promotional as well as political organizing activities. "Many members were skeptical about being involved in politics," recalled Kink.

He also recognized that if members were going to be involved in delivering campaign activities to candidates, they had to have a say in the Association endorsement process of those candidates. This would require major changes in the way WEA's political action committee, PULSE, decided on candidate endorsements.

Kink spent weeks in the Washington State Supreme Court library developing Political Action Manuals, eight in all. The manuals were designed so that each UniServ Council's political action committee had state-of-the-art campaign and technical information to successfully organize and deliver in all phases of campaign activities. He also created a political action newsletter, which was directed at local leaders to help them promote political action among their members. New membership brochures also were developed to encourage members to contribute to PULSE.

Kink remembers seeing the new PULSE brochures for the first time at a staff meeting. He went slightly "ballistic" when he noticed major errors in the copy. Due to a lack of editing and poor typesetting and other errors, it called for members to support candidates running for "pubic" office. Forty thousand were scrapped and new ones had to be printed. "This is a helluva start to the program," Kink said.

"We also created a new school at WEA's summer leadership academy [then called VIP]," said Kink. This school was open to anyone in the first year. "We urged UniServ Council leaders and staff to send political action committee members who were committed to working on campaign activities." Every year thereafter, the school was by invitation and open only to those involved in political action activities, particularly targeted campaigns. He also developed a training program on precinct analysis for those who would be working WEA-targeted legislative campaigns.

Armed with these new political skills, staff, leaders and members embarked on their first statewide effort in the primary and general elections of 1976. Kink was elated with the results of the program the first year. "These elections," he said, "proved successful from the national, state and legislative levels. Most of the UniServ Councils involved in legislative targeted campaigns won. Hundreds of member volunteers participated in campaign activities."

Council PACs were involved in an assortment of campaign activities. "Some," recalled Kink, "were more sophisticated than others." Generally, members did activities that were less threatening, such as putting up yard signs, sending postcards to relatives, doing mailing projects, encouraging relatives and friends to vote for endorsed candidates and conducting member voter registration. A few staff and leaders were major players on campaign committees of endorsed candidates and were involved in complex campaign activities.

These initial successes thrust the WEA onto the state's political scene. "The political establishment," recalled Kink, "realized there was a new kid on the block who had some juice." However, the 1976 elections only scratched the surface of WEA's potential political strength.

This sudden emergence into the system also made the WEA a target for groups that opposed the Association, individual legislators who were against WEA legislative goals and those who resented the Association's political power.

The Washington State School Directors' Association continually harassed the WEA in the Legislature. They went after the Continuing Contract Law, and with the help of Senate Majority Leader August Mardesich, eliminated it for a year. Later, Alan Gottlieb, a far-right conservative, filed an anti-strike initiative aimed at teachers and the WEA.

Governor Dixy Lee Ray, elected in 1976, snubbed WEA leaders on several occasions because WEA had not endorsed her. "She even went so far as to cancel a bill-signing ceremony because she found out WEA was going to show up," recalled Coe.

Vice President Bob Pickles, who was sent to a Dixy Lee Ray fundraiser, remembers another snub. "We were going through a reception line and someone introduced me to Ray as a WEA officer," he said. "She turned her back on me and refused to shake hands."

Ray never really accepted the idea of teachers being unionized. In her mind, teachers should not have both "tenure" and bargaining rights.

The Republican Party, which by now was controlled by far-right conservatives, opposed virtually all of WEA's major legislative goals.

While others in the Association saw these actions as major shortcomings, Kink viewed them as great organizing opportunities. "Each of these actions could be attributed to an individual political target," said Kink. The members finally had specific political enemies. This gave more members more motivation to become politically active.

WEA's policies had to be changed to meet these challenges from political enemies and to promote pro-education candidates and issues. Between 1976 and 1980, it became apparent that the Association's process for deciding political endorsements and for generating money for campaign contributions needed revamping. PULSE had a $10 annual dues structure and only about 8000 contributing members. It simply wasn't enough for WEA to be a major player in school board, levy, legislative and statewide political campaigns. Before 1976, Chief Lobbyist Dave Broderick, in reality, made all endorsements. Those who actually paid the dues and did the campaign work had little or no say in who was endorsed.

"To attract huge numbers of volunteers to campaigns, members had to have a greater say in the process," said Kink. He also knew that unless they had a voice, it would be difficult to generate additional PULSE dues for campaign contributions. He recommended an endorsement policy that allowed the UniServ Council political action committees (PACs) to have an equal say in legislative endorsements. If agreement could not be reached between WEA's PULSE Board and the UniServ Council, the Council PACs could veto the legislative endorsement in their legislative districts. Local PACs could endorse in school board, levy, municipal and county elections if they desired. That left the PULSE and WEA Board with the decisions on endorsements of statewide candidates and recommendations to NEA-PAC for congressional and presidential candidates. "This new policy gave all levels of the Association a piece of the action in deciding whom to support in various elective positions," explained Kink.

The next change to take place was around the PULSE dues. The dues were raised from $10 to $13. A process called "reverse dues check-off" was implemented, which meant that all WEA members would pay the $13 PULSE dues unless they specifically filled out an opt-out form indicating that they did not want to contribute to PULSE. Once this was in place, a portion of the PULSE dues was rebated to the UniServ PACs to use in organizing campaign activities and to make campaign contributions. These changes more than quadrupled the amount of money that PULSE collected. Now, the Association had viable campaign funds to compete at the local, legislative and statewide levels.

While the WEA looked like the real deal in the 1976 elections, it was clear it had not reached its potential. WEA would have to build on its expertise through additional campaign training, candidate recruitment, voter targeting, doorbelling, phone banks and campaign management. "In addition to expanding skilled member volunteers in endorsed legislative campaigns, the WEA needed to knock off a political powerhouse," said Kink. "The choice was an easy one."

For 1978, it would be WEA's arch-opponent, Senator August Mardesich from Everett.

Other factors were also in play during the 1978 campaigns. Because of the 1976 successes, endorsed candidates wanted more WEA volunteers in their campaigns and wanted to direct them as well. The candidates had a hard time adjusting to the concept that WEA's political volunteers were working in their campaigns for the Association first and the candidate second. WEA insisted on directing its own volunteers. "To address this problem," explained Kink, "we implemented the campaign contract system." He had representatives from every UniServ PAC attend the summer VIP political action school. Each PAC developed its own campaign contract that it would use in its legislative races. The contracts stipulated exactly what each council PAC would deliver in campaign contributions and activities for the endorsed candidate, how it would be done and who would direct it. Most council PACs could determine what they could deliver because they had already assessed what their members were willing and capable of doing.

Another factor prevalent in the 1978 elections was the collaboration of major public employee unions involved in political campaigns. The primary players in this coalition were the state employees union, the state firefighters union, the police union, the trial lawyers and the WEA. State leaders and their political action staff would meet to share information and identify potential legislative candidates, raise campaign funds and coordinate campaign activities for mutually endorsed candidates.

An ominous trend was also developing during the second half of the 1970s. Ultra-right conservatives were taking over the Republican Party in the state. The moderate Republican candidates were being run out. The popular moderate Republican Governor Dan Evans was even refused a seat on the state delegation to the Republican National Convention. "These new conservative leaders were well funded and trained in the newest campaign technology," said Kink. "They were beginning to exercise their political clout by taking over the party, identifying articulate candidates and becoming skilled in campaigning."

The 1978 primary election was pivotal. The full force of two years of political organizing would be needed to unseat WEA's major target — August Mardesich — and to get newly identified candidates through the primary. "All the energy and effort paid off in spades," said Kink. The WEA successes were spectacular. Ninety of ninety-eight WEA-endorsed candidates made it through the primary. The political blockbuster victory, however, was the defeat of the most powerful state senator of the decade, August Mardesich. This was the greatest measure of WEA's political action program. His defeat brought acclaim to WEA in political circles far and wide.

One other political event occurred in the late 1970s — Alan Gottlieb, a far-right consultant, filed anti-teacher strike Initiative 363. He decided that he wanted to expand a mailing list that already included conservative groups. He would use this list to solicit contributions for conservative campaigns. "By running an initiative, he could add those who signed the initiative to his growing list," explained Kink. Gottlieb decided that an anti-teacher strike initiative would be the one to generate the most names. It certainly would be a feather in his cap to deal a critical blow to the WEA by making it illegal for teachers to strike.

This was a huge threat to the WEA membership. It became a WEA priority to stop Gottlieb from attaining the signatures to qualify for the ballot. This was a two-part strategy. One, it would stop him from qualifying the initiative, and two, it would limit the number of names in his mailing arsenal. Kink was put in charge of the campaign. WEA hired Armand Tiberio to assist in the campaign. Kink and Tiberio went directly to the strength of the association. They created a campaign aimed at every member in every local.

Kink and Tiberio developed and delivered campaign materials urging members and others not to sign the initiative. They created informational brochures, postcards for members to send to friends and relatives, and bumper stickers. These were distributed in every local association for leaders and members to use in their communities. Some members confronted those trying to gather signatures. They challenged them about the real purpose of the initiative. It turned out that many of those gathering signatures were paid to do so.

WEA was successful in stopping Gottlieb from getting enough signatures to qualify for the ballot. He was very active in the 1980 elections using his mailing lists and supporting far-right Republican candidates. Then his political activities were interrupted. He pleaded guilty to filing false income taxes and served time in a federal prison.

Members, leaders and staff who worked in these initiative campaigns gained political expertise that would be beneficial in future initiative and levy election campaigns. They also had a lot of fun. At a WEA Board meeting, Kink was presented a gift from Ron Gillespie of the Olympic UniServ Council. "When I unwrapped this large, long present, I found a complete pickup truck bumper that had a 'Don't Sign Initiative 363' bumper sticker stuck to it. My theory about bumper stickers was 'once on, always on.' "

Between 1976 and 1980, WEA put together an unparalleled political action program. It trained a core of member campaign organizers, involved thousands of members in campaign activities, changed WEA policies regarding PULSE contributions and endorsements, had major successes in two rounds of legislative races, defeated the most powerful senator in the state and defeated an initiative campaign to outlaw teacher strikes.

Political action had become a major priority in WEA's program. This program was built from leadership at the state level but delivered throughout the field structure of the organization. Dozens of UniServ staff, hundreds of leaders, state and local, and thousands of members committed themselves to defeating anti-education incumbents and electing pro-education candidates. "I thought it was important to reward their energy and work," said Kink. He made sure that there was a WEA election center set up for every election. "We all had our assignments in the field to call in the election results to the WEA's election center," remembers Toni (Jenner) Graf. "We were in our local courthouses tracking all the returns. We would call in the returns to Kink and he would tell us how well things were going on a statewide basis. We had our role, but felt part of the bigger picture."

The election night party was a lot of fun for those who could attend. However, most of the Association political zealots were involved with the campaigns throughout election night. Kink and Coe decided that a bigger celebration was needed. After each general election, Kink provided a list of those members, leaders and staff who really had delivered during the campaigns, and Coe invited them to a WEA celebration dinner. These dinners involved three or four hundred people. "They were quite the thing," said Kink. "People dressed up and had a great time. We handed out award certificates and they really appreciated the recognition for the work they had done."

On the eve of the 1980 election cycle, there were ominous signs at the national and state levels regarding a power shift from the Democrats to the Republicans, from the moderates to the conservatives and regarding the insurgence of the religious far right into the political arena.

By 1980, the National Education Association was supporting Jimmy Carter for reelection. He had been a good president on education issues and, at NEA's urging, had created the United States Department of Education. Rampant double-digit inflation plus the Iran hostage crisis made Carter vulnerable. The NEA wanted all state associations to get involved in the presidential primaries to ensure that Carter would get the Democratic nomination at the national convention.

WEA President Carol Coe wanted the Association to have an impact on the delegate selection process for primarily the Democratic State Convention. She also wanted to pass an education plank in both the Republican and Democratic Party platforms. "I was opposed to draining energy from the preparation for the primary and general elections because every state office, half the state Senate, all of the state House, all the congressional seats and Warren Magnuson's US Senate seat were up for reelection in 1980," recalled Kink. President Coe prevailed and Kink was told to organize a precinct caucus program through to the national convention in addition to preparing for the fall elections. The precinct caucus program was to exceed every expectation.

In the 1980 primary election, the WEA had established a major political goal, to defeat incumbent Governor Dixy Lee Ray. Ray had managed to alienate many other organizations besides the WEA, but she especially disliked the WEA. She had publicly supported August Mardesich in 1978 and generally opposed WEA legislative goals.

WEA found a willing candidate to run as a Democrat against Governor Ray in the primary. The candidate was Jim McDermott. He was a liberal and appealed to the membership. He was viable and the membership was excited because they wanted almost anyone who could take on Ray. Once again, many thought she would be hard to beat. However, polling indicated that Ray was vulnerable and that was all the WEA needed to fully support McDermott. "I thought that Ray could be beaten in the primary," said Kink, "but I had major reservations about McDermott's ability to beat John Spellman in the general election." However, defeating Ray was the major goal and it would be a huge WEA win if successful.

Kink assigned Linda Peretti to the McDermott campaign on behalf of the WEA. She was a zealot in pushing for additional Association support for McDermott's campaign. Because of her, WEA played a major role in the strategy and the delivery of campaign activities. McDermott did defeat Governor Ray in the primary and WEA had its second colossal primary victory in just two years.

The 1980 primary campaign was the height of the WEA membership's direct involvement in political campaigns. Over 10,000 members actually were involved in some political campaign activity on behalf of a WEA-endorsed candidate. This was roughly one-fourth of the total membership. To this day, WEA has yet to beat this level of membership involvement in a comprehensive political action program.

August Mardesich Campaign

Nineteen seventy-eight was a critical year for WEA's political action program. After two years of political organizing and training, it was time to flex some Association muscle. The major target was Senator August Mardesich.

Mardesich was an attorney and commercial fisherman from the 38th Legislative District, primarily Everett and bordering precincts. He was officially a Democrat but voted on the side of big business and against many union legislative goals. He was the majority leader in the Senate. In the 1970s, legislation seldom passed without his approval. WEA lobbyist Bob Fisher was in awe of his power. "I was amazed at his depth of knowledge, gained through reading nearly every legislative bill that crossed his desk," said Fisher. Known as Augie, he was the most powerful person in the Legislature. The 38th Legislative District was a safe Democratic seat and Augie was considered "untouchable."

If he was "untouchable," why was Mardesich the WEA's target? Among other things, Augie supported severely reducing employee retirement benefits. He was responsible for creating "Plan II" retirement systems for teachers and other public employees. With his support, the Legislature eliminated the Continuing Contract Law, leaving teachers without any due process rights for a year until a somewhat weaker version could be reenacted. He gave big business what they wanted, usually at the expense of employees and the unions that represented them.

After the 1976 elections, Don Johnson, WEA's chief lobbyist, and Steve Kink, WEA's political action director, began meeting with other public employee union leadership. The primary unions involved were the state employees union (AFSCME), the state firefighters, the state trial lawyers and the police officers. The purpose of these meetings was to develop a campaign coalition working in coordination to elect jointly endorsed candidates throughout the state.

Johnson and Kink shared the WEA's desire to go after Mardesich. There was much skepticism expressed by the other unions about being able to beat him. "After much persuasion," said Kink, "we decided to go all out, and go all out we did!"

Even Kink's own parents urged him to be cautious. Mardesich was a distant cousin of the Kinks and part of the same commercial fishing community. They feared that he would retaliate.

WEA and AFSCME took the lead in the coalition. They assigned Steve Kink and Mark Brown, AFSCME's political action director, to organize the campaign against Mardesich. Doug McNall from Everett was the state firefighters union President. He volunteered to join the campaign organizers. Kink was chosen as the campaign manager, Brown would coordinate union volunteer activity and help with the campaign's public relations, and McNall would provide critical in-district knowledge and run the yard sign activities. From the very beginning, these three knew that they were involved in something unprecedented in Washington campaign politics. "We all respected each other and worked well together," said Kink.

The first problem that the team encountered was that they had no candidate who was willing to take on Mardesich. They consulted their local union affiliates for names of potential candidates. Everyone seemed afraid to challenge him. According to Kink, "All the local political potentials were afraid of Mardesich or they thought that he couldn't be beat." Finally, McNall saved the day by talking Larry Vognild into running. Vognild was a retired firefighter and a political neophyte. The one obvious plus to begin with was that with his gray hair and stately looks, he had the image of a good candidate. The strategy became clear. Vognild would run as a Democrat against Augie in the winner-take-all primary. The chance of a Republican winning in a general election in the 38th District was minimal at best.

Another major concern was the limited potential of the Everett Education Association (EEA) to assist the campaign. EEA might be on strike during the campaign. The Everett school district boundaries made up most of the 38th Legislative District. It could be a problem in two ways. One, there would be few volunteers to draw from during a strike, and two, if it were a nasty strike (which it turned out to be), it could have a negative impact on the campaign. Larry Vognild would have to support the EEA strike because he was the candidate supporting the unions and their members.

The coalition then filed with the Public Disclosure Commission (PDC) as a political action committee so that they could raise funds for the campaign. This would be a challenge because each union had to have enough campaign contributions for all their other endorsed legislative candidates in addition to funding the campaign against Mardesich. Augie would have all the money he needed from big business. Kink and Brown came up with the idea to do a raffle.

Kink and Brown met with the PDC staff and the Gambling Commission staff and got approval to move forward with a campaign raffle. This was a perfect strategy because the raffle amount was legally limited to one dollar per ticket. This amount would sell easily within the union membership. "This fundraising strategy had never been tried on a statewide basis within the coalition unions' membership," said Kink.

The coalition unions set about informing their memberships of the campaign goals and particularly the Mardesich target. They distributed information about the importance of the campaigns and goals. Union leaders encouraged members to participate. They solicited volunteers to work in endorsed campaigns. Every type of union and association leader sold campaign raffle tickets, and volunteers were trained for specific campaign activities. Raffle tickets were sold at nearly every WEA, UniServ Council and local association function. Thousands of members bought raffle tickets.

On the WEA's part, Kink met with John Morrill, the Pilchuck UniServ Director, to deal with the potential Everett teacher strike. Morrill insisted that the campaign not use any of the Everett members during the strike. Kink agreed but asked for several things in return. One, would the EEA make a major effort to get their members out to vote; two, would they take the picket lines down on election day in those schools that were polling places; and three, could the campaign have access to all the other Pilchuck local leaders and members in the Council? Morrill and Kink agreed, and then they identified key leaders through the Pilchuck UniServ Council's Political Action Committee to be major players in the Vognild campaign.

Kink then brought them and other Association political activists to WEA's Olympia office, where he trained them in precinct targeting for WEA's targeted campaigns. Through this targeting, it became clear how many votes, and in which precincts, were needed to win.

At WEA's VIP Conference that summer, Kink had all the UniServ PACs report on their campaign plans and contracts with endorsed candidates. Many of them had set aside volunteers who were on call at any time to work in the Mardesich campaign.

Kink and Brown set up meetings during the summer with coalition union contacts in the area. They were something, according to Kink. "Union reps would bring in large paper bags full of money and raffle ticket stubs. Each meeting would produce several thousand dollars accompanied by hundreds of member volunteer commitments."

The Vognild campaign office was established on Ruston Way in Everett. The campaign message was: Senator Mardesich no longer represented the voters in the 38th District. He sold out to big business and forgot about the employees who supported him over the years. It was time for a new voice that represented everyone in the district. This message sold well in the historically unionized 38th Legislative District.

Brown did most of the campaign literature and newspaper ads emphasizing these messages, by identifying Mardesich's voting record and his public statements and by specifically identifying his campaign contributors. The comparison was made between Vognild as someone who represented people inside the district and Mardesich, who represented big business outside the district.

Later in the campaign, Kink decided to visit a local radio station and grabbed John Chase, who was working the Everett strike, to go along. It turned out that the station producer hated Mardesich and was willing to donate his time and talent to help develop several campaign radio spots. "We saturated the airwaves in the last days of the campaign," said Kink.

One day during the campaign, Kink was mentioning to McNall that it would be great if they had some inside intelligence as to which precincts Mardesich was working and what campaign pitches he was making. The next day McNall showed up with a list of Mardesich's targeted precincts and one of his doorbelling packets. "I started to ask some questions of McNall and then decided that I really did not want to know how he got this valuable information," said Kink.

Voters were targeted in three types of precincts. In the No. 1 targeted precincts, each voter would be contacted by some campaign activity a minimum of five times. The No. 2 precincts would be hit four times and the No. 3 precincts three. All of this would be done in the four weeks before the September primary election. This was supplemented by a massive yard sign blitz run by the firefighters in the targeted precincts.

"I insisted that no work be done in those precincts that historically voted Republican," explained Kink. "It is wasted energy. If they voted Republican, then they will vote it again, and the true Republican in this campaign is Mardesich." These precincts turned out to be Mardesich's major support, and his campaign worked them hard.

WEA members and leaders were crucial during the campaign. Darlene Hensley, from Marysville, was assigned the responsibility of coordinating volunteers for the mass mailings. She ultimately helped coordinate volunteers for doorbelling. Connie Christman and Deanna Thorpe, from Snohomish, worked with Association volunteers in various campaign assignments. Lorraine Evans from Mukilteo assisted with office activities. They developed volunteer goals for each local association in Pilchuck, except Everett, and assigned them to campaign activities. Hundreds of Association members from Marysville, Snohomish, Mukilteo, Monroe, Sultan and Lake Stevens volunteered in mailing, doorbelling and other campaign projects. They also helped in the volunteer coordination of other locals outside the district that provided volunteers to the campaign.

"The hardest part of the campaign was coordinating all the volunteers," said Kink. "On doorbelling days we would have busloads of union members from as far away as Spokane coming to help. Off-duty firefighters and policemen from all over the west side of the state would show up to volunteer. State, county and municipal employees would come by the carloads to doorbell or do what was needed. Association members would fill in the nightly activities during the week. However, they would also show up for the weekend activities. A major expense in the campaign was paying for the pizza and beer following each campaign activity. It was truly a great thing to see, the variety of union employees pulling together for their common good and enjoying each other's company."

Initially, Kink and Brown agreed that it would be best to keep Vognild away from debating Mardesich. They thought Mardesich, with all of his insider knowledge and political savvy, would chew him up in any confrontation. However, Vognild insisted on debating him. After much preparation on Vognild's part, they finally met in a public forum and he held his own. He did it by staying on message and attacking Augie on his record.

There was some extra money to spend late in the campaign, so Kink designed a very controversial full-page newspaper ad. The ad brought Governor Ray into the campaign on the side of her friend, Augie.

The ad consisted of the page divided down the middle with Vognild and Mardesich depicted on each side. In the background, on Mardesich's side, were a huge dollar sign and a list of all the corporations that contributed to his campaign. On the Vognild side was a picture of a crowd of people and list of all the organizations that endorsed him. The inherent message: Augie was bought by the corporations and Larry was the people's candidate.

Governor Ray went ballistic and decided she wanted to help Mardesich by coming to the district to hold a press conference. Many thought that this would hurt the Vognild campaign. Kink disagreed. "This was great," he said, "because we knew that most of the voters supporting Vognild also disliked Governor Ray. This would solidify the Vognild voters and bring some fence sitters over to our side."

Sure enough, she came to Everett ranting about the newspaper ad and threatened to take it to the State Attorney General's Office for possible prosecution. Mardesich seemed like an afterthought during the media attention around the ad. Ray only succeeded in bringing more attention to the ad. "The headquarters phones rang off the hook the next day from people calling to volunteer," said Kink.

After a huge get-out-the-vote campaign in the Vognild targeted precincts, election day finally came. Vognild won the primary election in those targeted precincts by 600 votes above what Kink had thought they could pull from the No. 1, No. 2 and No. 3 targets.

Vognild's election victory set several state campaign precedents. First, no other campaign had brought the collective union and association membership to focus in a coordinated manner on a single campaign. Second, it set a record for legislative campaign expenditures. The raffle alone raised well over $80,000, and that did not count all the additional contributions made by individuals and organizations. This came at a time when the average legislative campaign expenditure was around $35,000. Third, this legislative campaign used more volunteers than were generated in some statewide races. Nearly 3,000 individuals volunteered for some campaign activity, and that did not count those who purchased raffle tickets for the campaign. Fourth, it proved that someone who was willing to take the risk could beat an "untouchable" incumbent in a primary.

For the WEA, the Vognild/Mardesich race and the 1978 elections were the high-water-mark for electoral successes brought about through the WEA Political Action Program.

1980 Precinct Caucuses

Early in the 1980 presidential campaign the NEA endorsed the reelection of Jimmy Carter. To ensure that he would be the Democratic nominee, they urged all the state education associations to become actively involved in their state's primary elections or precinct caucuses. Washington state had a precinct caucus system to determine who would be delegates to the Democratic National Convention and which Democratic presidential candidate they would support.

WEA's impact on the 1980 caucuses would catch the attention of *Seattle Times* political columnist Richard Larsen. "The call for help went out to state education associations. Washington's, one of the best organized and active in the nation, heeded the call," wrote Larsen in a June 29, 1980, article.

Kink created a two-part program. The first part involved developing an education plank for the Republican and Democratic Party platforms. He created one that matched WEA's legislative goals so that any candidate running on the party platform would theoretically be supporting education. It was printed and disseminated throughout the Association at all levels. It included information about caucuses and directions so that any member, Republican or Democrat, could take it to his or her neighborhood precinct caucus, introduce it, and speak for its adoption.

The second part of the program was to get as many WEA members as possible to the Democratic caucuses to support Jimmy Carter and get elected to the district, county and state Democratic conventions as Carter delegates. This was a little more difficult to pull off. Some members were not Carter fans, and most precincts would have more members wanting to be elected than there were positions.

Ken Bumgarner, WEA President and Summit UniServ Council Rep

Sheryl (Graham) Stevens, Central Kitsap Education Association leader and UniServ Rep in Olympic and Riverside Councils

Marline Rennels, Olympic UniServ Rep and WEA UniServ Manager

Bob Bell, WEA Director of Research and Deputy Executive Director

Joann (Slye) Kink Mertens, WEA field support staff and Research Field Rep

Ron Gillespie, Central Kitsap Education Association President,
Olympic UniServ Council President and WEA Board

Mike Schoeppach, Fourth Corner and Bellevue UniServ Council Rep

John Chase, Chinook UniServ Rep

WEA Chief Lobbyist Don Johnson (right) talks with State Senate Majority Leader Gordon Walgren, ca. 1980.

Reese Lindquist, WEA President 1981–1985

Terry Bergeson, WEA President 1985–1989

WEA Staff Attorney Faith Hanna

*Warren Henderson, Seattle Teachers Association
President and bargainer, Seattle Assistant
Executive Secretary, UniServ staff in Tacoma and
Edmonds, and WEA support staff organizer*

WEA awarded Seattle Post-Intelligencer *political cartoonist David Horsey this plaque with an etching of his cartoon ridiculing the 1982 Legislature for cutting Basic Education funding.*

"YUH SEE, THE LEGISLATURE WENT KINDA **HOG-WILD** CUTTIN' THE BUDGET BACK IN '82 AN' THINGS HAS JEST SORTA SLOWED UP EVER SINCE!"

WEA political action leaders celebrate their election victories in 1982. From left to right, facing the camera: Joann Christopher, Mead; Nancy Arlington, Cheney; Carla Nuxoll, Mead; and Virginia Dally, Bellingham.

Bob Pickles, Enumclaw and ACT President, WEA Vice President, and WEA Instruction and Professional Development staff

In the fall of 1990 Mukilteo teachers went on strike for thirty-three days, a record up to that time.

Tacoma's Leon Horne played many roles in his local and in the WEA, but he is best known for serving two terms on the NEA Executive Committee — the highest-ranking NEA office to be held by a member from Washington.

Pilchuck UniServ Rep Mike Wartelle addresses striking Mukilteo teachers in 1990. Seated is John Morrill.

Northwest Region local presidents hold a news conference prior to the February 13, 1990, demonstration. North Shore President Greg Waddle (at the microphone) was the group's spokesperson.

On February 13, 1990, Northwest Region members take a day off from school to rally at the Everett Stadium. This was one of many protest activities around the state that day aimed at Governor Booth Gardner's lack of action on school funding. It was part of the buildup to the 1991 Multi-Local Strike.

Facing page: In July 1990 over 6,000 WEA members and supporters rallied on Fifth Avenue in Seattle to protest Governor Booth Gardner's refusal to address school funding needs. The theme of the rally was "No More Hot Air." The centerpiece was a large hot air balloon. Gardner was inside the nearby Westin Hotel hosting the Education Commission of the States.

Over 20,000 WEA members and supporters fill the Capitol Campus in Olympia during the Multi-Local Strike in 1991. It was the largest demonstration at the Capitol up to that time in state history.

CT Purdom, WEA President 1993–1997

Summit UniServ Rep John Ward (center) confers with Fife President Maggi Kellso (left) and longtime local bargainer Jerry Steinkraus during their thirty-seven-day strike in 1995.

From right to center: WEA President Carla Nuxoll, Executive Director Jim Seibert, and NEA President Keith Geiger (suit) lead 6,000 WEA members and supporters down Fifth Avenue in Seattle to begin the Education Commission of the States Rally.

WEA members gathered at the Capitol by the thousands over several days in 1999 to urge legislators to raise school employee salaries.

Steve Paulson, North Central and Spokane UniServ Rep, Program Director for Eastern Washington Restructuring Network

Instructional staff member Patty Raichle (right) with
UniServ Rep Nancy Murphy (left)

WEA President Lee Ann Prielipp addresses a rally in
Olympia in 1999.

WEA members and supporters gathered over 300,000 signatures for Initiative 732 in 2000.

The WEA utilized local and UniServ Council PAC chairs and Presidents to carry the message about how members should implement the program. WEA distributed 10,000 "I'll be there March 11" buttons, designed by John Cahill, to members statewide. Some locals and councils conducted mock caucus meetings to get members prepared and even decided who they would support at the next level. WEA set up a phone bank and, using a match of WEA members and the voter registration list, called members to remind them to attend their precinct caucuses.

The program called for an assessment after each phase of the process. "We had to know," Kink said, "if the plank was adopted, which members attended and which members were elected as Carter delegates after the precinct, district, county and state conventions." Member political activists played a major role in this part of the program, as did the state Democratic Party providing WEA with this information. "After each level of the process, we would communicate and in many cases bring the elected member delegates together and strategize for the next level," said Kink.

"To our surprise," said Kink, "more than 4,000 members attended the caucuses and 1,800 made it to the next level. Of the 700 delegates to the State Democratic Convention, 300 were WEA members."

Jim Russell in the Olympic Council was proud that they got 58 delegates to the county convention right in the back yard of Joe Murphy, the head of the state Democratic Party.

"WEA's Precinct Caucus Program was the best in the nation," said Bob Pickles.

"We learned again to never underestimate the power of the membership when it is committed and directed!" said Kink.

The Precinct Program brought immediate gratification because in almost every precinct across the state, the education plank was adopted and members were elected as Carter delegates. In fact, the single largest group of delegates to every level of the process, including the state convention, was WEA members. For many, it was their first involvement in party politics. They were making history.

The 1980 state Democratic Convention was held in the Hoquiam High School gymnasium. WEA-member delegates descended upon the convention with exuberance and a mission. Their primary goals were to get the education plank in the state platform and to carry the state delegation for Jimmy Carter to the Democratic National Convention.

Several events highlighted the convention. The member delegate parties were fun and added to the sense of purpose for WEA members as they mingled with other delegates and enjoyed the full experience of the convention.

During the convention, incumbent Governor Dixy Lee Ray tried to appeal to the delegates, only to be greeted with resounding boos and hisses. "It was get-even time for four years of snubs," said Kink. She stomped off the stage and left the convention. Her primary opponent, Jim

McDermott, was greeted with cheers. He was, of course, WEA's endorsed candidate against Ray.

Then Warren Magnuson, the senior US senator, was introduced to a standing ovation. He was in great Magnuson form and rallied the delegates around Democratic principles. He got the loudest cheers when he chided Dixy Lee Ray for not being a Democratic team player.

Finally, the time came for the delegates to elect the Washington delegation to the national convention. This is when the Precinct Program paid off in full. There were so many member delegates that several state elected officials would have been shut out of the national convention. After some negotiating by John Chase and others, several member delegates actually gave up their seats so that some elected officials could attend the national convention. The Washington Democratic delegation to the national convention ended up with sixteen teachers and Association staff out of a total of fifty-eight delegates. Ronn Robinson, an NEA staff person and past Bellevue UniServ Rep, was also elected the chair of the state delegation, beating out state party chair Joe Murphy. "The Democratic state chairman, who obviously had no control over the convention at Hoquiam, last week saluted the teachers' forceful showing, which caught him by surprise," wrote Larsen. The Precinct Caucus Program was so successful that no other state in the country came close to the percentage of member delegates attending the national convention.

"In 1980, teachers of the state, their Washington Education Association and its parent NEA, are surging to a new high of political impact in Washington State," wrote Larsen.

This was another WEA high-water mark in party politics.

The state Democratic Party was so overwhelmed by the political force shown by the Association that they changed some rules so that one group would not be able to exert this kind of influence in the future.

On Top of the World

In the early fall of 1980 the Washington Education Association, by all indications, had achieved unprecedented power and influence in the state.

Its successes were many.

In collective bargaining, most locals had achieved strong and comprehensive contracts. The ability to organize and execute teacher strikes was well established. Because of a strong local bargaining program, unfettered by state salary limitations and the false promise of "full state funding," teacher salaries had climbed from fifteenth in the nation in 1972 to sixth and by 1981 would top out at fifth in the nation.

Organizationally, the WEA had modernized and strengthened its governance structure. The separate departments were gone;

administrative membership and influence was all but eliminated. Carol Coe had demonstrated what a strong WEA President could achieve. Locals had come a long way in the decade, some from "tea and crumpet" organizations to powerhouses within their districts.

WEA's legal program, always one of its leading member services, had become a powerful influence in its own right. Judith Lonnquist had strengthened the WEA Network Attorney Program and dominated her school director opponents in making the new bargaining law an effective instrument for teacher collective bargaining. New attorneys had been added to the WEA staff. Network attorneys were winning cases that strengthened teacher employment rights and security. WEA had beaten back attempts by the Legislature to limit teacher salaries. And WEA was winning education cases of statewide importance.

Conflicts within the WEA largely had been brought under control. Verduin was gone and Gregory generally had the confidence of the staff and the governance. Coe was a master at reducing conflict between staff and governance while at the same time building a strong presidency.

The UniServ Program was one of the strongest in the nation. Organizing was still its core tool. The program had bargained strong contracts across the state in five short years. And that staff proved it could shift gears and organize effectively in the political arena. The program was more firmly integrated into the WEA. More councils had become state option without any of the predicted dire results. UniServ had become the core program of the WEA, and fights over WEA funding were a thing of the past.

Legislatively, WEA had won its goal of a strong collective bargaining law for teachers. With what appeared to be a minor setback with the passage of Teacher Retirement System Plan II, teacher pensions remained strong. Besides, most members believed Plan II would not become an issue of concern until the next century! The Continuing Contract Law had been restored almost to its pre-1975 strength, losing only the right to have cases heard de novo in superior court. WEA had initiated a strong member-lobbying program under Coe's leadership, and it was tied to a robust political action program with heavy local association participation.

WEA had taken its bargaining organizing successes and applied them to political action. The successes in the 1976 and 1978 elections, capped with an unprecedented victory over Senate Majority Leader August Mardesich, made WEA a major player in the state's political arena. Successes in the 1980 precinct caucuses gave WEA the ability to dominate the State Democratic Convention in Hoquiam and ensure a teacher-dominated and pro-Carter delegation to the Democratic National Convention. In the September primaries WEA had helped Jim McDermott defeat Dixy Lee Ray. WEA political organizing for the November elections had picked up where 1978 had left off. Over 16,000 members, or well over a quarter of the Association membership, had worked in both the 1978 and 1980 elections.

All of this success had built a strong membership base of enthusiasm and participation in Association programs. Member energy was a driving force that seemed to foretell continued success.

Clearly, the ninety-one-year-old WEA, on the eve of the 1980 November general election, was at the peak of its power. Association leaders assumed its power simply would continue to grow.

CHAPTER FIVE

Response to Adversity

Even before most people in Washington had voted on November 4, 1980, all the major television networks had projected a landslide victory for Ronald Reagan. Incumbent President Jimmy Carter conceded the election hours before the polls closed on the West Coast. Just the night before, he had given a rousing campaign-ending speech in a hangar at Boeing Field attended by thousands of Democrats, including WEA members. A small group of local college conservatives, among them John Carlson, a future conservative talk radio host and a 2000 Republican candidate for governor, snuck in with Carter campaign signs and interrupted the rally with anti-Carter taunts.

Gil Gregory, Carol Coe and the handful of WEA stalwarts who had gathered at the Association's election-watch party at the Olympic Hotel in downtown Seattle could only watch in stunned silence as the Reagan landslide swept through forty-four states, including Washington. John Spellman handily beat Jim McDermott for Governor. Republicans swept the state House of Representatives by a margin of 56 to 42. Democrats lost several seats in the Senate, but hung on to power by a narrow 25-to-24 margin. Slade Gorton ended the Senate career of Warren Magnuson. Magnuson had been senator since the days of Franklin Roosevelt and was most recently President Pro-Tem of the US Senate.

Hired only weeks before the election, WEA staff attorney Faith Hanna attended the party. "It was depressing!" she recalled. Carol Coe, one of the architects of WEA's aggressive political action program and a WEA Carter delegate to the Democratic National Convention, was stunned by the defeat.

The election results were a blow to the thousands of WEA members who had worked so hard in the election. "It was devastating and we couldn't believe it," said Leslie Kanzler, who had run the Chinook Council's phone banks.

Toni (Jenner) Graf (her brother Bob Thompson was the state's Carter campaign coordinator) said, "We were really into political action, and we were used to winning. This shocked us."

According to Steve Kink, they had made over 200,000 voter identification phone calls, doorbelled some 500 precincts, put up 20,000 yard signs, polled 3,000 registered voters in twelve legislative districts, mailed campaign literature to 650,000 voters and distributed half a million other pieces of literature. It was not only difficult to understand the impact of Reagan's conservative movement; it was also difficult to comprehend how WEA would survive the legislative session coming up in two short months.

The Republicans who had taken over the House were not of the Dan Evans stripe; they were ultra-conservatives bent on putting WEA in its place. WEA would face the likes of Bill Polk, who would be Speaker of the House, and Ellen Craswell from Silverdale, who represented the new religious far right in politics. Bellevue Representative Rod Chandler drove home the election losses when he declared to a meeting of local WEA leaders, "We won and you lost!"

"He was really just telling us the truth," said Gil Gregory.

WEA's losses in the 1980 elections would prove to be just the first of several defeats for the Association in the early 1980s. WEA's response to these defeats would shape its fortunes for the remainder of the decade.

1981 Legislative Session

With a big majority of Democrats in the Senate in 1980, WEA had kept salary limitation legislation from surfacing, but 1981 was another story.

Smarting from losing to the WEA in the state Supreme Court over House Bill 516, passed in 1979 to cap teacher salaries, the House returned in 1981 with HB 166 carefully drafted to eliminate the legal flaws in 516. In addition, WEA faced a formidable list of anti-education legislation, most of it in the House. Bills included:

· Making teacher strikes illegal
· Prohibiting negotiation of the school day
· Placing all teachers in the state employee insurance program
· Establishing lengthy bargaining timelines and, as a last resort, submitting final offers to a vote of the people in the district
· Requiring the cost of fact-finding to be shared equally by the parties
· Requiring the equal treatment of "creationism" along with any teaching of evolution
· Requiring prior parental permission for sex education
· Requiring teacher competency tests

- No longer requiring private school teachers to be certificated
- Asking the President to abolish the Department of Education created under President Carter
- Allowing school districts to appeal hearing officer decisions in dismissals under the Continuing Contract Law
- Three-year probationary or provisional period for new teachers

Unlike the late 1970s, when the state had a budgetary surplus large enough to implement Basic Education without raising taxes, the state now faced a large deficit. Anticipated budget cuts were just one more piece of negative legislation facing teachers in 1981.

WEA clung to the hope that it could stop most negative bills in the Senate, and as a last resort seek a veto from Governor Spellman, a political moderate with whom WEA had built a relationship. "We had no ability to be on the offense in the Legislature," recalled Gil Gregory. For just over a month into the session, WEA's strategy held most harmful legislation at bay.

But on Friday, February 13, 1981, even that strategy would evaporate. Democratic Senator Peter von Reichbauer from Federal Way, and a friend of Spellman's, switched parties, throwing control of the Senate to the Republicans. Party control by the Democrats had been important. Even though a few Democrats supported HB 166, Majority Leader Ted Bottiger could bottle it up in committee and keep it from coming to the floor. Now Republicans controlled all of the committees and could move any bills they wanted to a vote. Even von Reichbauer's promise to WEA not to vote for HB 166 proved to be of no help.

On March 20 the Senate passed HB 166 by a slim margin and sent it to the Governor. The bill said in part: "School districts shall not grant pay increases in excess of amounts or percentages granted by the Legislature." The limitations applied not only to salaries but also to health benefits. And they applied to both certificated and classified employees. There would be no room for any challenge in the courts. WEA's primary argument against the bill was that by removing salary and benefits from the bargaining table, the Legislature was taking away the one ingredient — money — that made bargaining work. WEA's aggressive bargaining posture would be dealt a blow that would have devastating effects for years to come.

A few days later Governor Spellman had the bill on his desk, and Carol Coe and Gil Gregory made a trip to his office to ask him to veto it. "I tried to get him to not sign it," said Coe. He listened, but remained non-committal. As Coe and Gregory were walking back to the WEA Olympia office, Spellman signed HB 166. "That ended our relationship with him," said Coe. It was the second major defeat for a WEA that had been at the peak of its power just months before. The bill number "166" would live in the WEA vocabulary for decades to come.

The WEA lobbying team, including more than 150 member lobbyists, had managed to defeat most other negative bills proposed that session, but in the remaining days it faced a budget that proposed heavy cuts in education.

With the help of John Cahill, who was by now Assistant Executive Director for Communications, Carol Coe mounted an ambitious one-day, five-city news conference in April, using a chartered four-seat airplane. In Olympia, Seattle, Yakima, Wenatchee, Spokane and the Tri-Cities she spoke to reporters, urging the Legislature to fund Basic Education as mandated by the Doran decision and to abandon the pieces of negative legislation remaining before it.

But before the Legislature adjourned on April 26, it passed a budget that slashed education funding. Cuts included $154 million in Non Employee Related Costs (NERCS), $85 million in handicapped education, $45 million in school transportation and $15 million in substitute costs.

On May 5, some 2,000 teachers gathered in Seattle to protest. Democratic Senator Marc Gaspard from Puyallup called the budget "targeted misery."

In September, with schools struggling with tight budgets, the WEA filed an injunction in Thurston County Superior Court to stop legislative cuts in education funding. The shortfall represented about a 10 percent across-the-board cut in Basic Education. The WEA suit was based on Judge Doran's decision in the Seattle I or Doran I. Judge Frank Baker declined the injunction, deferring to the Supreme Court, which by now had Doran II pending before it.

Union Busting

The climate for successful union activity across the nation was dealt a severe blow early in the Reagan administration. The Professional Air Traffic Controllers Organization (PATCO), ironically one of the few unions to back Ronald Reagan for President in 1980, went on strike. These people were federal employees, and like teachers in Washington, they had no express right to strike.

Rather than negotiate, Reagan ordered them back to work. In a few days, with PATCO still on strike and with supervisors filling in, Reagan fired all of the striking air controllers and set about to permanently replace them. To the growing anti-union sentiment among the political right, Reagan was an instant hero. For unions and those who supported unions, Reagan's action had a severe dampening effect.

The PATCO disaster raised the specter of Timberline, New Hampshire, and Hortonville, Wisconsin, where teachers in those small rural districts had gone on strike in 1972–1973. In both districts the school boards had hired replacements and dismissed the striking teachers. Continued strikes in both districts proved futile. NEA organizers close to both actions wrote papers urging caution in similar districts. Now, state associations, including

Washington, began implementing strike approval processes and even, in some cases, intervening to avert strikes before they started.

The combined effect of the 1980 election results, the passage of HB 166, memories of the Timberline and Hortonville strikes, and the PATCO strike caused many local associations to pull back and take a more conciliatory approach in bargaining. WEA continued to do what it could to rally local associations from the state level, but for many at the local level, the energy for hard bargaining waned.

On March 28, 1981, WEA held a statewide bargaining conference in Ellensburg to prepare local associations for "hard bargaining" ahead. One hundred sixty-eight local bargainers attended. Jim Raines and others laid out many ideas for bargaining additional money that would not run afoul of HB 166, but despite the bravado, the response was muted.

1981 WEA Elections

By 1981 Carol Coe had served for five years as President. She had created the strong presidency in WEA and had overseen many of the Association's greatest successes. She ushered in strong political action and member lobbying programs. Contract bargaining came of age during her presidency. WEA's legal program became one of the strongest in the NEA family. And she restructured the governance of the organization.

Through these times she had united the Association around strong bargaining and political action programs and had little tolerance for those who would threaten that unity. Her supporters and detractors alike recalled getting phone calls from Coe pulling them back in line. She usually handled conflict behind closed doors, sparing the other party and protecting the unity of the Association. According to Coe, she never publicly aired conflicts between staff and governance because she believed it would appear that the Association was split. She kept the Association united and moving ahead at full tilt by her energy and force of will.

She developed a strong constituency among local Association Presidents and pulled many of them into leadership roles. Most of them were women, but that was never the focus of her efforts. She did work hard throughout her time at WEA, both in the Association of Classroom Teachers and as President, to bring people of color into active Association roles.

She counts Leon Horne, a Tacoma Elementary teacher, among those people she promoted into Association work. Horne had started teaching in 1972 and was active in both the 1974 and 1978 strikes in Tacoma. Horne was a six-foot-four-inch African American with a friendly personality. When he decided to run for the WEA Board in 1978, Carol Coe helped him out. He was running against two other TACT members in a board district that included Tacoma and Clover Park. "Carol Coe," he recalled, "said I should go to the Clover Park Representative Council to campaign. The other two candidates did not go there. Clover Park put me over the top. Later, she appointed me to the board bargaining team ahead of some more senior people."

Horne went on to be elected to Coe's Executive Committee. "We were Carol's army on the Executive Committee," said Horne. "She was a great President. She knew what she wanted to do and where she wanted the Association to go."

The 1981 elections for both President and Vice President would prove to be the most tumultuous in the Association's history. As they approached, Coe was very concerned about turning the reins of office over to someone she felt would be a strong leader and could maintain the unity she had built. Her second-term Vice President, Bill Miller from Lake Washington, was running against board member Jeff Wahlquist from West Valley of Yakima. Coe had recruited Wahlquist into Association work, and he had risen fast. Coe was concerned that Miller was not suited to be President. She was doing what she could to quietly help Wahlquist.

Less than two months before the election, word got to Coe that the Miller campaign was prepared to raise a personal issue about Jeff Wahlquist that would be detrimental to his candidacy. Coe was afraid that Miller would win the election.

That's when Horne played a vital role in the outcome of the 1980 elections. "I got a call from Carol about a month and a half before the elections," recalled Horne. "She told me to go to Yakima and tell Jeff [Wahlquist] that because of this information, he can't run. He has to step aside. I flew to Yakima and met Jeff's friend Rick Fulton (also on the board and, years before, Wahlquist's master teacher), and together we met with Jeff in a local bar. We told Jeff. He did not like it, but he decided not to run."

"I called Carol and asked her to pick me up at the airport. Then the wheels got in motion to run Reese Lindquist."

Reese Lindquist was then President of the Seattle Teachers Association, and Seattle had just completed bargaining a new contract that his members liked and that had given him wide visibility in the Seattle news media. For someone who had not been a WEA officer and had not even been on the board, he was well known and respected. He had been a teacher and football coach at Queen Anne High School and had become active in the Seattle Teachers Association following a dispute with his principal. He was active in the 1976 Seattle Strike and was Vice President and a zone coordinator in the 1978 strike. "I was the only top leader in that strike who stood up in the general membership meeting and recommended they stay on strike in the face of an injunction," recalled Lindquist.

Carol Coe knew he was the only viable candidate who could run successfully against Miller. "Reese was the only one with the power to win," said Coe.

"I agreed to run," said Lindquist. "Her support was critical. The next thing I knew, I had all these supporters!" He had but six weeks to mount a campaign. His campaign chair was Bob Maier, President of the Mercer Island Education Association, where his younger sister Mary was a teacher. His campaign chose to make leadership in troubled times its theme. His campaign signs read: "Reese Lindquist — A Leader Equal to the Challenge."

His first campaign stop in the Olympic UniServ Council was less than encouraging. "They took a straw vote," said Lindquist. "I got only one vote!" He did better, however, when he went to the Tri-Cities. "Toni Jenner took me out to the locals," said Lindquist.

"I met with Lindquist," recalled Jeff Wahlquist. "I agreed to support him if he gave me a couple of committee chairs." Board member Lee Ann Prielipp, a Coe supporter, said Lindquist was easy to support. "He acted very presidential," she said.

By the time of the Representative Assembly, Lindquist had closed ground with Miller and felt he would win, but he thought he still needed more votes. "I had to pick up three or four more votes on the floor to win," he recalled.

According to Lindquist, his campaign, besides carrying his large Seattle delegation, did well in Mid-State, Southeast Washington, Vancouver, much of the Puget Sound corridor outside of Lake Washington and Bellevue, Fourth Corner and the smaller units in King and Pierce counties.

When the votes were counted, Lindquist beat Miller 339 to 293.

The race for Vice President proved equally dramatic and had a long-range effect on the WEA. It was a three-way race involving Spokane President Judy Feryn, Federal Way Board member and past local President Lee Ann Prielipp, and Tacoma board member Terry Bergeson. Lee Ann Prielipp entered the race early and garnered the support of another Tacoma board member, Leon Horne.

"That's when Terry and I parted ways," said Horne. "I had become friends with Lee Ann. She asked me to support her for Vice President long before Terry decided to run. Terry was furious, and I told her I would not go back on my word. TACT President Elaine Miller told me it would make Tacoma look bad, so I gave Lee Ann quiet support."

Terry Bergeson, who had been on the WEA Board since 1976 and active in the Women's Caucus she had helped form both in Washington and at the NEA, had become a controversial figure with strong supporters and strong detractors. Jeff Wahlquist recalled meeting Bergeson at one of his first board meetings. "She had long hair, smoked up a storm and cussed. She never appealed to the mainstream. I didn't like her." But more importantly, "she was the best one-on-one organizer I've ever met." According to Horne, she was very confrontational. Lee Ann Prielipp also had an unfavorable opinion of Bergeson. "I remember Terry when she was Board Budget Chair," said Prielipp. "She flaunted being chair and had a reputation for being brash."

Bergeson's supporters liked her for many of these same traits and disliked what they saw as a double standard. For them Bergeson represented a much-needed challenge to the male-dominated Association. They saw her brashness as being nothing more than the way they saw the men behaving, especially the UniServ staff.

On the first ballot Feryn and Bergeson got the most votes, but neither had a majority. Lee Ann Prielipp went to the microphone and threw her support to Judy Feryn. "That's when I gave the best speech of my life!" said Prielipp.

The run-off balloting was conducted right after the lunch break. Bergeson won 294 to 280. What made the close outcome even more intriguing was that most of the large Spokane delegation had not returned from lunch in time to vote! According to Executive Director Gil Gregory, the vice presidential race had been overshadowed by the Lindquist-Miller race. "There wasn't the same follow-up (by the Feryn campaign) on the Vice President's race," said Gregory.

Organizing Classified Employees

In the late 1970s the issue of organizing classified school employees — secretaries, teacher aides, custodians, bus drivers, etc. — had landed on WEA's agenda. It would prove to be a controversial issue for many years to come. For almost ninety years WEA membership comprised teachers, other certificated employees (such as counselors, librarians, nurses, etc.) and their administrators, exclusively. Little thought had ever been given to opening up the ranks to anyone else.

But with collective bargaining now the centerpiece of the Association's program, more people began seeing advantages to representing all school employees. The issue was now being defined in terms of added bargaining power.

There were already a few precedents for classified organizing in Washington. Mercer Island represented both teachers and school secretaries. Stan Jeffers had organized school secretaries in 1969 just after Washington classified school employees had achieved a collective bargaining bill, RCW 41.56. In 1971 the Seattle School District was set to fire nearly all of its teacher aides. The Seattle Teachers Association, wanting to preserve them, mounted a card drive and gained bargaining rights for them. Warren Henderson negotiated their first contract and in the agreement changed the term for them to "paraprofessionals." In 1973 secretaries and nurses selected the Seattle Teachers Association as their bargaining representative. That year Seattle did something no other local had done. It bargained four contracts using a single bargaining team. In 1974 custodians and maintenance workers joined them at the bargaining table, though they kept their own union.

But the most dramatic example of how such organizing could demonstrate real bargaining power came about during the 1976 Seattle Strike. That strike was in reality three strikes with one bargaining table. Under the new negotiations law, nurses were now a part of the certificated bargaining unit. Besides teachers, Seattle's Office Professionals and Paras (for paraprofessionals) also were on strike. The shutdown of the District was absolute. No one thought of trying to open with strikebreakers.

In all of these cases classified employees were local members but not WEA or NEA members.

These seemed just anomalies until Roger Cantaloube entered the picture. At some point in 1978 he got a call from the Spokane Diocese asking him to bargain for its teachers. "I brought it up with Bill Hainer," said Cantaloube, "but he did not want to organize them." One important reason: organizing private school employees would require the WEA to come under the federal Landrum–Griffith Act, which had stringent reporting requirements. WEA was not prepared to go there.

Cantaloube was not ready to drop what he saw as a good idea. New Executive Director Gil Gregory had come from Pennsylvania where the Pennsylvania State Education Association had bargained for classified school employees. He, like Cantaloube, believed there was organizational strength in organizing "wall-to-wall." Cantaloube approached him with the idea. "I convinced him to organize classified employees, but I told him there would be no money in it," recalled Cantaloube.

Gil Gregory and Carol Coe convinced the board and the RA to allow classified organizing, and by 1979 the RA gave them affiliate status in WEA. The group came to be called the Classified Public Employees Association (CPEA), a name Cantaloube came up with because he felt it could serve as an umbrella name for organizing public employees outside education sometime in the future. It had its own board of directors, but was tied to WEA. It was clear that the CPEA would not have full membership rights including the right to vote and hold office in the WEA.

Gregory had been through all of the battles in the Pennsylvania State Education Association over classified bargaining and decided to proceed cautiously. "There was no intent at first," said Gregory, "to go for full membership."

"At a staff meeting Gil Gregory asked if anyone was interested in working with classified employees," said Cantaloube. "I raised my hand."

Cantaloube encountered resistance from both governance and staff. Some, like Summit UniServ Rep Ken Bumgarner, felt there was not a sufficient "community of interest" among teachers and other school employees. Others saw only added work and no real money for council bargaining programs, which by now had all the bargaining they felt they could handle.

"I just plowed ahead," said Cantaloube. "By the end of the first year I had thirteen new units and thirteen new contracts. All of the recognition clauses read WEA/CPEA. I was at the bargaining table in every new unit between Port Angeles and Finley. None of the local UniServ staff wanted to do the bargaining."

According to Cantaloube, organizing the Classified Public Employees Association proved to be "tough duty." "I put in a lot of windshield time," he said. It was tough in another way too. According to Cantaloube, both

Hainer and Bob Bell complained because the Classified Public Employees Association was costing the Association in staff time and not bringing in much money.

Because of these pressures, complicated by personal issues, Cantaloube left the WEA for a year and a half. Shortly thereafter WEA hired Kristeen Hanselman to fill the vacated post and classified organizing moved ahead. She was able to bring in some classified members temporarily to share the increased workload.

In 1984 Warren Henderson took over classified organizing and bargaining. Karen Hartman from Vancouver soon joined him, first as a temporary employee, then as a regular.

Pressures for full membership rights grew, and at the 1980 Representative Assembly, a constitutional amendment was presented that would give classified members full rights in WEA. It failed to pass. In the 1981 RA the amendment was back again. In the regular balloting it had failed to get the two-thirds vote required for passage. Constitution and by-law amendments are done by a secret paper ballot election, but it was not unheard of to reconsider and bring up a failed issue on the floor, where voice votes are taken. After the tension-packed elections for President and Vice President, the issue was on the floor for debate.

Reese Lindquist, a staunch supporter from his roots in Seattle, sought a united front in support of the amendment. Carol Coe, in her last RA, was pushing it hard but needed strong support from the floor.

This was the start of an open break between Reese Lindquist and Terry Bergeson.

"I went to Terry and asked her to speak for it from the floor," said Lindquist. "She turned me down. She said her supporters would not understand it."

According to Terry Bergeson, she declined because she objected to using a voice vote to replace the secret ballot. "After that, I never got into any inside decisions," said Bergeson. "There was nothing I could do to get back on his right side."

The final vote that year was only 62.7 percent in support. It would have to wait until the next year.

At the 1982 Representative Assembly, Reese Lindquist was better prepared. "I used my campaign committee, headed by Bob Maier, to be the Committee for Full Membership Rights," said Lindquist. The campaign started well before the RA. "We had to work on it all year," he said. The Communications Division created a brochure to be used by organizers for the amendment.

In 1982 Bergeson also supported Amendment 1.

On the first vote Amendment 1 fell just two votes shy of passage. It was reconsidered and brought to the floor. On that second vote it passed 421 to 187 or with 69.25 percent of the vote. When the vote was announced, eighteen

CPEA delegates, who up to this point had sat in the visitors' gallery, were immediately seated on the floor as delegates with the full right to debate and vote. A few minutes later, in an emotionally packed scene, Lindquist recognized a classified member from Shoreline waiting her turn at one of the floor mikes to debate a motion. She began simply by introducing herself. "I am Josie Merns — delegate," she said. A rousing round of applause interrupted her.

In the mid-1980s no-raid agreements with competing unions slowed the rate of acquiring new locals, as did the practice of organizing very small locals. But by the late 1980s UniServ Councils were doing most of the classified organizing and bargaining. The Classified Public Employees Association was closer to being totally integrated into the normal WEA structure.

Although some of the controversy over organizing classified school employees would linger, CPEA, later to be renamed Educational Support Personnel (ESP) after the name NEA used, continued to grow and prosper in WEA.

"A Nation at Risk"

In April 1983 the education establishment all across the country was shaken by the release of the Nation at Risk report written by a prestigious group of educators and sponsored by the Carnegie Foundation. In dramatic terms it laid out what it felt were the failures of public education across the country. It was a ringing call for educational reform.

When the report was closely examined, it was not only a call for structural changes and for placing a greater emphasis on educational excellence; it was also a call for greater resources. However, government leaders tended to overlook that aspect of the report.

Instead, the report became a focal point for those who wanted to declare public education a failure. "It focused a lot of negative energy on education," recalled Reese Lindquist. "The opportunity to do something about education was never taken. I had a meeting with Reagan's first Secretary of Education, Terrell Bell. He wanted me to speak to [NEA President] Willard McGuire to work with the Department of Education on issues. It did not last long. Bell couldn't deliver. Reagan did not want to do anything. Bell fell out of favor with the Administration. At about the same time, McGuire was going out of office."

On top of everything else that had rocked the WEA in the early 1980s, the Nation at Risk report was just one more blow. Reese Lindquist wanted to use the report in a positive way and turn it back on the critics. With board approval, WEA created a fourteen-member commission of its own called the Washington Commission on Educational Excellence, jointly chaired by Lindquist and Highline Community College President Shirley Gordon, who had been a member of the national commission. Bergeson was also on the Commission. WEA appropriated $85,000 for the work.

The Commission produced a comprehensive report entitled "Reducing the Risk: Educational Renewal for Washington's Future." It outlined needed changes in Washington's public education system, including a call for the state to provide the resources necessary to carry out the recommendations.

The WEA report was printed in an impressive-looking book and distributed widely across the state. Copies were sent to the Governor and to every legislator. For the next several years, that report served as the basis for WEA's legislative agenda with respect to educational excellence. But the mood within the state Legislature and in the Reagan administration was not favorable to spending any additional money on education.

Looking back, Lindquist did not see WEA's efforts to respond to the Nation at Risk report as very significant. "I don't consider it to be one of my greatest accomplishments," he said. He did not see WEA's response itself as leading to anything tangible.

Fault Lines

Compounding the 1980 election setbacks, the passage of HB 166 and later the impact of the Nation at Risk report, the split between Lindquist and Bergeson was to divide and paralyze the WEA for most of the decade of the 1980s. It was a bitter time in the memories of many people.

Relations between President Reese Lindquist and his Vice President, Terry Bergeson, were not great to begin with, but they only grew worse during the four years he was President. Her refusal to speak on the floor of the 1981 RA in a unified front in support of full membership rights for classified members was only the beginning.

"She did not help me at all," said Lindquist. "Terry avoided taking any stands she could avoid."

In some ways Lindquist was not prepared for the job. He had never been a WEA officer, let alone served any time on the WEA Board. In Seattle he had been used to having a Vice President who gave him 100 percent backing and helped him secure votes when necessary. He did not know the fine art of assuring his base and counting his votes ahead of time, as Coe had done. Floor strategy was not his forte. Old board hands stepped in to help. "Lee Ann Prielipp, Toni Jenner and I took it away from Reese," explained Wahlquist.

In this situation, Reese Lindquist felt he got no help from Bergeson, who had been on the board for many years. "She took advantage of the fact that I was new to the inside of WEA," he said.

Feeling frozen out, Bergeson looked elsewhere to advance her agenda. "I went out and did my own thing," said Bergeson. "I built a cadre of people to support me, and I spent time talking to the management side of education [Washington State School Directors' Association, Washington Association of School Administrators, etc.]."

Gil Gregory said the fragmentation began shortly after they were elected. Having worked with Coe since coming to WEA in 1977, Gregory valued unified governance, especially in difficult times. "I tried to deal with Reese to involve her [Terry Bergeson] more," said Gregory. "He had a lot to learn. He believed Terry was undercutting him."

According to Gregory, the split came to a head at the 1982 NEA-RA in Philadelphia. "Reese asked me to come to his room, and when I arrived, Terry was there," explained Gregory. "He reamed her out [strongly berated her]. I had to step in to break it up. After the Philly thing she just went out and did her own thing. I was going to be loyal to the President. This was not what you would call a fun experience!"

According to Reese Lindquist, Terry Bergeson told him she was going to run against him for President in 1983. "We were not on good terms, so I encouraged a candidate to run against her for Vice President. She realized the odds were against her and did not run for President."

On the surface the policy differences between Lindquist and Bergeson were never sharply defined. The differences were more along the lines of personality, trust and power. Those closer to the situation saw Lindquist in strong support of bargaining and political action, while Bergeson leaned toward shifting the emphasis to instructional issues.

"I ran on a platform of repealing HB 166," said Lindquist. During his term most of his editorials supported a strong bargaining and legislative issues. "I wanted instructional strength," said Bergeson. "I wanted WEA to be the most important educational institution in the state. For me it was kids and a system that would help me do it for them. I was not hot for bargaining and salary, but I spoke for them."

Their differences were never talked out or accommodated in any way. Lindquist supporters feared Bergeson would back away from the Association's commitment to collective bargaining and WEA would lose the gains it had made in the 1970s. Bergeson supporters believed, as did she, that they were being denied a significant voice in the Association. Members tended to line up with whom they liked or with a particular group that supported one or the other officers.

In part, the split was over two philosophies of governance. Reese Lindquist was of the Carol Coe tradition of basing organizational strength on always presenting a united front to the members and the public. He believed the Vice President should be a supportive part of the President's team. That did not leave any room for the Vice President to have an independent voice, let alone one that was in opposition. As Vice President, Bergeson felt she was entitled to have an independent voice and to air those differences. After the initial split, she spent much of her time building an independent and competing constituency, mostly composed of members who felt they were without a voice and on the outside of the organization.

The split began to take its toll on the Association and its ability to mount a united front on the issues of restoring bargaining rights and achieving adequate funding levels for public education. Progress seemed to grind to a halt.

Gil Gregory, in his role as Executive Director, tried to keep the staff together. "I advised the staff not to get in the middle of this," said Gregory. "Some did, however."

In the early 1980s Leslie Kanzler was President of the North Thurston Education Association and had gained a great reputation for her years of hard work in the Chinook Council's political action program. In one election Kanzler recalled involving all but 100 of her 450 members. According to Kanzler the splits at the state level carried right on down to the local level.

"It shifted all of the relationships in our council," said Kanzler. "We became very unfocused. At the leadership level it created a situation where people stopped talking to each other. As President I was always being challenged."

Kanzler was critical of Terry Bergeson's role in the disputes. "What she did was take discontent and expand it," said Kanzler. "If you were on the other side, you were targeted. Things were still happening, but where the energy went was in disagreement over inconsequential things."

Kanzler summed up the 1980s from her viewpoint: "It was the decade that split the organization!"

Bergeson Elected President

When 1985 rolled around, Bergeson had built up a campaign and a constituency to back it. It was part Women's Caucus and part people who felt they were on the outside of the organization. Also going for her were the previous four years which had seen little obvious progress in the core areas of bargaining and legislation. Her ideas on instructional advocacy, though not sharply defined, seemed to many to be the best course for the WEA.

Her opposition was Bob Maier. Maier had been a successful President of the Mercer Island Education Association and most recently chair of the WEA Legislative Commission. He'd been Lindquist's campaign chair and his point person on full membership rights for classified, and that put him clearly in the Lindquist camp. He inherited much of Coe's and Lindquist's political base and had a charisma that made him appealing to many members. He placed a greater emphasis on bargaining and on political action.

The campaign was bitterly fought, and Bergeson dominated the voting at the 1985 Representative Assembly. A stunned Bob Maier mustered less than 40 percent of the vote. The split in the Association was as wide as ever and destined to grow. Throughout Bergeson's terms there would continue to be references to the "Terry Camp" and the "Maier Camp."

Maier supporters were heartened by the election of Carla Nuxoll as Vice President. She beat out John Zavodsky from Evergreen, who some believed ran as a Bergeson partisan. Nuxoll not only had built up a good campaign organization of her own, she had gained fame for leading opposition in the Mead School District to several attempts by right-wing inspired parents to get books like the teenagers' coming-of-age book *The Learning Tree* banned from the schools.

The 1985 elections gave Bergeson a strong mandate, but they did nothing to heal the split in the WEA. Right away she tried to change the emphasis of WEA's summer leadership training program. "We have to take charge of our future," she wrote in *Action*. She advocated a more "holistic approach" rather than specific skill training like bargaining and political action. She said it should stress "networking with communities, business and administrators."

Bergeson attempted to pull the sides together at the board's August retreat. "I asked Andy Griffin to facilitate my first board retreat," said Bergeson. According to Bergeson, he agreed, but with some tough conditions. "He said I had to bring in the four people in the WEA who hated me the most and spend four hours just listening to them." She recalled they were Darlene Hensley from Marysville, Leon Horne, Lee Ann Prielipp and Bob Maier.

"What I discovered they hated about me was not what I thought it was," Bergeson explained. "It had been as much my fault as theirs." Bergeson recalled in part what they told her. "Don't discount what we believe in," they said. "You don't even hear us. You can't do much about education without collective bargaining. Stop judging people just because they don't agree with you." Griffin facilitated the parties airing these same concerns before the full board and the WEA management staff. However, Griffin's help proved to be too little too late. The fault lines just widened.

The following September Bergeson conceptually outlined her program in an editorial in the WEA *Action*. The four points of the program were:

1. Image

2. Economic Power

3. Professionalism

4. Instructional Leadership

"My goal was to change the educational system to give kids and teachers a chance," said Bergeson. "I wanted the WEA to have an education goal."

In April 1986 Bergeson held a goal-setting conference at which the following statements were adopted for consideration at the RA:

1. Organize at the local level to become decision makers in the educational process.

2. Increase money in the system.

3. Restructure the school funding system to restore free and open collective bargaining.

At the RA the goals were put on large sheets of paper on the wall, and delegates were given stick-on "dots" to register their priorities. They were adopted but the order was reversed, putting bargaining rights first. The split between those advocating bargaining and those advocating Bergeson's instructional priorities continued throughout her time in office.

Bergeson Fires Gregory

By 1986 the gulf between the major forces or "camps" was wider than ever. WEA was not having any success in the Legislature. Bargaining had stagnated in most parts of the state. UniServ had lost much of its vitality. Washington's average salary rankings had dropped precipitously in the wake of HB 166. Members were increasingly critical of the Association. A cynical joke at the time likened the WEA to a "circular firing squad" in which the members all formed a circle and fired inward. Joann Kink Mertens said, "We became our own Donner Party."

Lee Ann Prielipp, who was an NEA Board member and on the WEA Board at the time, put it succinctly: "With so many defeats, where do you go? You turn inward."

Julie Green, President in Edmonds for four years during the 1980s and later a UniServ Rep in Lower Columbia, said it was "such a political thing. There were fights all the time. It got down to who had the most votes. Going to board meetings was turmoil."

As bad as this situation was for WEA, it was about to worsen, dramatically.

According to Reese Lindquist, relations between Terry Bergeson and Gil Gregory were not particularly good. "During the last year of my term I knew Gil was in trouble with her," said Lindquist. "She never said why. I think it was more personal than anything."

Lindquist tried to give Gregory a degree of security. "I knew Terry would try to get Gil, so I gave Gil a contract that would not expire until Terry's terms were up, and I got it passed by the board," explained Lindquist.

Though Bergeson says she felt relations with Gregory were good her first year, the subject apparently had been discussed between them. "I had an agreement with Gil that he would leave if it didn't work out," said Bergeson.

By her second year in office Bergeson had decided Gregory had to go. "I felt we didn't have as strong an Association as we could have," she concluded. But she ran into several obstacles. First, Gregory decided he was going to remain as Executive Director. Second, Bergeson could not get the necessary support from the Executive Committee, which handled management personnel matters. "I couldn't get Carla and the Executive Committee to help me, so I went to a lawyer," said Bergeson.

Another obstacle for Bergeson was Gregory's contract, which she was unaware of. "Reese had a second contract, and Gil had it locked up," she said. The contract had a rollover clause and some due process rights she did not expect. The Executive Committee required her to come up with a performance evaluation process.

Bergeson made her first attempt to dismiss Gregory at a 1987 spring Executive Committee meeting held at the Renton Sheraton. According to

Wahlquist, he and Nuxoll stopped her temporarily. "She told the Executive Committee she was going to fire Gil," said Wahlquist. "She said she couldn't stand him. Carla and I ran the bluff of our lives. We went to her and told Terry she did not have the votes. I said we know how to count votes, and I said we have the votes. She believed us. About a week later she figured out we did not have the votes!" Wahlquist and others left the board that spring and were replaced by people more supportive of Bergeson. At the Representative Assembly that year both Bergeson and Nuxoll were reelected to another two-year term.

By fall the management staff, or cabinet, openly split with Bergeson, mostly over what they perceived as a lack of fairness. They distributed a letter to board members opposing Gregory being fired. Bergeson took them out in the hall, strongly expressed her displeasure with what they had done and told them to stay out of it. "We got taken to the woodshed," said John Cahill.

The October 24 board meeting began normally enough. Jim Aucutt gave a report on the successful thirty-day Edmonds strike in which he was the organizer, and the meeting proceeded up to the lunch break. Immediately after lunch Bergeson took the board into executive session and excluded all of the managers, including Gil Gregory. This time she had the votes. Bergeson had been meeting secretly with the Executive Committee over a period of time. Nuxoll had been excluded from those meetings.

According to Gregory, his contract "had a little wiggle room in it." He was relieved of duties but continued to receive pay and benefits until it expired. Gil Gregory had been Executive Director for a month short of ten years.

"It was a shocker of a vote," said Terry Bergeson. "A lot of people hated me for it. I felt it had to happen. I was responsible."

The following Monday morning Bergeson called the entire headquarters staff together to explain the situation. An obviously angered Carla Nuxoll used the occasion to read a letter to the staff condemning the board's action to fire Gregory.

Deputy Executive Director Steve Kink reluctantly agreed to serve until January 10 as Executive Director until an interim Executive Director could be found. Bergeson went to Washington, D.C., and talked to NEA Affiliate Services Director John Hein. Hein appointed James Seibert, who was then Director of the Southeast Region and formerly Executive Director in Missouri. Like Gregory, he'd gotten his start in Pennsylvania.

Seibert arrived in December and immediately brought an air of calm to the Association.

Terry Bergeson finished out her final term as President unable to complete what she had started out to do. She pointed to the controversy over Gregory. "It really diminished what I could do about my educational reform agenda," she said. "It was our response to the Nation at Risk report." Many of her supporters wanted her to hang in there. "People tried to get me to seek a change in the constitution to run for President again. It was time for me to go do something else." She explored several job opportunities before becoming an Executive Director in the Central Kitsap School District.

The Bargaining Front

From 1976 to 1981 WEA's bargaining program had been one of the most successful in the country. Washington went from having a handful of real contracts at the beginning of that time to a state virtually blanketed with teacher contracts. By 1982 Washington had the fifth-highest teacher salaries in the nation.

The 1980s was a time of decreased bargaining activity in many parts of the state, despite continued urging from WEA to continue a policy of hard bargaining. With some notable exceptions it was a time of decreased strikes. And it was a time that saw experiments with alternative forms of bargaining.

The decrease in bargaining activity in the early 1980s was a result of the passage of HB 166, the levy lid, a bad economy and a hostile political climate in the state and nation. Many felt it was a time to hunker down until things improved. Some reasoned that bargaining had accomplished most all that was to be gained. Other felt it was time to turn to the Legislature for economic gains.

Some voices cautioned against that approach. One was Executive Director Gil Gregory. "I always opposed full state funding," he said. "It's best to fight your battles at home."

Pilchuck UniServ Rep John Morrill said it was a conflict between resolving issues locally versus resolving issues through legislation. "Watch out; you may get what you asked for," he said. "State funding and salary controls did not solve the funding problem. They only eroded or put bargaining on the back burner."

HB 166 convinced too many locals that bargaining for improved compensation was all but over. "We did a good job of convincing people that salary bargaining was over," said Julie Green, who feels too many members gave in to the idea too easily. "We let people slide into apathy: 'Poor us! The state did this to us. Since the state did this to us, we'll just roll the contract over.' "

"The state created a box and we accepted the boundaries," recalled Joann Kink Mertens.

It was now a matter of making sure that all of the money appropriated for salaries went to that purpose. Some school districts tried to keep some of the salary pot for other purposes. A WEA Research report in May 1984 showed there were sixty-three school districts holding back $20,000 or more in salary and fringe benefit monies. The Seattle School District held onto $536,000 in salary monies, and Tacoma withheld $303,000 in fringe benefit dollars. In many districts, administrators robbed the salary and fringe benefit pools to get higher salaries and benefits for themselves. In November 1982

WEA reported that 154 of 300 superintendents had taken fringe benefits higher than the $121 per month allowed by the Legislature. One topped the list at $399.42 per month. That meant that teachers were paid less to make up for this superintendent's greed. That led to WEA's seeking legislation in 1984 to provide for separate pools. These battles were soon won or at least reduced to the level of petty disputes.

When the state finally distributed salary monies according to an allocation formula that on paper looked like a salary schedule, many members saw an opportunity to get more money for themselves, at the expense of other members, by adopting the allocation model as their salary schedule. What ensued were internal battles that tore some associations apart. It was just one more split in the Association during the 1980s. Locals turned from the local bargaining table to the Legislature for salaries, a strategy that proved to be unsuccessful. Some locals, tired of the conflicts of the late 1970s, were relieved that they no longer had to engage in a conflict with their districts over compensation. In that was born the myth that locals could no longer bargain salaries.

But some locals, like North Shore, heeded WEA's call to stay tough at the bargaining table. In 1982 teachers there refused to give up a previously bargained 10.5 percent salary increase to avert a threatened Reduction In Force. "A salary deferment," said NSEA President Tom Carter, "would have resulted in what I believe could have been the largest loss of teacher salary money in the history of this state."

For some small locals the early 1980s was a bright time for compensation. These locals had not bargained hard for money, or some felt they could not. Many members of these locals were some of the highest paid in their communities and were reluctant to ask their boards for higher pay. The state Legislature's strategy on salaries was to bring up the lower-paid districts while providing the traditionally higher-paid districts little or no increases. For the low-paid districts it was a temporary windfall. "For three years they had received 10 percent raises. I was a hero to these districts," said Reese Lindquist. They apparently were unaware that he had run on a platform of doing away with HB 166. For the state as a whole, it meant a decade in which teacher salaries fell dramatically.

By 1985 Washington's average teacher salaries had dropped to eighth in the country, and in 1986 they fell to fourteenth. In the school year 1985–1986, Washington was dead last among the fifty states and the District of Columbia in the percentage of salary increase, at a mere 2 percent. Massachusetts led all states with a 15.8 percent increase.

Each year WEA held bargaining conferences for locals, and the theme was always the same: bargain hard for money! Locals were urged to seek other ways "to put more money in members' pockets." And some areas of the state, keeping the spirit of the 1970s alive, responded.

In 1982, almost by accident, the Kennewick Education Association discovered that locals could bargain around the restrictions of HB 166 by negotiating pay for extra days. Local association President Diane Schmidtke recalled that they had finished the year by paying salaries in excess of the limits imposed under HB 166. Accounting for salary compliance was chaotic in the early days. Teachers faced the prospect of having to repay excess salary out of their remaining summer paychecks.

Both the Association and the district were unhappy about doing that. Schmidtke said that she and UniServ Rep Ken Landeis went to the district and proposed that they settle it by having teachers work another day. The District agreed. Neither HB 166 nor any subsequent legislation up to that time defined the length of a teacher's work year, beyond the required 180 student days, for salary limitation purposes. Kennewick crossed its fingers and hoped the State Auditor's Office would OK what they had negotiated. It did. The news spread across the state, and local negotiators saw their first real opportunity to breach a supposedly iron-clad HB 166.

Some locals picked up on the idea and began to bargain contracts that added extra days of pay beyond state salary limits. Some began to reduce the length of their teacher work years back closer to the 180-day student year. In 1985 the Legislature caught up with established bargaining practices by passing ESB 3235, which allowed bargaining of extra days.

But many members felt that legislation did not go far enough. Like UniServ Rep Roger Cantaloube, they argued that added days at the going daily or per diem rate did not constitute a pay increase. In 1987 the Legislature passed the so-called TRI legislation, which had allowed locals to bargain additional pay for Time, Responsibility or Incentive. For salary compliance the work year was set at 180 days. An earlier version of the bill supported by the Governor's office was called TRIP. The P stood for Performance, which was a wide-open invitation to merit pay.

During the mid- to late 1980s three areas of the state, in particular, took an aggressive posture in bargaining salary increases beyond the limits of HB 166. Others followed suit.

The most successful was the Pilchuck UniServ Council. John Morrill believed in collective bargaining as the best strategy for long-term gains. Pilchuck started its own coordinated bargaining program in 1983 after most councils had abandoned it. In 1983–1984 Pilchuck bargained its first optional days contracts, and by 1987 had translated them into shadow steps on their regular salary schedules. Their early success resulted from emphasizing TRI bargaining every year. The result was that by the 1990s Pilchuck locals had the highest rates of pay in the state when TRI pay was included.

In Summit, UniServ Rep Ron Scarvie also emphasized bargaining compensation. "I always put salary bargaining first," he said. He pushed TRI bargaining in all four of his locals but had the most success in Fife, which by the mid-1990s had salaries rivaling those in Pilchuck.

Roger Cantaloube came to Tacoma in 1984 and began to aggressively bargain TRI. Tacoma already had extra days, but Cantaloube pushed hard for pay for the hours of work teachers did beyond the school day. By the time he left Tacoma in 1994, Tacoma had one of the highest TRI salary schedules in the state. He did one other thing to emphasize that TRI pay was just like regular salary. He and the Tacoma bargainers were able to convince the District to put regular pay and TRI pay on one combined schedule. From then on, salary was just salary. It was split out only for reporting to the state.

The 1980s was also a time when alternative forms of bargaining were explored and used.

Pilchuck's coordinated bargaining was called PUB for Pilchuck Unified Bargaining. One of the tactics employed was to create bargaining teams in which chief bargainers of each local also sat at the bargaining table of another district. Morrill also sat on all teams. This emphasized the commonality of bargaining goals. Districts may not have liked it, but there was nothing they could do, because one principle of labor law is that each side has the right to choose its own representatives.

In the November 1984 WEA *Action,* Pilchuck Unified Bargaining reported that the program in its first year achieved added days in all districts, as well as just cause and sick leave cash out. In the second year all locals achieved maximum salaries and fringe benefits. At one time in the program Pilchuck achieved settlement of seven contracts in seven days.

While Pilchuck built a more sophisticated bargaining program based on traditional models, others looked at newer approaches.

In the early 1980s Marline Rennels, now a veteran UniServ Rep in the Olympic UniServ Council, took a class at Antioch College from a person from Harvard named Bill Lincoln. Lincoln introduced her to win-win bargaining, which after several name incarnations became known as interest-based bargaining. It stressed that more progress could be made when there is a strong working relationship between the parties. His approach emphasized "interests" as opposed to "positions." It was bargaining more akin to mutual problem solving.

Rennels convinced him to come to a two-and-a-half-day retreat attended by many UniServ staff. Out of that was born the Labor-Management Consortium, consisting of a group of UniServ staff and superintendents. She remembered Mike Schoeppach from Bellevue, Rick Oglesby from Seattle and Cory Olson from Kent. Steve Kink, now Deputy Executive Director for Field Services, also participated for a few years. According to Rennels, they met about once a month for a while. She remembers taking Peninsula School District Superintendent Tom Hulse with her to those meetings. Bill Lincoln continued to provide training. Rennels chaired the group when she left UniServ to come into WEA management in 1987.

Her assessment was mixed. "We went from hard-core bargaining to interest-based bargaining," said Rennels, "but it went too far to the other end. Many locals wimped out."

Perhaps the most successful long-term relationship was that built by Mike Schoeppach in Bellevue. He and the Assistant Superintendent not only used Lincoln's teachings in bargaining, but also incorporated the state's strongest and most comprehensive site-based decision-making language into their contract, and through it made Bellevue teachers authentic partners in educational policy-making in that district.

Many districts also adopted various interest-based bargaining models. Even the Federal Mediation and Conciliation Service (FMCS) got into the act. FMCS concluded it could not mediate every bargaining dispute that came along in the private sector, let alone a growing workload in the public sector. It began to provide training in interest-based bargaining.

Many districts reported success with various forms of interest-based bargaining, but it had its problems and its detractors.

In 1986, Steve Paulson developed the Spokane Unified Bargaining Program. He developed a bargaining team that bargained for eleven different bargaining units. "We had 2,700 items on the table," he said. The strategy worked and he reached agreement for all the units. This was hard work, but it put the members in the different bargaining units on common ground.

It sometimes broke down, and the results were strikes. Two notable examples were long strikes in Seattle in 1985 and in Edmonds in 1987.

In many locals inexperienced bargainers embraced interest-based bargaining because of the relationships with school management it built at the expense of solid gains at the bargaining table. They valued the lack of conflict. They avoided making any large demands on management for fear of damaging the relationship. School management often embraced it for the same reason. They also saw it as a way to avoid having to make major concessions. Those bargainers who understood that all forms of bargaining are based on power tended to be more successful.

Another weakness was that often the relationships did not go deep enough into the structures on both sides. Too often the relationship existed between two "enlightened" people, and whenever one of them left, such as a key UniServ Rep or a superintendent, the relationship evaporated and the parties resorted to more traditional forms of bargaining.

Strikes in the 1980s

It was not at all unusual to expect a large number of strikes between 1976 and 1980, when the bargaining law was new and locals were bargaining first contracts. By the time those contracts were in place, one could have expected a natural decline in the number of strikes. HB 166 and the economic and political climate, however, exacerbated that trend in the early 1980s.

Starting in the fall of 1981, there was a brief one-day strike in Richland and a thirteen-day strike in Evergreen. What made Evergreen unusual was that the Superintendent there declared a lockout for the first five days. When he announced that school would open, the teachers remained on strike.

In 1982 the only strike was a successful one-day affair in Steilacoom.

That year, however, the WEA *Action* ran an article commemorating the tenth anniversary of the first K–12 school strike in the state, in Aberdeen. Editor Jeanne Giardina interviewed Sharon Amos, who along with Harry Cartham and Mike Poitras were the bargaining team in 1972. A photo of the team being interviewed by then KOMO TV reporter Rod Chandler accompanied the article. Amos recalled then that the school board had reneged on a promise made two years earlier to pay teachers in future years for teachers agreeing to take no increase.

John Chase, who had been the strike organizer, paid Aberdeen teachers a tribute for their courage in being first. "The Aberdeen teachers are the toughest, meanest, nicest, most beautiful people in the world," he said.

The year 1983 saw an increase in strike activity. Five strikes occurred: Clover Park, Renton, Snoqualmie Valley, Cheney and Stanwood. The longest was Clover Park at twenty-one days, followed by Snoqualmie Valley at eighteen, and Stanwood at thirteen.

KIRO commentator John Miller, later a Republican member of Congress from the First District, saw this increase in strikes and figured it had something to do with a failure of HB 166. He met with John Cahill, and what followed was an editorial blasting HB 166. He called it "a state law that has backfired" and said it had not speeded up bargaining. "Instead of more peace and harmony in the schools, there's more anger and ill-will." His conclusion was that it had made negotiations worse. "I think we are discovering that when it comes to collective bargaining in education, the more limited the stakes, the more bitter the negotiations," he wrote. The Washington State School Directors' Association objected, but Miller's point was made.

In 1984 only Longview was on strike, and only for two days.

The year 1985 belonged to Seattle. Bad feelings remained from the 1978 strike, when teachers returned to work under a court order. And in the spring Seattle teachers had successfully boycotted a reading program the District had tried to impose on the teachers.

One of Seattle's greatest Presidents, Carol Reed, was not only tough and very charismatic, but also a superb organizer. Key issues were TRI (Time, Responsibility or Incentive) pay for teachers and classified employees alike, and money for class size and "class mix." Class mix was a term used to describe the impact on a classroom of the high level of diversity present in the district. A third issue was money for teachers to purchase classroom materials and supplies not otherwise provided by the District. The strike became one of the longest in the state up to that time.

Mayor Norm Rice, SPI Frank "Buster" Brouillet and Governor Booth Gardner tried to settle it, but it was PERC Executive Director Marvin Schurke who brought the parties together. The Seattle Teachers Association, which changed its name to the Seattle Education Association shortly after the strike, simply outlasted the District.

In 1986 three districts were on strike. Strike efforts were hampered that year by a WEASO (WEA staff union)–management labor dispute in which WEA and State Option UniServ Plan staff worked to rule, which meant they would not work outside the contractual workday.

North Kitsap, which had come under the rule of a conservative superintendent and school board, mounted a successful five-day strike.

Bellevue Community College was on strike for seven days, during which they bargained salaries above limits set by the state.

Steilacoom again went on strike, this time for fifteen days. What was significant here was that it was the last strike in which a district successfully employed scabs to try to break the strike. WEA's new general counsel, Kathy O'Toole, took the issue of "super pay" for scabs to the Public Employment Relations Commission. Since 1974, districts employing scabs traditionally paid them well in excess of what substitutes made and often offered them travel pay and lodging in nearby motels.

PERC ruled that these scabs were "replacement employees" and districts could pay them no more than what they would be paid if placed on the existing salary schedule. PERC also put an end to other forms of compensation for them. Now that districts could no longer offer extra pay to entice people to scab in a district, Steilacoom was the last district to successfully employ scabs.

There were three strikes in 1987: Renton, Lower Columbia College and Edmonds. Lower Columbia withstood an injunction under the state's recently passed Community College Bargaining Act, which specifically banned strikes but gave judges the ability to consider a district's bad faith bargaining before issuing any injunction.

The big strike in 1987 was in Edmonds. It lasted a record thirty days. The big issue was class size. The Edmonds Education Association, now with UniServ Rep Nancy Murphy on hand, had thoroughly surveyed its members the spring before, using the sophisticated WEA Issue Identification Survey. It confirmed the members' deep outrage over large class sizes. The EEA had even taken the results of its survey and presented them to the school board in an open meeting. The board, in deep denial, simply chose not to believe the survey's findings.

According to Murphy, after the strike, stunned district officials decided to do their own survey, which confirmed what the EEA had been saying all along. What ensued was a coming together of the parties into a relationship that was to last for many years. It also helped that the District soon hired a new superintendent and the EEA recruited and helped elect several new school board members.

There were no strikes in 1988. Moses Lake and Bellingham went on strike in 1989. Both were in areas of the state that had not seen strikes up to that time.

By 1990 members across the state were becoming increasingly upset with a decade of lagging salaries. In February of that year several areas of the state, led by the Northwest and Central regions, had closed schools for one day to stage a protest centered on compensation. It was a prelude to the 1991 Multi-Local strike.

It came as no surprise that there was a sharp increase in strike activity in the fall of 1990. Mukilteo, Lake Washington, Castle Rock, Yakima and

University Place were on strike. The Lake Washington strike was eleven bitter days long. The personality of Superintendent Bud Scar was the motivating factor. Pay was the top issue.

Yakima's one-day strike was bizarre in that the superintendent had a grand scheme to break the strike by using televised lessons. The District promptly settled.

The Mukilteo strike was a record thirty-three days long. Their issues included pay and class size. UniServ Reps John Morrill and Mike Wartelle did something new in Washington teacher strikes. They borrowed a page out of private-sector strikes when they asked the members in August to authorize the Mukilteo Education Association Action Committee to call a strike on the first day of school if there was no settlement.

Midway through the strike the District challenged the Association to let the members vote on its offer. With television and news media present, the members voted it down 405 to 28. When the Snohomish County Superior Court handed down an injunction with threatened fines of $100 per person per day and $500 on the Association, members voted 322 to 65 to remain on strike. With the help of three state mediators, settlement came in early October.

By the end of this decade WEA members, particularly in Western Washington, were ready to take action over basic issues of compensation and school funding.

Legislation and Political Action

After the disastrous 1981 legislative session that saw the passage of HB 166 and severe cuts in Basic Education funding, Democratic legislators were quick to commiserate with WEA's plight. Representatives Wayne Ehlers, Denny Heck and Dan Grimm issued a statement that was reprinted in part in the WEA *Action*. "The Republican majority stripped away teachers' collective bargaining rights. . . . They rammed through House Bill 166, which transfers control over teachers' salaries from local school boards to the Legislature."

The clear implication of this statement was that the Democrats, once back in control, would reverse these actions and give teachers a better deal. However, the reality was to fall far short of these lofty promises.

Following the election defeats of 1980, and seeing the ability of business and far-right groups to raise almost unlimited funds for campaigns to defeat pro-education candidates, WEA decided to go on the offensive to the people with a campaign finance limitation initiative.

Initiative 401 was a comprehensive approach that limited all groups and individuals but was especially aimed at the big contributors in the business world. Steve Kink put together a campaign for WEA members to collect 175,000 signatures statewide. That year initiatives needed 138,472 valid signatures to qualify for the ballot.

Each UniServ Council was given a quota of signatures based on the population in each council. I–401 gained a lot of editorial support; if it could just qualify for the ballot, it seemed to have a good chance of passage.

But disappointment was again to hit WEA. By the deadline in July, WEA was able to turn in only 141,282 signatures, too few to assure validation. Several councils excelled. Tacoma led the signature-gathering effort with 134 percent of its quota, followed by Pilchuck at 110 percent, Northline at 109 percent, Soundview at 102 percent, Bellevue at 101 percent and Highline at 101 percent. However, these efforts could not overcome shortfalls in other areas, such as MidState at 17 percent and North Central at 33 percent.

The passage of I–401 could have prevented passage of the anti-union I–134 in the 1992 session. I–134, also a campaign finance limitation measure, was written by conservative forces and was aimed at restricting the power of unions such as WEA.

After the 1981 legislative session WEA leaders were expressing doubt about the benefits of state funding of education. In an editorial Reese Lindquist wrote: "As we are all well aware by now, so-called state funding has created a whole new set of problems that must be resolved. Those problems are local control of schools, preservation of teacher collective bargaining rights, and, of course, adequate funding." Lindquist went on to encourage locals to bargain aggressively for salaries and benefits. "In short," he concluded, "we must bargain hard in order to preserve bargaining. We can't afford to lose our bargaining rights through lack of use."

The 1982 Legislature cut education funding further, and moderate Republican Governor John Spellman labeled conservatives as "troglodytes" when they objected to raising revenues for education and other needs. The following April Judge Doran would not require the state to repay funds cut in 1981 and 1982 even though he ruled that the Legislature could no longer shortchange Basic Education to balance the budget.

The 1982 Legislature passed SHB 782, the so-called "Quick RIF" bill, making it easier for community colleges to reduce instructors. It required all of those RIFed to appeal or no one could appeal. Other than that, WEA was able to avert passage of any further negative legislation.

The funding cuts led to a scathing editorial cartoon by David Horsey in the *Seattle Post-Intelligencer*. In it he pictured a rundown town full of ignorant people and a dilapidated school. The caption read: "Yuh see, the Legislature went kinda hog-wild cuttin' the budget back in '82 an' things has jest sorta slowed up ever since!"

Horsey won a WEA Friend of Education award for that editorial cartoon at the next RA. He was given a plaque with his cartoon etched on it.

Writing about that session, Lindquist said: "Public education, which we serve and for which we advocate, stands on the threshold of a dark age — an educational dark age in which fewer and fewer resources are to provide less and less education."

In November 1981 Steve Kink, who had organized WEA for the 1976, 1978 and 1980 elections, became the WEA Assistant Executive Director for Field Services. Organizing for the 1982 elections was turned over to Dick Iverson. Iverson's task was no small one. He was charged with taking back the Legislature so the Dark Age Lindquist foresaw could be averted.

In a preview of the 1982 elections, in an off-year election in 1981 the WEA gave the Republicans a close scare in Wenatchee, one of their traditional strongholds. Steve Paulson, who had been on the Evergreen bargaining team during its 1973 strike, was now the UniServ Rep for North Central. He volunteered to run the campaign of Democrat Betty Shreeve against Earl Tilly to fill a vacancy. The only campaign he had ever run was for his colleague Virginia Oliver for a WEA office. And he lost that one. "We just made it up as we went along," said Paulson. On election night Shreeve led Tilly, only to lose when the absentees were counted

Iverson and WEA members proved they were more than up to the task in 1982. They exceeded what they had done in previous elections. Some 15,000 WEA members helped in legislative campaigns that saw WEA win 73 out of 104 endorsed races. And in a sharp contrast to the Reagan landslide of 1980, Democrats won control of both the state House and Senate.

WEA also changed its strategy with regard to campaign funds that year by working more closely with the Democrats. "I gave Kink the green light to turn the organization over to the D's," said Lindquist. "We folded the money through Denny Heck, Ehlers and Grimm."

Lindquist also worked the Republican side, but with limited success. "I set up a meeting with John Spellman and the state labor leadership," said Lindquist. "I worked through Phil Rockefeller. We told Spellman that we would support his reelection if he would support us. But because it would put him in conflict with House Minority Leader Bill Polk, he backed out. I was mad at him."

In 1983 it was time to take up the Democrats' promises to do something about HB 166. But in December incoming Speaker Wayne Ehlers sounded a cautionary note. "You may see some modifications in HB 166, but I don't think you are going to see outright repeal of the law."

Representative Denny Heck from near Vancouver led the charge to nullify HB 166. He sponsored HB 21 that would "hold harmless" the Legislature when school districts bargained salaries in excess of monies appropriated by the Legislature. "The right to bargain salaries is the grease that makes collective bargaining work," said Heck.

HB 21 passed out of the House Education Committee on an 8-to-6 party-line vote, but six Democrats joined the Republicans to sidetrack the bill to the House Ways and Means Committee. Eventually it got out and passed. It went over to the Senate and, after some amendments, it passed there too.

Now back in the House for concurrence with Senate changes to the bill, it languished until the closing night of the session. An anxious Lindquist sat in the House gallery as the clock moved to adjournment. Ehlers did not bring the bill up for a vote. He just let it die. "We had the votes," said Lindquist. He left the gallery angry. "[Representative] Bob Williams came up to me and said, 'You must feel pretty good about this session. I said 'Bullshit! We got nothing!' " The result was that WEA refused to support Ehlers in the next election.

Spellman dealt a blow to some pieces of WEA legislation that did pass in 1983. He vetoed a Higher Education Collective bargaining bill and a bill restoring community college instructors' rights under the Quick RIF bill passed in 1982. He vetoed a portion of the budget that allowed school districts to exceed salary limitations by up to 5 percent, but he also vetoed penalties for districts exceeding the limits.

Spellman vetoed SHB 126, which would have allowed teachers to buy back retirement credit they had cashed out when they interrupted their teaching service. This veto hurt mostly women who had left teaching to raise children.

The Legislature did restore school funding back to 1980–1981 levels, as required by Judge Doran. The budget contained single salary increases for all teachers rather than the differentiated increases of past years.

The Legislature restored the sick leave cash-out legislation that had been nullified by the state Supreme Court because of a faulty title. This time, however, the bill made it bargainable with school districts.

In the 1984 session WEA was successful in passing the Martin Luther King, Jr. holiday, but support in the Legislature for modifying HB 166 waned. Spellman vetoed another Higher Education Collective Bargaining bill and the House failed to bring to a vote an Educational Excellence bill that had passed the Senate. "We can't count on the House Democratic leadership to pass key bills," declared Lindquist at the end of the session.

Insurance coverage for classified school employees who worked 1,440 hours a year passed.

The 1984 elections were nearing. Walter Mondale visited the WEA, and the Association was looking for someone to challenge Spellman for governor. Lindquist turned to his old friend and UW fraternity brother Booth Gardner. Gardner, a former Democratic state senator, was then Pierce County Executive. "I told him he should run," said Lindquist. "Eventually he decided to run. I asked what it would cost to run a campaign. He said it would cost $2.6 million. I asked him how much he would put up. He said he was willing to put up $2.6 million! I pledged our support." In September WEA endorsed Gardner for Governor and Buster Brouillet for another term as Superintendent of Public Instruction (SPI).

In September WEA had another legislative problem to fend off. The 1982 Legislature, wanting to deal with several education issues, created a committee to do a study and make recommendations. Officially it was named the Temporary Committee on Educational Policies, Structure and Management. Commonly it was called the "3609 Committee" after its bill number. It had thirteen citizen members, all appointed by Spellman, and none of them were teachers. It was not hard to figure they were up to no good.

The committee floated a draft report and set up a schedule of twelve hearings around the state from October 8 to 30. The initial report had an overt interest in collective bargaining and the Continuing Contract Law. WEA flooded the hearings to voice its concerns on these and other issues.

Spellman, now in an uphill race with Gardner, ran a series of ads throwing mud at the WEA. Lindquist termed them "outright lies."

The final report of the 3609 Committee dropped all of its recommendations on collective bargaining and agreed with much of what WEA had to say about educational excellence. But in a move that was to characterize the educational excellence debate for the rest of the decade, the report made no mention of salaries and was silent on where the money to pay for excellence would come from. With regard to class size, it spoke only to reductions in K–3. It also recommended a three-year provisional period for new teachers. In the end, 3609 had little impact.

In November Gardner beat Spellman, and Democrats retained control of the House and Senate. Maybe the bad times in Olympia were over.

To fend off merit pay proposals by the 3609 Committee and the Boeing-dominated Business Roundtable, WEA came up with its own plan to allow teachers to spend a part of their careers working in other areas of education. The term "career ladder" was all the rage with 3609 and the Roundtable. WEA weighed in with "career lattice."

Meanwhile, the Professional Education Advisory Committee (PEAC) was looking at a number of recommendations, including an entry-level skills test for teachers, along with concepts like "endorsements," "program units," "beginning teacher assistance," and continuing education requirements for teachers. PEAC was composed mostly of teachers. Members at that time were Lee Ann Prielipp (Federal Way), Betsy Brown (Federal Way) and Virginia Birkby (Clover Park).

WEA's legislative agenda for 1985 included the following:

· Raising the levy lid to 20 percent
· Modifying 166 to allow local bargaining
· Salary schedule credit for district in-service
· Increasing the funding formula to 55/1000
· Full funding of NERCs
· Comparable worth study (comparing male/female pay disparities)

WEA began the 1985 legislative session with a new chief lobbyist, Michele Radosevich, a one-time state senator from Wisconsin and highly recommended by the Association Executive Director there.

By April 1985 Gardner was in hot water with the state's teachers. He had run as the "Education Governor," a term that haunted him for his time as Governor. He had proposed a budget that had no salary increases for either year of the biennium and he had ignored educational excellence. He made an unscheduled appearance before the WEA Board and was unable to appease angry members.

The board voted without dissent: "That the WEA prepare its members and organization for a possible work stoppage and/or other collective actions to respond to the Legislature if our members' needs have not been significantly addressed."

Near the end of the legislative session, many local areas across the state erupted in protest against the Governor and the lack of legislative action. In the Vancouver School District 850 members held a rally, as did 500 in Olympia, 500 in Kennewick, 500 in Shoreline and 1,000 in Bellevue. Central Kitsap, Tacoma and White River staged one-day walkouts, as did Issaquah, which packed up and took its protest to Olympia.

The biggest single demonstration was that staged at the Tacoma Dome. Some 4,500 members in Pierce County, south King County and Kitsap County staged a well-publicized rally replete with banners, signs, empty seats for invited legislators who did not show up and stirring speeches. Jerry Steinkraus, President of Fife, delivered the keynote address. These demonstrations were a dress rehearsal of what would take place in the early 1990s.

The Legislature adjourned without addressing members' needs. Even the passage of ESB 3235, which allowed bargaining of extra pay for extra days, did not make a dent in teacher feelings. Another attempt to pass a Higher Ed collective bargaining bill failed. The best WEA could get on levy lid relief was a freezing of the phase-down to 10 percent.

In May Terry Bergeson was elected President, and implementation of the board's motion fell on her shoulders. Though Bergeson did not say it publicly, it was clear to most that she did not favor a walkout. Despite a growing demand for a statewide walkout, a plan for a vote was delayed until the next February. WEA did what it could to discourage a walkout by holding a mail-in ballot. Articles were run pro and con on the issue, but when the votes were tallied, some 23,000, about half, responded. It failed by a margin of 25 percent for, 75 percent against.

In 1986 WEA went to the Legislature as part of a fourteen-organization coalition asking for a 5 percent salary increase. Higher Ed collective bargaining and class size relief were also on WEA's want list. WEA limped away from the session with a 3 percent salary increase and no class size money or Higher Ed collective bargaining. By this point in time it was becoming difficult to get WEA members interested in endorsing or helping any candidates for the Legislature, Democrat or Republican.

In 1987 Governor Gardner proposed his own education reform package. It proposed a 200-day school year by 1990–91, a requirement that all teachers get an MA by 1992–1993 and a 2.5 percent salary increase. The Legislature talked about a statewide salary schedule for all teachers. The Governor actually cut a deal with administrative groups for such a schedule. TRIP (Time, Responsibility, Incentive or Performance) also was proposed.

WEA was able to beat back the statewide salary schedule, settling for the Allocation Model for distributing salary dollars to districts. WEA did make some important gains. TRIP became TRI, and administrators and classified employees no longer were subject to HB 166. A 2.77 percent salary increase was passed, as was Higher Ed collective bargaining. One hundred and eighty days became the standard for the teacher work year. The funding formula separated teachers from administrators, which would prevent administrators from raiding the pot to enhance their own salaries and benefits. The 20 percent levy lid, with flexibility for grandfathered districts to stay between 20 and 30 percent, passed. An MA would not immediately be required for all teachers; rather, they would be given seven years to attain one.

In early 1988 the state was predicting a future teacher shortage. Projections said that by 1994–1995 Washington would be able to fill only 34 percent of teaching vacancies. Hardest hit would be science, math and special education.

By 1988 school employee health benefits had been frozen at $167 per month for the past four years. A study showed that Washington's teacher earning power had fallen 2.21 percent between 1976–1977 and 1986–1987.

The Legislature that year did raise health benefit dollars to $224.75 per month and passed SB 6600, which required school employees to report suspected child abuse and be protected from any liability for doing so. By June of that year, the NEA reported that Washington's average teacher salary had dropped from seventeenth the year before to twentieth, putting the state fourth in the Pacific Region and below the national average for the first time.

WEA was desperately looking for a strategy to put more money in Washington's education system. WEA teamed up with the Alliance for Children, Youth and Families, the League of Women Voters and the Committee for Affordable Health Care to sponsor what came to be called the Children's Initiative. Initiative 102 had going for it a great set of objectives, with 50 percent of the money going for education and 50 percent going to children's services. Early polls supported it.

However, when voters took a closer look at its complexity and taxing measure, they voted against it. Safeco, Boeing and Longview Fiber spent $50,000 to defeat I–102. Failure left WEA members looking to themselves and their collective strength for a solution.

In January 1988, WEA, with the help of an NEA grant, had initiated what it called the Compensation Project. Steve Kink led the effort, and he brought in people from all parts of the Association including Research, Communications, the Organizing Team and others.

Unlike earlier efforts to raise member awareness about salaries, this project was a full court-press on the issue. WEA Research amassed a wealth of data about teacher pay, cost of living, pay in other professions and the like. WEA put the data into easily understood charts and graphs and distributed it to all UniServ Councils and locals. And they kept it going. School employees began to understand what almost a decade of state control of salaries coupled with years of legislative inaction had done to them. Putting this wealth of data and information in the hands of the locals was just what was needed for the locals to be the force to revitalize the Association.

But WEA had to take it further. The public had to know too. WEA polls showed there was more support among the public than teachers realized. Again, a grant from the NEA helped spur that effort. Initiated in 1989, it was known as the Awareness Project. It worked hand in hand with the Public Awareness Campaign. The 1988 RA voted a $1 per-member assessment to fund the campaign.

Sylvia Skratek headed the campaign. An advertising agency was hired, and the first products of the campaign were a series of dramatic posters and smaller newspaper ads. The first poster pictured a life-size specially built sardine can packed with children. The theme was class size, and the caption read, "Give Our Children Room to Grow!"

The second poster, a few months later, was a dramatic picture of a scruffy older teenage boy sitting in an alley, smoking. The caption read, "Without Good Schools, Johnny Looks Elsewhere for Role Models."

The third poster was the famous "Peanut Poster," which for the first time took the teacher pay issue to the public. It was a close-up photo of a lot of peanuts. The caption read, "In Washington We Don't Give Our Teachers Apples."

By 1990 Washington's average teacher salaries had dropped to twenty-third and were now behind Oregon's.

UniServ Fights

As if other splits and fights in WEA during the 1980s weren't enough, UniServ became just one more headache for the Association to resolve.

By 1982 some of the original UniServ Reps who had sparked a revolution in WEA and made bargaining and the field operations the top priorities in the Association were gone. John Ward had left in 1978 to go to Colorado. Steve Kink, one of the early driving forces, was now in WEA management, and John Chase, who had provided much of the daring and genius in the 1970s, had left to take a job with the NEA. And after the bargaining battles seemed won, UniServ became more institutionalized and less the rebel force in the WEA.

Without strong issues to keep UniServ united, it came as no surprise that it too began some internal fights.

At the 1982 Representative Assembly there were three New Business Items dealing with UniServ. NBI 11 called for a study on a UniServ intern program. NBI 25 would study a scarcity grant for rural UniServ Councils. But NBI 39, concerning the funding of UniServ Councils, if passed, would have the greatest impact.

Since the adoption of the State Option UniServ Program (SOUP), the funding rates between it and the Local Option UniServ Program (LOUP) had drifted apart. Some of the councils that had become SOUP councils did so because their small numbers made it difficult to sustain any kind of program. WEA fully funded those programs. The result was that those SOUP councils received more money per member than did LOUP councils. One of the drawbacks of Washington's UniServ Program was that it never had any mechanism or process, as in other states, for WEA to "redistrict" the councils to ensure relatively equal numbers. And the culture of UniServ strongly resisted giving WEA that authority. The boundary changes that took place were strictly voluntary. That created rich and poor councils and councils that were on the verge of going under unless subsidized by WEA.

NBI 39 required that the funding for all councils, LOUP or SOUP, be done on an equal, per-member basis. SOUP councils suspected that it was anti-SOUP inspired. There was a scramble among WEA leadership as to how to handle the New Business Item. If it passed, Soundview, with a declining membership, would not be able to survive.

Leadership was able to get the item amended to delay implementation until 1983 and to give WEA a chance to come up with a set of "objective, written criteria" that could make exceptions to the equal funding mandate. These would have to be reported to the 1983 RA. A UniServ Task Force was created to study and make recommendations on all three New Business Items. Lindquist appointed Bergeson to chair the task force. This set in motion one study after another for the next six years to solve the UniServ problem.

At the 1983 RA, New Business Item 11, creating an intern program, from the previous year was voted down. Items 25 and 39 were adopted, but were essentially put on hold because NBI 21 passed, creating a UniServ task force to study and report to the next RA on UniServ dues, boundaries and scarcity grants.

By 1984 UniServ was becoming an issue that delegates were unwilling to deal with in finality. As chair of the task force, Bergeson moved that all of the previous new business items on UniServ passed in the last two years be put on hold and that an independent consultant be hired to study the issues of boundaries and efficient service delivery. The consultant's report was to be presented to the board by February 5, 1985, allowing plenty of time to be digested by the 1985 RA. In the meantime, funding for all councils would be maintained.

The WEA hired Paul Phibbs and Associates of Dublin, California. His report to the board in February was largely procedural. It did recommend boundary changes but called for a single UniServ Program, either all LOUP or all SOUP. The board came up with a series of recommendations that were nearly all procedural. One substantial recommendation, for regional offices, was voted down by the 1985 RA. A boundary change process was adopted, as was a directive for the board to come up with a new UniServ Program by the next year. In effect, everything of substance regarding UniServ was put off until the next year. Out of all this came the UniServ Structure Steering Committee, chaired by Carla Nuxoll.

In the meantime, the NLRB ruled that the UniServ Councils and the Wisconsin Education Association Council (WEAC) constituted a joint employer of UniServ staff. That decision brought Washington's UniServ Program into question.

The Committee reported to the 1986 RA, but the RA directed the WEA and the UniServ Councils to negotiate "one or more" contracts for employment of UniServ staff in a new UniServ Program, with an interim report to the 1987 RA and a final report to the 1988. Now, Nuxoll's committee was called the Transition Team. It had thirty members. Kink was assigned to be the staff consultant.

WEA's staff union, WEASO, in the meantime filed a claim similar to Wisconsin's with the NLRB. The purpose was to determine who was the employer of UniServ staff in Washington.

Nuxoll reported the Team's progress in 1987, and a motion was presented by Peter Bogdonoff of Bellevue that the new UniServ Program require "element(s) of shared management authority between the Washington Education Association and the UniServ Council(s)."

In 1988 UniServ finally was resolved. The report was lengthy, but the most important outcome was a third UniServ option called "Designated UniServ Councils." In addition to LOUPs and SOUPs, DUCs were added to the WEA lexicon. DUCs were councils in which the WEA and the councils became joint employers of UniServ staff. Eight previously LOUP councils became DUCs. This plan satisfied all parties as well as the NLRB.

In addition, a boundary change process was adopted, but no boundaries were changed. A funding formula with enough objective factors to suit everyone was adopted. By now, six years later, the agony of UniServ was over, and it would be a long time before any RA would revisit the subject.

UniServ continued to expand during the 1980s to match a huge growth in students and educational employees, certificated and classified, across the state. Second and third UniServ Reps were added to councils like Olympic, Chinook, Fourth Corner, Northline (which became Cascade with a merger with Edmonds), MidState and Eastern Washington. Renton and Highline merged to form Rainier.

After the slow start in hiring women UniServ Reps, now many were added to the ranks. Mary O'Brien came from Oregon to MidState. Jan Genther from Renton went to Northline. When Nancy Murphy went from Seattle to Sammamish, Seattle hired Donna Lurie to replace her. Later, Karen Davis from Montesano replaced Steve Paulson in North Central, Sheryl Stevens was hired in Riverside and Toni Jenner from Kennewick went to MidState. Leslie Homer was added to Riverside. In 1988 Julie Green from Edmonds replaced Dick Anderson in Lower Columbia. And after almost two years in Omaha, Leslie Kanzler would come to MidState in 1989.

By 1989 UniServ had expanded to forty-five UniServ Reps in twenty-two councils. It would continue to expand in the 1990s.

Research — Expanding the Horizons

In March 1974 Joann Kink Mertens, then Joann Slye, began as an entry-level secretary working as a floater on the switchboard, in the Records Center and in the Personnel Office sorting employee records. She recalled that she faked the shorthand test required for hiring in those days. She began college at age 16 at Western Washington University and she had just graduated from the University of Washington. She also had a night job at the King County Juvenile Center. She applied for an opening at WEA because she needed to have more of an employment record to qualify for a home mortgage.

In 1975 she was working with Meeting Planning and bargained WEA's first hotel meeting contract with the Renton Sheraton.

When an opening for a secretary in Field Services came up, she applied. She got the job because transfers did not have to take the shorthand test. She began working with Dale Troxel, Jim Raines and Wes Ruff.

Her earliest "research" experience came from collecting and compiling negotiation settlement reports. She had the data on what had been bargained in the early days. "We tracked everything," she said. "We compared and contrasted. I did charts and graphs. In our meetings we traded and analyzed contracts." The regions came to depend on her. She began attending regional meetings and even became Ruff's assistant in the 1975 Clover Park strike.

Joann Kink Mertens remembers the vitality of the first regional structure set up to promote and coordinate bargaining. "The staff made commitments to each other," she said. "They held each other's feet to the fire. Meetings were focused and productive. If you weren't a team player, you weren't treated very well. We were making incredible gains."

She said the early UniServ Reps were like "pirates." "We joked about tying down our staplers, because John Gullion would take anything that wasn't nailed down," she said.

When Bob Bell became Deputy Executive Director, Don Murray was put in charge of WEA Research. Kink Mertens was assigned to work with him. In those days, analyzing a school district budget for a local needing bargaining assistance was a several-day job done with paper, pencil and a calculator. This was a promotion to "Level B," and she decided then to quit her night job.

When WEA got one of its first computers for budget analysis, it was located in a closet-like room in the basement and hard-wired to the NEA. Kink Mertens was put in charge. In this job she got some of the earliest computer training in the Association.

In Research, Kink Mertens collected data for WEA's legal team in some early court cases. When WEA moved to Federal Way in 1979, she began to help build WEA's modern Research Department. Local demand for complex budget analysis grew, and Kink Mertens' work with computers put her in the position to be indispensable to the Association.

Joann Kink Mertens takes a dim view of the Basic Education Act and state control of salaries and education in general. "It was the beginning of the Legislature micro-managing the schools," she said. "Every dollar the Legislature appropriates comes with a string attached. It created a box we began to operate in."

When the state allocation model came along, and locals began adopting it at a great loss and burden to many of their own members, she was one of the loudest critics. "The Levy Lid was just another side to the box," she said. "When HB 166 passed, we spent our time and energy explaining the system. Then we became part of the system."

Research grew in importance in the 1980s and promotions followed for Kink Mertens.

How was Research changing in the 1980s and 1990s? "Bigger, faster, better," said Kink Mertens. Every school district budget and all personnel data for the state is on computer. WEA can spit out sophisticated budget analyses overnight. Tacoma's former Assistant Superintendent Dan Barclay, the District's chief bargainer, remarked once that when Kink Mertens did a budget analysis, Districts had better listen. Districts didn't like seeing her at the bargaining table, because she knew where every one of their dollars is. "Many districts have huge cash reserves," said Kink Mertens. "We should be going after it."

She also took a fledgling member and public polling capacity and built it into one of the best in the country. At first she used members to do the polling. That moved into contracting with a professional firm. "What I've found over the years is that we have a lot more support from the public than we want to believe," said Kink Mertens. "Every morning after we'd get poll results in, the Executive Director couldn't wait to see them. I just wish we would make more use of the polls."

Instruction in the 1980s

WEA's instructional program in the 1980s was aimed at fulfilling a very real professional need of the members. As an outgrowth of the old Teacher Education and Professional Standards program of the late 1960s, headed by Vern Archer, and the "improvement of instruction" program of the Association of Classroom Teachers Department in the 1970s, WEA under the leadership of Bob Pickles built a program of classes that most teachers found missing in their college preparation.

When the position of Second Vice President for Instruction was eliminated, Pickles was hired to head up WEA's instructional program. Teachers wanted classes that taught them better ways of dealing with such things as classroom discipline, new instructional strategies and approaches to teaching special needs students. And they wanted to get college credit for the courses so they could advance on their salary schedules. The classes had to be taught at times and places convenient to teachers.

Pickles put this together in an instructional program that became the largest teacher continuing education program in the state. Classes like Project Teach (a classroom verbal skills course), Pride (a performance learning systems course) and LEAST (Least amount of discipline, End the action, Attend more fully, Spell out the consequences and Terminate the behavior) became common offerings for teachers. The classes all helped teachers improve their instructional and discipline techniques. Pickles found instructors, mostly teachers, set them up in locations around the state and contracted for a college or university to sponsor the classes. Some institutions declined to sponsor classes because they did not like the competition. However, some like Western Washington, Central Washington and especially Seattle Pacific did. Tuition was in a range that teachers could readily afford. Washington teachers were being exposed to leading-edge ideas in education and increasing their advancement on their salary schedules as well.

Pickles aggressively marketed the programs through a quarterly multi-page insert in the WEA *Action*. As the offerings increased, so did the size and complexity of the insert. By 1982 WEA *Action* reported that more than 2,000 teachers were taking WEA classes. Pickles said, "We were bringing in $25,000 a year to the WEA budget by the various classes we were running. We had over 250 teachers teaching teachers about topics they wanted help with."

Eastern Washington Network

In 1989 several WEA and UniServ staff in Eastern Washington took coursework from Dan Leahy, at Evergreen State College Labor Studies Center, that stressed the need for associations to look beyond the boundaries of their bargaining relationships with their school districts, reach out to community groups and embrace a wider range of social issues. People like Dick Iverson and Steve Paulson were convinced that the Association could not make more than marginal progress without this approach.

They distinguished between "public opinion" that might be reflected in a public opinion poll and a deeper and more durable "public judgment" that could be built over time. The approach went beyond narrow educational issues. It meant that local associations would focus on wider social issues. Bargaining was played down, and they advocated abandoning political action as a means of creating an education-friendly climate in Olympia. They stopped endorsing candidates for the Legislature.

It was a more long-range approach to getting out of the stagnation WEA felt in the late 1980s, and it appealed to teachers in Eastern Washington, who by then saw no hope in electing education supporters from their side of the state to the Legislature and no immediate hope of getting the Legislature to solve any of education's problems. Many of them lived in small communities where salary and other compensation issues seemed less compelling than on the west side, where the cost of living was higher.

Eastern Washington UniServ Councils used their regional structure to form an Eastern Washington Network to promote this community-based approach. Alliances with community groups sprang up all over Eastern Washington. In a clear increase in support for schools, local levies began to pass with substantially higher margins in Spokane and surrounding areas.

But many leaders and staff in Western Washington were skeptical. They saw the approach as an abandonment of collective bargaining and of any meaningful involvement in the political process. They saw it as turning over control of locals to interests outside their memberships. It soon became another fundamental split in an organization that had suffered a decade of splits. The rift became more severe in 1991, when Western Washington locals heavily participated in the Multi-Local Strike against the Legislature, and Eastern Washington made the decision not to participate.

In July 1989, the tumultuous presidential term of Terry Bergeson ended. "I wanted to change the public education system to work better and the association to be a force for kids and members," Bergeson said of her presidential goals. "I'm proud I left the association with better management, brought new viewpoints into the Association, was a force for women's equity and never lost integrity with the members." While the goals were admirable, many throughout the Association felt that her methods were divisive, confrontational and lacked focus. But others, like UniServ staff person Mary O'Brien, felt that "Terry was the best thing that ever happened to the WEA."

The WEA ended the 1980s suffering from a decade of defeats and internal splits. It had exhausted its available energy on organizational infighting. Progress had come primarily in locals and regions that organized despite what the state organization was doing. This local initiative would catch fire at about the time Carla Nuxoll became President in 1989. It would take over the state organization and drive a more aggressive agenda into the 1990s.

CHAPTER SIX

Finding Focus

The decade of the 1990s would continue to be a challenging one for the Washington Education Association. This was a decade in which the WEA struggled to redefine itself. It was a decade of massive confrontation with the Legislature. The decade saw the implementation of an educational reform movement only talked about in the 1980s. Most of all, it was a decade of revitalization for the Association.

In April 1989 Carla Nuxoll was elected President and CT Purdom from Naches Valley was elected Vice President. The same RA that elected them passed New Business Item 89–11, a vote of no confidence in Governor Gardner.

Locals Set the Agenda for Action

On April 27, 1990, all hell began to break loose. The Northwest Region, long a hotbed of activism, held the first of several major mass protests that would lead to the 1991 Multi-Local Strike. "Pilchuck was the engine that drove the Northwest Region," said Research staff person Joann Kink Mertens, who was assigned to work with the region. "There was lots of energy." The region consisted of the Pilchuck, Cascade and Fourth Corner UniServ Councils and all the locals they represented. North Shore President Greg Waddle, Everett President Mike Sells, Edmonds President Dave Wood and Herb Sargo of Fourth Corner were the key governance leaders in the region. Janet Genther of Cascade, Mike Wartelle and John Morrill of Pilchuck and Box Bond of the Fourth Corner UniServ Council were the key staff organizers.

Teachers from Northshore to the Canadian border packed the Everett High School Auditorium that night. Waddle chaired the meeting. The event was "Report Card Day" for the Legislature. All local legislators were invited, but only a few attended and stood in the wings. What they got was an earful on how they had utterly failed to address the needs of education, including salaries, class size and a host of other issues, mostly ones requiring money. The media covered the event.

By now teachers were armed with all the information they needed. Dramatic testimonies from teachers and a panel grading the Legislature on each issue dramatized the issues in ways the Legislature and the public had never before seen. Those few brave legislators who attended listened, received their failing grades and heard horror stories from outraged teachers to take back to their colleagues in the House and Senate. The assembled teachers called for a statewide strike. The question was, could it really happen this time?

The Central Region put on a similar "Report Card Day" at Seattle Center, and got even more media coverage.

These events in a few parts of the state recalled the vitality of the early UniServ days of the 1970s. The "action" had the support of WEA, but the energy was member driven and locally organized. After nearly a decade of defeats, organizational splits and discouragement, it was fun again to be a WEA member.

Many looked to the new President, Carla Nuxoll, to restore unity and to provide focus for the WEA. As Vice President under Bergeson, Nuxoll often had been the mediator and peacemaker between the divided camps within the association. She provided a collaborative approach to the job that many staff and leaders were ready to follow. According to Jim Seibert, "The camps continued until Terry left." Most staff were fed up with Bergeson's my-way-or-the-highway approach. "Most of the management staff of the Association were relieved. Now, they could concentrate on some consistency instead of dealing with the programs du jour proposed by Bergeson at various management meetings," explained Kink.

Carla Nuxoll was a high school English teacher from Mead, a community just north of Spokane. She was a bright and articulate leader with an expressive face and sharp features that made her equally adept at speaking in front of large gatherings and one-on-one with friends and colleagues. She was well liked and trusted within the WEA. Nuxoll got her first taste of union work as a picket captain in the 1974 Mead teachers strike. Later, when conservative parents began to challenge the use of certain controversial books, such as *The Learning Tree*, she organized her fellow teachers and school librarians to meet these challenges head on. Before getting into WEA elective politics, Nuxoll was active in the Eastern Washington UniServ Council.

Many looked forward to the change in WEA leadership, Report Card Day and other events, and the previous spring had proved that local leaders were poised for action and had high expectations. After all, the decade of the 1980s produced very little for members in salary or fringe benefits. In the beginning of the 1980s, the average teacher's salary ranked sixth in the nation and by 1990 it ranked twenty-third, and Washington's average class size ranked forty-eighth in the nation.

The state had seven consecutive years of economic growth, and 1989 was the largest. By 1990, the state had nearly $1 billion in unanticipated revenue.

However, Booth Gardner, the self-proclaimed "education governor," insisted that none of the surplus be spent on teachers' salaries.

In the early 1980s, the K–12 share of the state general budget was just over 50 percent. Members saw it decline throughout the 1980s and 1990s to less than 45 percent. This translated into public education being shortchanged hundreds of millions of dollars.

According to Nuxoll, "Bergeson was not that interested in bargaining or legislation." While the WEA staff was trying to get Association members and leaders to concentrate on compensation, the WEA President had been a reluctant follower.

The Compensation Project, along with the Public Awareness Campaign and Report Card Day, set the stage for Nuxoll's first major meeting of her presidency. The meeting was called by local leaders in August 1989 and held at Bellevue Community College. "It was a come-to-Jesus meeting," recalled Nuxoll. Local leaders were frustrated and took it out on the new President. They wanted to know WEA's "specific" plan for getting money from the Legislature. The Public Awareness Campaign was not enough for these leaders. During the meeting, Mike Schoeppach told Kink in an understatement, "It appears they want action and they want it now." What WEA was doing was not enough for them and Nuxoll was caught flatfooted. According to the Executive Director, Jim Seibert, "That meeting set the stage for organizing the Association around compensation."

WEA staff rallied, under Nuxoll's leadership, to develop "specific plans" to address local leadership concerns and the issue of education funding. The Compensation Task Force, with the support of WEA's Research and Communications Departments, issued a newly researched WEA Compensation Packet to Association leaders and staff. This publication clearly portrayed the funding crisis through charts and graphs comparing Washington with other states. The data was produced in a format leaders could use in presentations to members, legislators and the public. Local leaders and members now had the information and rationale to justify increased state funding for education. According to Kink, "It gave the UniServ staff and local leaders the tools to organize in their locals and their communities. The compensation movement was on a roll."

The WEA program delivery system was organized in regions of the state. As in the 1970s when contract bargaining was the goal, each region had a WEA staff person assigned to it as the coordinator. The "specific plan" of the WEA was to give leaders the information and to challenge them to do something about it.

The Northwest Region was the first to respond. The region plan was to have an Awareness Day to hold legislators accountable for their lack of action. They set February 13, 1990, as the day to have a one-day strike to protest and deliver their message. Other local associations agreed on the same date for their activities. Each local and region staff and leaders made their own decisions as to which actions they would take to voice their displeasure with the Legislature. WEA's role was simply to provide whatever assistance was needed to help make the activities successful.

And successful they were! On a crisp sunny day with snow on the ground, the Northwest Region held a rally at Everett Memorial Stadium. More than 7,000 members attended the rally from the Northwest Region. These and other members went on strike for one day, for as Greg Waddle put it to the rally, "One decade is long enough of diminishing salaries, of ignoring pensions and of higher class sizes." NEA Vice President Bob Chase delivered a high-powered speech. The members wrote postcards and signed petitions directed at Booth Gardner and the Legislature to respond to education needs.

Throughout the state, more than 25,000 participated in Awareness Day activities of their own choosing. Of those, 13,000 went on strike for the day and the other 12,000 either dismissed school early or rallied after school.

In Seattle, SEA President John Carl Davis led a 3,000-member march down Fifth Avenue pushing a wheelbarrow full of peanuts to illustrate what the governor was proposing for education. Bellevue wrote 3,000 letters to legislators. In Olympia, 1,500 rallied from Chinook, Tacoma and Soundview UniServ Councils. In the Lower Columbia UniServ Council, members doorbelled their communities and left 11,000 voter brochures and 10,000 flyers explaining the lack of legislative attention to education. Local leaders Bill Green and Dave Struthers, along with their UniServ Rep Julie Green, organized the action.

MidState UniServ Council sponsored a march and 600 members participated. Another 400 marched in North Central UniServ Council.

Olympic UniServ Council members picketed the ferry terminals with signs reading, "Pay the toll, Booth." They also sent broken-hearted Valentine's Day cards to the Legislature during one-day local rolling strikes between February 26 and March 2.

Other locals throughout the state did a variety of activities on Awareness Day such as putting ads in newspapers, holding marches and communicating with parents.

This frustration of educational employees had been building for a decade. Awareness Day actions were just the beginning. These actions would soon lead to an unprecedented event in Washington history.

In the spring of 1990, the WEA held its annual Representative Assembly. Members and leaders, who were hot off the Awareness Day activities, wanted more. The RA approved the recommendation to create a Crisis Action Plan and Team. The purpose of the plan was to develop and recommend a plan of action to support WEA's legislative package in the 1991 session. Steve Pulkkinen was put in charge of the Crisis Action Team. The team began working on the plan.

By the fall of 1990, plans were in place for the upcoming legislative session. However, in September, other events grabbed the spotlight. Local strikes in University Place, Yakima, Lake Washington and Castle Rock, capped by Mukilteo's thirty-three-day strike, demonstrated that locals were ready for a fight.

Another event in July 1990 added fuel to the members' fire of frustration. The Education Commission of the States was holding its annual meeting in Seattle. It just so happened that the chair of this meeting was none other than Booth Gardner. This was his chance to shine as the so-called "education governor." This was just too good to pass up and the WEA organized a rally on the opening day of the meeting. More than 6,000 WEA members, led by President Nuxoll and Vice President Purdom, marched with balloons and banners chanting, "No more hot air! Schools deserve solid solutions." The throng anchored a huge hot air balloon. The delegates to the meeting quickly learned that things were not well in Chairman Gardner's own state. One newspaper headline described Gardner's situation this way: "Gardner is wearing educational robes, but lacks thesis."

In December, the WEA Management Team decided that the WEA needed to provide resources to locals in the area of community organizing. Rod Regan was hired as a WEA community organizer. He had political action skills and was utilized in both program areas. He developed a community organizing school at WEA's summer leadership training conference (now named the WEA Leadership Academy or WEALA) and began to work with leaders and councils who were interested in reaching out to their communities.

The Funding Task Force was formed to develop a new education funding formula for introduction in the 1991 legislative session. This group was co-chaired by Mike Schoeppach and the Edmonds President, Dave Wood. They created a formula that utilized the number of Full Time Equivalent Students, the Staff Mix, the number of Support Staff and the Student Mix. This new formula provided a fairer method of allocating education funding to school districts. The Legislature would take no action on it.

Multi-Local Strike

By late fall of 1990, the Crisis Action Team had developed a process to call for a Multi-Local Strike against the Legislature. The name was carefully chosen so as not to offend locals that would not participate. The process included a review of data such as public opinion polls, state budget information, and local association readiness, among others; a recommendation to local associations regarding a strike; local association confirmation of the recommendation; and rules and procedures for the Legislative Bargaining Team. The team also developed a process to settle a strike that included the following steps:

- A tentative agreement

- A majority of striking locals accepting the agreement

- Calling off the strike

The team recommended that a strike be authorized but that the Legislature be given a few months to realistically deal with the issues. By the end of January 1991, more than seventy local associations had authorized a strike following the Team's recommendations.

Many UniServ Councils went all out to prepare their locals for a strike. In Pilchuck, Mike Wartelle developed a *Multi-Local Strike Manual*. The *Manual* included sections on Leaders and Roles at the State and Local Levels; Checklists for Organizing; Recommended Activities; Work Instructions; Picket Captain Activities and Instructions; and Reporting. This *Manual* was shared with other UniServ Councils to help other locals prepare.

During March, local leaders were asked to share the information and the issues with their communities. The issues were simple: more education funding for salary, reduction in class size, education restructuring, benefits and retirement. They told their communities that the strike action was not against them or their school districts but against the Legislature.

During the legislative session, newspaper and radio ads were run saying, "Every day, thousands of Washington children are abandoned. But not by their parents — underfunded schools hurt kids." "The ads really got to the legislators," said WEA Communications Director Teresa Moore. "They made the point and they didn't like it."

The WEA was also preparing for the confrontation. A new structure was put into place to manage the Multi-Local Strike. Jim Seibert and Carla Nuxoll made staff and governance assignments for strike responsibilities. Seibert assigned himself to head Legislative Bargaining. Nuxoll chaired the Legislative Bargaining Team that consisted of staff and members representing those on strike. A Coordination Team was co-chaired by Seibert and Nuxoll. Its job was to make sure things ran smoothly between the strike activities and the legislative activities. Steve Kink was assigned to be the overall Strike Manager, and the Operations Chief was Steve Pulkkinen. A Strike Strategy Team was co-chaired by Kink and Vice President CT Purdom. The Strategy Team consisted of staff representatives from the five regions of the state and others who coordinated strike activities in Olympia. Rod Regan put together phone banks all across the state. The phone banks were used to call school levy voters and encourage them to contact legislators.

On Friday, April 19, 1991, more than 13,000 WEA members flooded the Capitol grounds in Olympia. The Multi-Local Strike was on! Mark Matassa of *The Seattle Times*, reporting on April 21, called it "one of the nation's largest" and *The Everett Herald* reported on April 20, "Teachers' rally called Olympia's biggest." On the 27th, more than 21,000 striking members rallied in Olympia, eclipsing the previous record set just eight days earlier. For twelve days, more than 30,000 members were actually on strike. More than 370,000 students were affected by the action.

"We set up a strike headquarters in Olympia to manage the strike activities," said Kink. "The logistics were awesome. Moving that many people into and out of Olympia was a challenge. For the most part, it went smoothly. The staff and leaders did an excellent job getting members to the right place at the right time. It was no easy task with hundreds of buses and cars to manage. Event planning was a huge organizational challenge over the 12 days, and Pulkkinen's operations plan was masterful."

On April 29 in front of 15,000 members, Nuxoll delivered a powerful speech. "And look what you have done on a more personal level in your communities," she said. "In ten days you've made more than 40,000 calls from phone banks to parents and voters. You have distributed hundreds of thousands of leaflets. You have held countless neighborhood meetings with parents, talked to thousands of citizens at restaurants and grocery stores and shopping malls, waved picket signs at about a million cars!"

What was Governor Gardner's response? He simply let the Legislature adjourn without dealing with any of the issues and told them to come back on June 15 for a special session because there would be a new revenue forecast. When asked if he was willing to commit any new revenue to education, he said, "No promises."

Whatever this action or inaction by the governor appeared to look like, as Teresa Moore said, "He turned tail and ran." It had a quelling impact on the strike. Legislators abandoned Olympia. WEA members had made their statement in Olympia and across the state in every local community. School would be out in many districts by June 15, and many members felt there was little more to gain beyond the school year. Several school districts had sought court injunctions against locals who were on strike, and those locals were not going to defy them while the Legislature took a walk. The strike was temporarily suspended and the activities ended with a thud. There was much debate in the Association as to how it could have ended differently, and its ending did not meet the expectations of many of the staff and leaders.

The Legislature did return for the special session in June. However, Booth Gardner did not prevail in his budget proposal. The Senate Republicans stood fast and added $200 million more to his budget for education. They reversed some of Gardner's cuts and added some new money for certain categories within the education budget. When all was said and done, about $9,200 was added to the budget per striking member. Time would prove that WEA had emerged more successful than was immediately apparent to most when the strike ended.

Another internal problem emanated from the Multi-Local Strike. Those on the west side of the state, who actually went on strike, felt that Eastern Washington locals and UniServ Councils did little to support the cause. This caused an internal rift between leaders and staff that took several years to mend. That part of the action was a setback for a WEA that was recovering from the internal fights of the 1980s.

G-CERF

The Governor demanded that a new appointed body be formed to look at education reform and funding. He called it the Governor's Council on Education Reform and Funding (G-CERF). This appointed committee was to come up with recommendations to the Legislature regarding educational accountability and funding. Nuxoll was appointed to G-CERF, as was one other teacher from Vancouver who had little connection to WEA. The G-CERF appointments were heavily weighted toward big business and politicians.

"I was the lone wolf on the committee," said Nuxoll. "It was hard to work with them because there was little interest in what teachers thought. Their primary concern was accountability, and they had no interest in fixing the funding crisis. They wanted us to do more for less money."

The WEA formed a Support Team to assist Nuxoll in representing educators' interests. Donna Dunning chaired the team. The team's job was to provide information that would assist Nuxoll in her efforts to provide sound educational rationale to G-CERF. Dunning was well connected to education experts in and out of state. Her team provided volumes of information for G-CERF. "They were more interested in what Frank Shrontz, of Boeing, thought than what was educationally sound," said Nuxoll.

According to Nuxoll, she spent her last year as WEA President fighting a defensive posture with G-CERF. "I was able to get some things modified, but in the end they took the Business Roundtable's recommendation."

After the 1991 session, which ended in June, the WEA settled into preparation for the 1992 session. Of course, the Instruction and Professional Development Division under Dunning was involved with G-CERF activities. Approaching the 1992 session, WEA took this message to the Legislature: "No Cuts — Raise Revenue." Even though the state budget shortfall amounted to $900 million, the WEA was not backing down from what it had not gotten in the Multi-Local Strike. Governor Gardner kept true to form by introducing a budget that eliminated the promised 3.5 percent salary increase and cut non-basic education programs across the board. The WEA advocated raising revenue by rescinding some of the tax breaks given to big business.

By the time the WEA Representative Assembly rolled around, WEA's Chief Lobbyist, Bob Fisher, called the legislative session "the most successful WEA has ever had." WEA lobbying resulted in, among other achievements, a 3 percent salary increase, increased health benefits, higher education increments, restoration of block grants to $57.7 million, a one-time early retirement, expansion of the levy lid and levy equalization. On the down side, new teachers were given a two-year probationary period.

"It was dynamite," Fisher said, "and it was because of the Crisis Action Plan and the Multi-Local Strike." The real benefits of the Multi-Local Strike came to fruition about one year later for WEA.

Strategic Planning

The WEA spent much of the decade of the 1990s attempting to improve the Association's planning processes and organization.

During the 1992 WEA Representative Assembly, the delegates took a major step toward changing the WEA. They reviewed a recommendation to adopt a thorough WEA strategic planning process. For many inside the WEA, it seemed as if the Association could not, alone, resolve the major issues that affected public education. A WEA public opinion poll of registered voters done in 1955 was discovered. The respondents had felt that the biggest issues facing Washington were: education 24 percent, highways 23 percent, state budget 17 percent and taxes 17 percent. What was their biggest criticism of public schools? Crowded classrooms, at 26 percent. Why didn't people want to be teachers? For 81 percent, salaries were too low. Which services need more money from the state? Seventy-six percent said public schools. These issues facing the WEA in 1955 were the same ones facing the Association in the 1990s. Some thought the time had come to look at what the WEA represented and how it might be more strategic in meeting the challenges facing public education. The RA delegates agreed and passed a motion setting WEA's strategic planning process in motion.

In April 1993, WEA's drive and successes in increasing Educational Support Personnel membership was rewarded when NEA chose WEA to host the largest-ever National Education Association Educational Support Personnel Conference in Seattle.

During the late spring and summer, Nuxoll appointed a committee to develop a WEA Strategic Plan. President Nuxoll and Vice President Purdom co-chaired the committee and assigned Deputy Executive Director Steve Kink as coordinator. The committee consisted of fourteen staff and governance people from around the state who represented various programs and divisions within the WEA.

The WEA Strategic Planning Committee continued to work during the 1992–1993 school year. The WEA hired the consulting firm of Deloitte & Touche to assist the committee in developing a strategic plan. It was decided to do an external and internal scan. The purpose of the external scan was to identify the strategic issues that WEA would face in the next five years and how various community leaders viewed the WEA. For the external scan Deloitte & Touche conducted twenty-three interviews of political, labor, media, institutional, religious and business leaders.

The internal scan was to determine what the members, leaders and staff thought WEA's purpose, goals and core values should be. The WEA trained a set of leaders and staff facilitators, who conducted thirty-six focus groups of randomly selected members, including classified, certificated and higher education members. They also conducted focus groups that included the associate, professional and management staff of the WEA, and they developed two questionnaires for the WEA Representative Assembly delegates and the Student WEA. All in all, more than 1,300 members and staff participated in the process. In May 1993, a group of seventy-five key staff and leaders retreated in Bellingham to finalize the strategic issues, the new core values and the mission statement. Another retreat was held in September to finalize the strategic goals. A membership poll was done in December to seek final input.

Carla Nuxoll's two terms ended in July 1993. When she became WEA President there were 43,000 members, and when she left there were 60,000. According to Teresa Moore, "It was a dream working with Carla. It was like working with an actor. She was a quick learner, took direction well and was an outstanding spokesperson for the WEA."

Nuxoll said, "I tried to be a voice for public education and educators. I tried to be a positive force in the Cabinet meetings and let the managers accomplish their work. Seibert was a hardworking administrator who had brought stability and unity to the WEA. Kink brought the ideas to the table, the other managers did their jobs well and they were a great support system for me."

After a decade of WEA being on the defensive, the Nuxoll years had put the Association on the offensive. WEA activities during her term were open and aggressive, and set the stage for the great growth in public support for education that would last beyond 2000. Nuxoll would go on to become this region's US Department of Education Representative for President Clinton's administration.

CT Purdom took office as WEA President in July. CT, as he liked to be called, had been Carla's Vice President. He had been an Association leader and principal in Naches Valley before returning to teaching. According to Jim Seibert, it was an easy transition from Carla to CT. "Carla involved CT and kept him informed, so he was ready to take over the job," said Seibert

"CT and I had a good relationship, and he was loyal to me and the position," said Nuxoll.

According to Kink, CT was more of a systems guy. "I think that his background in administration gave him a greater appreciation for how things operated," said Kink. "I think that is why he was so committed to the Strategic Plan and reengineering of the WEA. He wanted the WEA to be more efficient and more responsive to the membership."

Lee Ann Prielipp was elected Vice President. "CT was a quiet person," said Prielipp, who really did not know him well. "There were not a lot of people out there to run. It seemed like a leadership gap. The organization helped me grow and there were still some reform issues I wanted to address, so I ran."

The WEA Strategic Planning Committee presented its report to the WEA RA in 1994. The delegates overwhelmingly adopted a new Mission Statement, Goal, Objectives and Core Values for the Association. With the adoption of the new mission and goal, the WEA is charged "to build confidence in public education and increase support for Washington's public school system." In addition to advocating for member needs, the new objectives also called for WEA to champion public education throughout the state and in local communities. The result was more a clarification of what WEA believed rather than any real change in direction.

Strategic Planning — Phase Two

In the summer of 1994, the WEA entered into the second phase of its strategic plan. The Strategic Planning Committee adopted a process modeled after the concepts found in the book *Reengineering the Corporation* by Michael Hammer and James Champy. A twenty-five-member Reengineering Team was appointed to monitor the process. Steve Kink again was assigned the coordinator role. The team decided to create three Change Teams. Thirty people were appointed to the Change Teams, which would develop recommendations to change the Association. They were to address the Association's governance structure, the program and staffing structure, and the finance structure. CT appointed the governance members. The WEA management staff in collaboration with the staff union, WEASO, appointed the staff to the Change Teams. The Change Teams were to create an Association structure designed to implement the new Mission, Goal and Objectives. In November, the Reengineering Team held a meeting with 200 leaders and staff and shared their working documents. The Reengineering Team gave a status report at the 1995 Representative Assembly and made some recommendations to appoint two task forces to explore membership expansion and a new policy about defending the habitually in-trouble member — the member who year after year required Association assistance for various infractions of school district rules and regulations or for difficulties with job performance — and report to the WEA Board for their consideration.

By the end of 1995, the WEA had 65,000 members in 400 local associations and 150 WEA employees in twenty-two offices around the state. It had been conducting the business of the Association, albeit much larger, using the same basic delivery structure that existed in 1971. There were more programs, more staff, more members and more offices than in 1971, but the structure was essentially the same.

Reengineering

In the spring of 1996, the WEA RA was presented with the Reengineering Team Report. The process that started in 1992 had led to the adoption of a new WEA Mission, Goal and Objectives, and now was about to consider major organizational infrastructure changes. According to Kink, "The Reengineering Team spent the last year determining the basic functions of the organization and then trying to create the best structure to deliver them." Purdom said, "It's about bringing WEA closer to its rank-and-file members. The structure is outmoded and must be changed, and the recommendations are logical and functional."

The Reengineering Team recommended, among other things:

·   Eliminating Committees and Commissions, to be replaced by Task Forces with sunset provisions
·   Eliminating conferences and meetings that did not support WEA's Core Functions

- Eliminating the Department structure and moving AHE (Association for Higher Education), SWEA (Student Washington Education Association), ESP (Educational Support Personnel) and WEA-R (WEA-Retired) into program functions instead
- Develop Consulting Centers in lieu of UniServ offices with no fewer than two UniServ staff (consultants) per office
- A single UniServ Program to replace the SOUP, LOUP and DUC structure
- Reducing the size of the WEA Board of Directors with the Consulting Center Presidents serving on the board

The RA acted on some of these items, and all those up for approval passed by a super-majority except the reduction of the Board of Directors, which failed with a 61.8 percent majority. Other items were referred to work teams for further development and implementation.

Up to 1996, only a few WEA staff members would retire each year. During the 1980s several of the original staff leaders like Jim Raines, Dale Troxel and Don Johnson retired. They had made significant contributions to the Association and its members. The WEA was able to work through the changes as new staff people assumed their roles. However, in 1996, fourteen management, UniServ and associate staff retired at once. They represented 300 collective years in Association work. "We had made our contributions to the cause, of which we were proud," said Kink of these retirees. "It was time to make room for new and younger staff who could relate to the growing number of new members. This group of retirees did make a difference in the lives of many members over four decades of service."

From Steve Kink, the Deputy Executive Director, to Mydra Caldwell, the WEA receptionist, they represented all levels of experience in the Association. Some, like Helen Ortiz in Field Services, had started in the old WEA building in downtown Seattle. Dick and Jeanne Johnson both left the Communications Division. Don Maekawa, WEA comptroller, was among them. Kink was given a half-time contract to complete the Reengineering implementation and to lead Organizing for Public Education (OPE) Team activities. The OPE Team, consisting of staff and governance leaders, expanded community organizing training and focused on establishing local projects and training in specific association, school district and building teams.

Political Struggles in the 1990s

After the successful 1992 legislative session following the Multi-Local Strike, the patterns in Olympia seemed to return to the usual struggle just to keep up. Despite having more Democratic governors and mostly Democratic Legislatures, there were no great breakthroughs in the 1990s.

Many WEA members had soured on the political action process because of a succession of endorsed candidates who had failed to produce on their promises.

Hoping to revive interest in the candidate endorsement process, WEA held the first PULSE (Political Unity of Leaders in State Education) Endorsement Convention. For the first time, PULSE members would vote at the convention to endorse statewide candidates and choose congressional candidates to recommend to the NEA for endorsement. More than 400 members came to the convention. Among others, they endorsed Mike Lowry for Governor and Christine Gregoire for attorney general. They did not endorse WEA's past President Terry Bergeson for Superintendent of Public Instruction but instead endorsed Judith Billings. They also chose Patty Murray as their recommendation to NEA for endorsement in the US Senate race. "I think for the first time around, the convention was a resounding success," said WEA Governmental Relations Field Representative Bob Maier.

1992 Elections

Riding Bill Clinton's success in Washington and across the country, the 1992 elections went well for WEA. Gardner was finally out of the picture. WEA had endorsed the winning candidate for governor. Mike Lowry, a liberal Democrat, gave WEA leaders hope that he would stand up on education issues unlike Gardner, who had let them down. "Except for Initiative 134, we were very successful in getting endorsed candidates elected," said Maier. Because of the election successes, the expectations for a legislative response to education issues ran high. But WEA would be, yet again, disappointed.

The passage of Initiative 134 would prove to be a major headache for the Association. It was an anti-union campaign finance initiative opposed by WEA and many other organizations. WEA's failure to get its own campaign finance measure, I–401, on the ballot in 1981 loomed all the larger now. Like I–401, I–134 was also about campaign finance reform, but anti-union advocates wrote it. WEA's political action committee (PULSE) had used a system to collect political funds from members called a reverse dues check-off or automatic dues deduction. PULSE contributions would be automatically deducted, as WEA dues were, from members' paychecks unless they stipulated that they did not want to contribute. Initiative 134 ended this practice, and it required members to sign up annually. The effect was to greatly reduce WEA's political action funds. It also limited campaign contributions to candidates and was not well written. This would soon cause WEA huge problems.

During the 1993 legislative session, a big issue was health care reform. Between the 1983–1985 and 1991–1993 budget years, the budget for educational employees' health care declined 7 percent while everyone else enjoyed a 7 percent increase. Annual insurance rates were in the double digits and the industry was under fire from a variety of fronts, including WEA. The Democrats and the newly elected Governor Lowry wanted to move this agenda. WEA assigned Rod Regan to work the issue inside the Association, and Karen Davis was working it in the Legislature. It was controversial because it put educational employees in a large insurance pool as opposed to their own district pools. Davis was able to get a provision in the bill allowing locals to bargain above the state's coverage. The bill passed. However, in the very next session the health care industry got the bill repealed, except for the right of locals to bargain additional benefits.

The Legislature provided no salary increases for school employees for the 1993–1994 school year. This would become the subject of a rallying cry in later years.

The 1993 Legislature also adopted the report from G-CERF by passing HB 1209. They recommended a variety of education reform measures costing a little over $1.5 billion. They dealt with the reform items only, and made no recommendations to deal with the current funding problems facing public education. They did not even provide a recommendation as to where to get the revenue for the $1.5 billion in reform costs. They did recommend that the Legislature create — yet another — committee, called the Student Learning Commission, to work out the details of the reform recommendations. After a stint as a Central Kitsap School District administrator, Terry Bergeson was chosen Executive Director of the Student Learning Commission.

CT's first major challenge as WEA President was Initiatives 601 and 602. Initiative 601, backed by Vancouver's Representative Linda Smith, was a state government spending limitation, and 602, a somewhat overlapping measure, would also remove taxes from alcohol and tobacco. WEA worked against 601 and 602 primarily because they reduced revenues to the state. Less revenue for the state would exacerbate the existing lack of education funding. The initiatives had some popular support because a couple of TV stations were running a series of waste-in-government-spending stories.

A coalition was put together to help defeat the initiatives. WEA participated in the coalition. Kris Hanselman from the WEA staff and Sondra Williams from the NEA staff were assigned to work with it. Rod Regan and Steve Kink were assigned to run the internal membership campaign out of the WEA office. WEA's theme was "Know to Vote NO on 601 and 602." WEA cranked up the phone bank operation and called its pro-education voter lists. Members, leaders and staff all had assignments to contact friends and relatives urging them to vote no. Initiative 602 was defeated, but 601 passed by about 51 percent. The Legislature took this as a huge public mandate and for years gave it priority over other initiatives that had much higher public support.

The 1994 legislative session provided few positive results for education. The Legislature, shell-shocked from the passage of Initiative 601, had yet another excuse to say no to needed education funding. It was interesting to note that the consumer price index from 1973 to 1993 went up 242 percent while legislative salaries increased by 619 percent. The salary increase for public school employees from the Legislature for 1994–1995 was another 0 percent added to the 0 percent provided a year earlier.

The WEA took another route to deal with the lack of education funding. Rod Regan began working directly with local associations in levy elections. He developed a levy campaign program. The program utilized and expanded the pro-education voter lists started during the Multi-Local Strike. He did precinct analysis, along with absentee voter and pro-education voter phone contacts. He worked with UniServ staff, encouraging them to add bargaining contract language to provide money from the approved levies. WEA was building its pro-education voter files with community connections throughout the state via levy elections. WEA has since expanded the list to more than one million names.

In the summer of 1994, WEA was again challenged by two more initiatives. Fortunately, Initiatives 608 and 610, both restricting gay rights and the teaching of the "gay lifestyle," failed to make the ballot. WEA opposed these initiatives because, as WEA President CT Purdom stated, "They would erode academic freedom and citizens' rights regarding sexual orientation." WEA's message to members was, "Decline to sign," and the Association made a sizable contribution to the campaign against the initiatives.

In December of that year Bob Fisher told the WEA Board that the coming session would be the toughest in his twenty-seven years with the WEA. Following the pattern of the national elections, which saw President Clinton losing party control of both houses of Congress, Washington's fall elections provided a swing of twenty-seven seats in the House, putting the Republicans in control. The Democrats had the Senate by one vote. Fisher anticipated anti-strike legislation, repeal of the duty-free lunch and little if any salary money.

When the Legislature adjourned, WEA had made out much better than Fisher had predicted. The budget included a 4 percent salary increase and funding for higher education increments. WEA was able to fend off anti-bargaining legislation but lost the bill to reduce school levies to a simple majority vote. With the help of WEA-R, WEA's retired member organization, SSB 5119 passed. It provided a cost of living allowance for retired school employees.

On that achievement Bob Fisher, who began work for WEA in 1967, retired.

In 1995, Rod Regan was assigned full-time as the Political Action Director, leaving the Community Organizing program without staffing. Steve Kink, with his new half-time contract, assumed responsibility for the Organizing for Public Education (OPE) Team created to implement community organizing activities.

The fall of 1995 brought yet another challenge to the WEA. Initiatives 173 and 177 were filed. If passed, they would create school vouchers and charter schools in the state. Initiative sponsors and others attacked public schools, and WEA responded to the attacks. The WEA held its Restructuring Conference and invited David Berliner. Berliner was a professor at Arizona State University and had studied the American public school system. He gave his "Exploding the Myths About Public Education" presentation. He said, "Today's students are better than they have ever been." He provided factual data that disproved right-wing claims about public education.

The year 1996 began with what was described in the WEA *Action* as a "Gloomy Session." WEA's Governmental Relations staff introduced the legislative package with a new twist. They put all the proposals in terms of what was best for students, such as safe schools, appropriate learning environments, active parent and guardian responsibilities and having qualified teachers and support staff. However, the lobbying staff found itself fending off voucher and charter school legislation and ended up with another 0 percent in the budget for school employee salaries.

In February, an event that had occurred in a few other states took place in Moses Lake. It would come to influence WEA's legislative proposals for the next few years. At Frontier Junior High School, a disturbed student shot and killed a teacher and two students and critically wounded another. The entire state was taken by surprise. Teaching colleagues from across the state offered their condolences and support to the staff at Frontier. WEA pushed even harder for legislative assistance in making schools a safer place to work and learn.

The 1996 state elections would bring another set of changes that would impact the WEA and its members. Terry Bergeson took another run at the State Superintendent of Public Instruction office and, unlike her first attempt, she got WEA's endorsement and won. The Republican candidate for governor was conservative Ellen Craswell. The Democrat was Gary Locke, who was King County Executive and a former state representative. Locke crushed Craswell, and again WEA leadership hopes were high for additional education funding.

In the fall of 1996, a conservative organization called the Evergreen Freedom Foundation (EFF) alleged to the Public Disclosure Commission (PDC) that the WEA had misspent over $4 million in WEA dues monies for political action purposes. The EFF was headed by Bob Williams, a former conservative Republican House member and an unsuccessful candidate for governor. The board of the EFF consisted of former Republican legislators, most of whom had poor WEA voting records. The EFF received funding from a few out-of-state right-wing contributors and had support from the National Right to Work Committee.

"EFF took an enormous amount of time," said Executive Director Jim Seibert. "Williams used the WEA as a test case to go after the NEA. The EFF charges created a cloud over WEA with the public."

"We never did anything we thought was wrong," said Lee Ann Prielipp. "You could call the PDC on two days and get two different answers as to how to meet their reporting requirements. It was very expensive but after all the legal challenges, we prevailed 90 percent of the time."

There were several legal charges and countercharges filed by the EFF and the WEA over several years. "We were finally vindicated by the recent EFF court decision," Seibert said in 2003, when all was said and done.

In January 1997, the WEA entered yet another year hoping that the Legislature and new governor would finally address education's funding needs. The legislative package was framed around standards for schools and students. The theme which ran in the form of public ads, was "Washington Schools: Working Today for a Smarter Tomorrow."

During the legislative session, WEA was proposing cost of living increases of 2.5 percent for the next two years. Soon the rallying cry became "Don't Crush COLAs." WEA also supported some of the education reform issues coming from the Student Learning Commission such as the Essential Academic Learning Requirements (EALRs), which were standards for certain academic areas. The WEA supported the funding for Standard Learning Improvement Grants, also known as SLIGs, designed to help school districts deal with reform issues. The WEA ended up helping to veto the budget and kill several bad education bills. On salaries the WEA again came up short, with a one-year 3 percent raise for school employees.

January 1998 rang in another familiar situation for the WEA. The Legislature was once again rolling in money. It had a $900 million surplus. WEA characterized the situation as "Booming Budget — Bulging Classrooms." Washington state had consistently ranked near the bottom of the nation in class sizes. In 1998, it ranked forty-eighth (third highest) in the nation. The state had done little to address the issue, and it would have cost $467 million for Washington state to reach the national average. Governor Locke was uninterested in any significant spending to address the issue. WEA brought out the "Student in the Sardine Can" ad and ran it during the session. A large group of parents held a "Parent Power for Lower Class Size" rally in Olympia.

The EFF made a crucial error in attacking the WEA. They created an ad for distribution in major newspapers across the state. The ad depicted a crisis in the classroom by showing a masher robber, identified as the WEA, taking money from a woman teacher's purse. The League of Women Voters and the State Labor Council ripped the EFF, and it lost what little public credibility it ever had.

In June, WEA's Representative Assembly met and the delegates were angry. Once again the Legislature and Governor had failed to deal with the funding crises. School employees again got another 0 percent for salary increases. The delegates made it loud and clear that the WEA's top priority for the next session was compensation!

In the fall of 1998, a couple of things occurred on the political scene. The WEA targeted ten legislators to defeat. They were successful in eight of the ten races. The State Labor Council and others were supporting a minimum wage initiative. The WEA also supported it, and it passed.

Jim Seibert appointed an Action Task Force (ATF) to prepare for the upcoming legislative session. Rod Regan headed it up and Lynn Macdonald from University Place was released from her position as President of the Soundview UniServ Council to serve full-time on the ATF. A public opinion poll was commissioned in December. Tom Kiley, of Kiley Inc., located in Boston, had been doing WEA internal and external polls for many years. He was chosen to do the poll. The poll results showed popular support for an annual automatic cost of living adjustment (COLA) for teachers and for reducing the local maintenance and operation school levies passage requirements from a super majority to a simple majority.

In January 1999, the legislative cry was "Catch Up and Keep Up." WEA's legislative package included a salary increase of 15 percent. This was based on what members had lost to the cost of living for the past six years when they received 0, 0, 4, 0, 3 and 0 percent increases. Locke offered 4 percent over the next two years. WEA responded with ads that said, "2+2 = 2 little." The ATF developed plans for local associations to hold local meetings and demand that legislators attend.

The WEA and the locals kept on the pressure for higher salaries. Meetings were held mostly in Western Washington. Frank Chopp recessed the House of Representatives so legislators could attend the meetings. More than 500 people showed up at the Greek Orthodox Church in Seattle demanding fair pay. A Garfield High School teacher said, "The economy's up and teachers get nothing. I feel like a chump." Then a strike chant began.

Pilchuck held a rally at the Everett Civic Auditorium. Over 2,500 people showed up and shared stories as to how it felt to be taken for granted and the financial hardships the Legislature had caused. Twelve hundred staff walked out in Northshore. Rallies of school employees and supportive parents and students were held for ten days on the Capitol steps in Olympia. More than forty districts either walked out or rallied after school during the session.

Kevin Teeley from Lake Washington and Lynn Macdonald representing WEA debated legislators on KOMO TV's *Town Meeting*. Everett teacher Jared Kink, who is Steve Kink's son, went on the conservative radio station KVI to make the case for higher salaries.

At the 1999 WEA RA the delegates were set to take some action. The Legislature had done little to respond to their cries to "Catch Up and Keep Up." A poll showed that the public was in favor of teachers having an automatic COLA. However, the WEA leadership was gun-shy from recent EFF challenges and feared that sponsoring an initiative might qualify the whole WEA as a political action committee. They failed to share the findings from the poll with the delegation. The delegates ended up following the leadership and voting down pursuing a COLA initiative, but there was a big split with around 40 percent voting to sponsor the initiative.

When the Legislature finished, they added $200 million over Governor Locke's salary proposal. However, it was a far cry from the 15 percent that was the "Catch-Up" needed to make up for the lack of past legislative actions.

Later in August, Superior Court Judge Thomas McPhee issued a ruling that entirely favored the WEA over the EFF. The EFF had tried to stop the WEA from organizing and lobbying for compensation issues. McPhee said, "EFF failed to prove its case. Participation in the political process to obtain economic security is a hallmark of every public-sector labor union."

Governor Locke followed Gardner's suit and appointed only one teacher to the Academic Achievement and Accountability Commission. The other eight are mostly business people and administrators. The Commission is charged to oversee the new academic goals for schools.

Legislators and other elected officials were granted salary increases. The Legislature got a 13 percent increase for the next two years. The education employees' 3 percent for one year was a far cry from what the politicians voted for themselves.

During the winter, WEA leaders and staff were told by legislative leaders that there would be little change in salaries in the upcoming session even though the state had yet another surplus. Despite the recent small salary increase for teachers, they fell behind inflation by 9 percent by the 2000–2001 school year. A *Seattle Post-Intelligencer* poll showed that 45 percent of those polled thought that the Legislature should use the surplus to improve public schools and 35 percent wanted affordable health care.

Bob Maier was chosen as WEA's Chief Lobbyist. After serving in a variety of political action and lobbying roles and what Bob called "an inter-galactic search," he was given the position three days before the session started.

In March, "The Drive Is On" started. This was a cross-state bus tour that drove home the link between fair pay and quality education for students. Lake Washington started it and other locals joined in as the message spread.

The WEA undertook a member and public advertising campaign that picked up where "Catch Up and Keep Up" left off. The theme was around providing salaries that would "keep and recruit" quality teachers, and it paved the way for WEA's greatest ballot success since the 1930s.

Strikes Continue in the 1990s

It was no surprise, following the Multi-Local strike, that there were no local strikes in 1992. With a few dramatic exceptions, the decade of the 1990s would see fewer teacher strikes. Those that did occur would keep collective bargaining very much alive and allow locals to once again make local money for salaries a viable bargaining issue.

In 1993 Kennewick went on strike for three days over teacher evaluation, student discipline, assignment and transfer, and site-based decision-making. Pateros, also in Eastern Washington, saw both its classified and certificated employee units on strike for eight days over a long list of issues including agency fee for both units.

In January 1993 Shelton secretaries struck for a day. This was the first purely classified school employee strike in the state.

In 1993 the only local to strike was Soap Lake. Again both classified and certificated employees joined ranks. It lasted for seven days and involved a long list of issues for both units.

The number and intensity of strikes increased in 1994. Federal Way teachers were on strike for the first time since their successful 1974 strike. It lasted eight days and resolved issues concerning school violence, student discipline, PE specialists and control of optional days.

The Bremerton strike lasted longer, twenty-one days. The issues, including district take-aways, school violence, discipline and weapons, class overloads and site-based decision-making were familiar bargaining items for the mid-1990s, but the overriding issue, one familiar in all decades, was the dictatorial superintendent DeWayne Boyd. A year after the strike this contentious superintendent "resigned."

From November 1 to 11 Concrete teachers, known as the "Fighting 49," again proved that very small and isolated locals could strike successfully. A number of money issues led to the walkout.

In October 1995, the state's longest teacher strike to date would start in the Fife School District. It lasted for thirty-seven days and was ultimately settled by submitting the remaining issues to an arbitrator. It was a very difficult strike to settle because it involved essentially a single issue, TRI (Time, Responsibility or Incentive) pay. Fife over the years had bargained one of the higher TRI pay schedules in the state, and the District wanted to take away a large portion of it. The District had just changed its superintendent under questionable circumstances and maintained that it did not have the money to pay for the TRI schedule.

The grim weather of October and November tested Fife's 126 teachers, led by Maggi Kellso, who inspired them and urged them on even as they set a new record for the length of strikes in Washington. After thirty-seven days, with a partial settlement achieved, the Fife Education Association and the District agreed to submit the remaining issues to binding arbitration. This was a first for strikes in Washington (except for makeup days in West Valley in 1975), and it was a risk to put the outcome of the strike into the hands of a neutral third party.

The District's main contention was that it did not have the money. However, WEA Research Director Joann Kink Mertens successfully disputed District claims. Network Attorney Mitch Cogdill, who had interest arbitration experience, helped prepare Fife for the hearing. In the summer of 1996 the arbitrator ruled in favor of the Association and restored all the disputed TRI money. She awarded Association members $295,000, money the District was shown to have through the work of Kink Mertens.

The next strike occurred in September 1998, at Lake Stevens. Among twenty or so issues, teachers were seeking increased TRI pay to bring them up to what other Snohomish County locals were making, along with teacher control of optional days and class size. The strike lasted for sixteen days.

There would be no more school employee strikes in Washington until 2001, but grievous conditions in the Riverside School District near Spokane caused teachers there, with the help of UniServ Rep Roger Stephens, to mount a community organizing drive equal in intensity to any strike. Superintendent Jerry Wilson had tried to take away funds the Legislature had allocated for salaries and for years had tried to silence the professional voice of the District's teachers. Riverside teachers viewed him as a despot whose dictatorial style had terrible effects on students and teachers. Though not considered on strike, they did take a day off to do a "Walk for Democracy" around the superintendent's office. The REA President, Marv Sather, also the Washington State Teacher of the Year, announced that he would resign from teaching unless the superintendent left, and he did resign before the board acted. The board finally saw the light and dumped the superintendent. In the aftermath, six more administrators and three school board members lost their jobs. Roger Stephens said, "Whenever you think all is lost, you can come up with creative solutions and strategies."

Eastern Washington Restructuring Network

In May 1994, the Eastern Washington Restructuring Network was launched. The network consisted of six UniServ Councils, two Educational Service Districts and twenty school districts throughout Eastern Washington. After much discussion since 1989, staff and leaders put form to their ideas and created the network. The core organizers were Dick Iverson and Steve Paulson of WEA, Joan Kingery of the Spokane School District and Bill Mester, the Mead Superintendent.

The network had three parts. An instruction part developed a League of Schools, the purpose of which was to work with Washington State University to share best practices in instruction. The network would hold conferences showcasing successful instructional practices to other network members. Hundreds of members would attend the conferences to learn what was working well in different schools. Washington State University's role was to collect and promote these best practices — innovative classroom strategies to enhance student learning and performance.

Another part of the network was restructuring. The network utilized Patrick Dolan to lead them in systemically restructuring school districts. The basic premise in this effort was to develop an oversight committee in each district consisting of representatives from each school board, the administration and the local association. The purpose of the committee was to provide permission and parameters for freedom within the system to meet instructional needs and to function creatively at the building level, to take such actions as changing the schedule, changing staffing ratios, adding specialized staffing, and utilizing parent assistance differently.

The third part of the network was parental involvement. For leadership here, the network turned to Joe Chrastle of the Industrial Areas Foundation. The purpose of the parent piece was to work with parents at each school building to help them become active participants in the decision-making process at the building and district levels.

According to Iverson, the network's efforts to get those education stakeholders working together dovetailed with the collaborative bargaining move throughout the state. The network provided training for hundreds of education stakeholders, parents, teachers and administrators. Some districts made significant operational changes and developed better working relationships.

"The network began to break down for several reasons," said Iverson. "Dennis Ray at WSU never really bought into what we were trying to do and did not see the need to systemically change the school structure. The parent organizing part never was integrated into the system. Standardized testing really killed it because teachers had to refocus on tests due to pressures from the administrators. Where once teaching professionals were creators, testing turned them into test implementers."

In 1999 the Washington Network for Public Education (WNPE) was developed primarily in Eastern Washington. It replaced the Eastern Washington Restructuring Network, in a sense. The WNPE was a systemic approach to restructuring schools based on continuing research, creating flexibility in the system, engaging parents and advocating democracy in the classroom environment. According to Steve Paulson, who headed the project, "It's about finding solutions outside the adversarial union-management model. It answers the question, how good do you want your school to be?"

The Prielipp Era Begins

CT Purdom exited as WEA President in 1997 on a somewhat sour note. According to his successor, Lee Ann Prielipp, Purdom was frustrated that he was not more successful with Reengineering. In his farewell speech to the RA he chided the delegates. "New Unionism [a term coined by NEA President Bob Chase] means it's time to take a chance!"

Other factors were to explain Purdom's parting demeanor. "CT was tough with the Legislature and not diplomatic," said Seibert. "He also had a bad taste after the last round of WEASO bargaining. He was more hands-on and opinionated about personnel items."

Lee Ann Prielipp, along with her new Vice President, Tom Morris, took over the reins of the WEA in July 1997. She was a longtime activist who had begun her Association involvement around the time of the 1974 Federal Way strike. Carol Coe had been an inspiration for her.

She had climbed up through the governance ranks and became a major player in the Coe-Lindquist-Maier camp. She was very active at the NEA level as a board member, on a committee dealing with AFT/NEA mergers and on the Blue Ribbon Task Force on Education Reform. Prielipp was an education reform advocate.

Tom Morris was a local and UniServ Council President from Renton. He was a hard-core union advocate who championed member compensation and rights. Prielipp and Morris represented the major sides of Association advocacy.

Events of Note

Throughout the decade of the 1990s WEA diversified its programs. It had many things to be proud of that went beyond the major programs of UniServ, bargaining and political action and legislation.

In April 1993, as we have seen, NEA recognized WEA's successes in increasing Educational Support Personnel membership by choosing WEA to host the largest-ever NEA ESP Conference in Seattle.

In November 1993, WEA's Minority Leadership Training Program (MLTP) reached a milestone. They had just trained their 2,000th member in the program. MLTP, started many years earlier, had been a popular program to bring minority and women members into leadership levels of the Association.

The 1994 Representative Assembly adopted the Children's Fund, WEA's nonprofit foundation to raise funds to help needy kids in schools throughout the state. The foundation has continued to receive grants since its inception. Hundreds of students have received everything from instructional materials to clothing from the Children's Fund.

The WEA had revised its major publication, WEA *Action*, and it really was the state Association's voice to every member. Jeanne Johnson had been editor since 1980 and tried to reflect what the members wanted in the publication. Despite fluctuations in WEA leadership philosophies, Johnson was able to keep the *Action* as an advocate publication. Her efforts were rewarded in 1995 when she received the National Education Association's Editor of the Year Award.

During the late winter of 1994 and the spring of 1995, two instructional issues were reported in the WEA *Action*. Four teachers in Vancouver were the first in the state to qualify for and receive National Board Teaching Certificates. They were Shelly James, Patricia Simonds, Kathy Kirkland and Edri Geiger. WEA's Patty Raichle would soon head up a program to facilitate and train other teachers across the state in how to achieve this prestigious credential.

The second instructional issue reported was Seattle's Staff Training and Review program, or STAR. STAR was a joint program of peer assistance between the SEA and the school district that had been implemented in the early 1990s. The program had two purposes. It gave added peer assistance to teachers in their first two years of teaching, and it gave remedial assistance to experienced teachers who were struggling with their teaching.

In 1995 the *Action* reported two different organizing events. The first was the Community Organization for Yakima County (COYC), which was organized around identifying and addressing youth issues in the county. Les Hall, UniServ Rep Leslie Kanzler and Rick Rodden of the MidState UniServ Council were instrumental in its inception. Program activities included organizing the Hispanic community to pass a much-needed levy in Toppenish with COYC support.

The second organizing event was a first for WEA in more ways than one. In April the faculty at Eastern Washington University bargained their first collective bargaining agreement. It was the first four-year institution in Washington to bargain a contract. No state law mandated such bargaining. The school's United Faculty organization was a joint affiliate of the WEA and the AFT. WEA organizer Steve Pulkkinen was instrumental in the merger and in bargaining the contract.

In September 1997, the WEA, working with the Washington Federation of Teachers, created the United Faculty organization that won bargaining rights at Central Washington University by a vote of 236 to 84. It was the second four-year higher education institution to have union representation for its faculty.

In October 1997, WEA invited Jamie Vollmer to a fall instructional conference. Vollmer was a CEO from Iowa and on the Iowa Business and Education Roundtable. An outspoken public education advocate, he said, "Every single standard measure of your work shows you have never done a better job." Earlier in September, Washington State's SAT scores were released and students' scores were up 12 percent in verbal and 11 percent in math.

In December, the WEA Research Department continued its work in getting money to members who had been mistreated at the school district level. In Bremerton, they identified $125,000 that was due and then paid to teachers in the district. In Darrington, they identified $150 for new teachers and $240 for veteran teachers that was due and paid.

WEA's Organizing for Public Education (OPE) Team reached a crucial point in its existence. The team leader, Steve Kink, was about to conclude his part-time contract and leave the WEA permanently. The team developed recommendations regarding the future of the program. A key recommendation was to create a full-time staff position. Later, OPE team member and MidState UniServ staff Leslie Kanzler was chosen for the position. The recommendations included a summary of the team's activities. In three years, the team had provided training to fifteen UniServ Councils and six local associations. They had created an "Issues in Education" presentation that was delivered to twelve community and education coalition groups inside and outside the association, to the entire staff of eight school districts on opening day of school, and to the staff of six school buildings. The team also conducted five Future Search Conferences (a group dynamics process for communities to design the future for their local schools), trained at three WEALAs and held three OPE seminars that showcased other community/ education organizing projects.

Kink also wrote a Network Report that encapsulated the major activities that related to WEA's objective to "forge partnerships with parents, business and community groups." He identified four kinds of coalitions and networks that evolved on both sides of the state at state and UniServ Council levels:

· Single Issue Coalitions, such as the WEA Learning Space, WEA-OSPI Para-Educator Project and the Fourth Corner Masters Certification Project

· Dispute Resolution Networks, such as the Fourth Corner and Cascade Mediation Networks and the Joint Dispute Resolution Consortium in Eastern Washington

· Cooperative Coalition Networks, such as the Fourth Corner P-SUP, the MidState Coalition and the Coalition for School Improvement

· Educational Change and Improvement Networks, such as the Eastern Washington Restructuring Network and the Soundview UniServ Council's Union School Project

In February 1998, John Gullion died of a brain tumor. Gullion was one of the original UniServ representatives who came to Washington in 1971. He was the first staff person jailed in a strike (in Elma). Gullion was a pioneer in his field, a risk taker and a successful advocate for member and bargaining rights. He served the members of the Puget Sound UniServ Council from 1971 to 1998.

On August 19, 1999, the WEA sponsored "Tomorrow's Classroom: Teaching in the New Millennium." They rented the Kingdome in Seattle and 10,000 visitors observed school projects from around the state. WEA's Donna Dunning said, "For a first-time event, this was just incredibly successful."

WEA supported two other events during the winter. The first was the Children's Festival 2000, which supported the appreciation of world cultures and mixed fun with learning. The second event was Read Across America Day. WEA has participated in this *Cat in the Hat*–themed event since its inception. Mike Holmgren, the Seattle Seahawks coach was chosen Advisory Chair for the event.

One of WEA's efforts in the instructional area was the Keys to Excellence for Your Schools (KEYS) Program. The program provided a school's organizational profile, assessing its climate for teamwork, community support and the like. Once the data was identified, staff, parents and administrators could focus on what issues they want to address together and what they want to change. "KEYS provides the vehicle for schools to come together to have deeper, more focused conversation on issues that truly impact student learning," said WEA's KEYS Coordinator Pat Steinburg.

Initiative 732

If the unprecedented 1991 Multi-Local Strike was one giant event of the 1990s, the campaign for Initiative 732 in 2000 was the other. It would prove once again that the WEA had the ability to mobilize school employees and their supporters to accomplish what few organizations were capable of doing. It would be the culminating event of Lee Ann Prielipp's four years as WEA President.

After a year of frustration for many leaders and internal political pressure from the Sammamish UniServ Council, among others, the WEA Board approved filing a COLA (Cost of Living Adjustment) initiative. The initiative language called for the Legislature to provide for a COLA for all school employees every year. The WEA had gotten nowhere with the Legislature on this, so went directly to the people for a mandate. The board also supported Initiative 728, known as K–12 2000, which would provide, among other things, additional state funding to lower class sizes. WEA needed to generate 240,000 valid signatures by July to qualify for the November ballot.

The 2000 WEA RA convened and heard that the Legislature had allocated nothing for salaries. "There was around $100 million that they could have allocated to salaries but the supplemental budget had zero," reported Bob Maier. The delegates were more than ready for action.

The COLA initiative was numbered I–732 and was printed in full in the May 2000 edition of the WEA *Action*. The WEA organizing plan to get the signatures was to establish goals for every level of the association. It was an all-out emphasis at the grass-roots levels. "There was a natural and friendly competition among many of the councils," said Rod Regan.

Prielipp called it "crunch time." The campaign established a 732 Club that had an exclusive membership made up of individuals who personally gathered 732 signatures. The first members were Vice President Tom Morris, Jared Kink, Dan Brown and UniServ staffers Leona Dater and Lisa Raine. Regan estimated that 25,000 people worked the initiatives. In July, WEA turned in around 300,000 signatures, far more than required for validation.

What was Governor Locke's role in the process? At first, he would not commit to 732, but he changed his mind and became a "Johnny-come-lately" to the bandwagon. It could only be surmised that he could read public opinion polls that favored the COLAs.

WEA geared up for the 2000 general election. Members were encouraged to get the word out to friends and relatives regarding I–732 and I–728. Kris Hanselman was put in charge of the campaign at the WEA level. WEA spent a substantial amount of money on a simple public advertising and word-of-mouth campaign.

After sixty-nine of eighty-eight WEA-endorsed candidates won in the election, Bob Maier said, "WEA members played a big role in electing pro-public education legislators." Gary Brown, the Chinook UniServ Council President, said, "Governor Gary Locke will play an even bigger role in improving public education. He'll be more willing to work with us. He values education a lot." Unfortunately for Brown and Maier, these words would come back to haunt them.

The greatest win for WEA was the passage of I–732 and, to a lesser degree, I–728. The I–732 campaign was one of the greatest organizing efforts in WEA's history. It was a shining moment and proved that success comes when members are committed to a cause, motivated and organized to get results.

The WEA set a national precedent in passing an automatic annual COLA for all school employees. The initiative passed in every county in the state. Where the Legislature had failed to act, the public rose up and demanded that they do what was right for school employees. I–732 passed by over 60 percent, and the class size reduction initiative, I–728, passed by over 70 percent. The public had spoken with thunderous approval. It supported the initiatives far more strongly than it had I–601, which the Legislature had used for years as an excuse not to provide salary increases for teachers.

The WEA held a Special Representative Assembly in December. The Special RA came about due to an internal debate raging around a WEA position on compensation. Local leaders from the west side of the state wanted to propose a housing allowance factor in state funding as a means to address cost of living differences throughout the state. After a lively debate pro and con, the concept passed. This RA also adopted the goal that by 2010, Washington public school employee salaries should rank in the top five nationally. If achieved, it would return them to where they were in 1981.

WEA introduced its Campaign for Quality Schools to the newly elected 2001 Legislature. It called for:

· Fair compensation to attract and retain quality teachers and school employees

· Smaller class sizes

· Safe schools and more parent involvement

· Higher academic standards

· Sufficient school funding

· Respect for the education profession

The Academic Achievement and Accountability Commission finally released its legislative recommendations. Its measurement tools for achievement were centered on the Washington Assessment of Student Learning (WASL) tests. Their accountability recommendations were, among others, to withhold funds, reconstitute the district's personnel, appoint a trustee to administer the district, abolish or restructure the district, and authorize student transfers to other schools or districts.

They proposed to reward successful schools and districts, provide assistance for students and schools, and offer intervention strategies for schools and districts with persistent low performance. The process would center around WASL as the measuring tool to determine the success or failure of a school or school district.

The WASL became a single high-stakes test that concerned the WEA. After several problems arose in the format, delivery and grading of the tests, WEA lobbied against the sole use of the WASL as the decision-making criterion. They instead proposed the use of multiple assessment methods to determine student learning and success. WEA continued to push legislation that addressed the financial needs required to meet the new education reform recommendations, which seemed to be an afterthought of the policy makers.

By April, the Governor and the Legislature had proposed not only to ignore the public mandates of I–728 and I–732, but to cut existing education programs by some $85 million. They decided that the word "all" in the phrase "all school employees" as defined in Initiative 732, didn't really mean that the Legislature was responsible for providing COLAs for some 25,000 school employees hired with local and federal funds. Legislators left it to districts to fund those COLAs. The state feebly contended that "all" meant only those employees it had funded traditionally. One legislator told Olympic UniServ leaders that they "may have to sue the state to get full funding for the initiatives." Later, the WEA did sue the state over the definition of "all" in the initiative, and won.

Local association leaders and members, school district administrators and parents reacted to legislative inaction. Community rallies, votes to walk out, votes of "no confidence," newspaper ads, multiple press conferences, e-mails, letters and phone calls were all directed at the Legislature. The bottom line: After a 105-day session plus a thirty-day special session costing approximately a million dollars, they shortchanged the cost-of-living increases, underfunded health insurance and cut existing education funding. They did virtually nothing to seek additional revenue sources.

Transition

In May 2001 the start of a major historical transition took place at the WEA. A new President and a new Vice President were elected at the WEA RA. Lee Ann Prielipp and Tom Morris completed their leadership terms, leaving behind them the legacy of I–732.

Charles Hasse, a fourth-grade teacher from Highline, was elected WEA President and Dave Scott, the Edmonds Education Association President, was elected WEA Vice President. Jim Seibert, WEA Executive Director since 1988, decided to retire. WEA hired Armand Tiberio, former UniServ and WEA staff person, as its new Executive Director. These three people have the opportunity to begin a new history beyond the years covered in this book.

Conclusion

The year 1965 divided the old WEA of Joe Chandler from the WEA that has emerged in the 21st century as the largest and most influential public-sector union in the state. The ups and downs in the fortunes of the Association are a very product of the activism that had its birth in 1965 with the passage of the Professional Negotiations Act, which signaled to Washington's teachers that they had a legitimate voice in their own profession.

WEA was at its finest when it had clear and concrete objectives and a leadership that turned to the membership, both locally and statewide, to be the driving force for achieving victory. More often than not the impetus began at the local level, as with Seattle to achieve the first PN Act or with the Northwest Region at the end of the 1980s to press for greater state support for school funding. Not only have local strikes been major milestones in WEA history, they have strengthened all locals across the state.

Often great strides were made because of a handful of people like the core of the original UniServ staff, who propelled a reluctant state organization into becoming a powerful and influential public-sector union, or a President who united the members around a key political objective.

Eight major achievements marked the growth of the WEA. Each in its own way made the Association stronger and gave the state's teachers a greater voice in education. All of these happened because WEA members, leaders and their staff broke out of old constraints, dared to take risks and had the vision to take advantage of fortuitous circumstances.

These eight major events were:

1. 1965 — Passage of the Professional Negotiations Act
2. 1970 — UniServ Program
3. 1972 — First K–12 teacher strike in the state in Aberdeen
4. 1973 — Evergreen teacher strike
5. 1978 — Mardesich campaign
6. 1980 — State political caucus program
7. 1991 — Multi-Local Strike
8. 2000 — Initiative 732 campaign

If this book achieves anything, we hope it will provide some useful lessons for the state's newer teachers, who will inherit, for better or worse, what we have handed over to them. For them we see four key lessons.

First, the power and strength of the WEA is its members who, when informed, motivated and organized, can be a tremendous force to achieve great gains for public education and the teaching profession. To abandon power, even in the most collaborative of relationships, is a mistake. To ignore this truth is to court defeat.

Second, WEA is at its best when it supports its local associations to fight battles for education at the local level. That does not preclude statewide efforts, but those efforts have to be built on a network of strong, well-organized local associations.

Third, expect defeats from time to time, even much of the time, but rely on the Association's core tools and a faith in the strength of the membership to seize new initiatives and move forward. The fear of losing could be more fatal to the vitality of the organization than assuming new risks and daring great deeds. A loss is not fatal. The WEA has been serving the education community for over 112 years, and it has proven that adversity can't destroy it.

Fourth, don't allow adversity and the lack of a clear agenda to devolve into destructive infighting such as occurred in the 1980s. There will always be conflicts. They have occurred between the field and the state organization, between the staff and governance, between governance factions within the WEA, between geographic factions such as Eastern Washington and Western Washington, between philosophies such as "professional" and "union" and between WEA and external forces such as the Legislature and the Governor. But when there has been leadership committed to bringing disparate factions together in a united front to achieve clear objectives, the Association finds a way to pull together and move ahead to greater achievements.

The WEA through its history has played a major role in the history of education in Washington. It has become a strong and dynamic organization because of strong leaders from all parts of the organization who have had the freedom to dare great things.

Since 1965 the WEA has become a strong voice for Washington's teachers and other school employees and a staunch advocate for public education. We are proud to have been a part of WEA's history.

Appendixes

APPENDIX 1

Professional Negotiations Act

State of Washington Chapter 143, Laws of 1965
(As Amended by the 1969 Legislature)
SCHOOL DISTRICTS — EMPLOYEE ORGANIZATIONS

AN ACT Relating to education; recognizing the right of employee organizations to represent certificated employees in their relations with school districts.

Be it enacted by the Legislature of the State of Washington

Sec. 1. It is the purpose of this act to strengthen methods of administering employer-employee relations through the establishment of orderly methods of communication between certificated employees and the school districts by which they are employed.

Sec. 2. As used in this act:

"Employee organization" means any organization which includes as members certificated employees of a school district and which has as one of its purposes the representation of the employees in their employment relations with the school district.

"Certificated employee" means any employee holding a regular teaching certificate of the state and who is employed by any school district with the exception of the chief administrative officer of each district.

Sec. 3. Representatives of an employee organization, which organization shall by secret ballot have won a majority in an election to represent the certificated employees within its school district, shall have the right, after using established administrative channels, to meet confer and negotiate with the board of directors of the school district or a committee thereof to communicate the considered professional judgment of the certificated staff prior to the final adoption by the board of proposed policies relating to, but not limited to, curriculum, textbook selection, in-service training, student teaching programs, personnel, hiring and assignment practices, leaves of absence, salaries and salary schedules and non-instructional duties.

Sec. 4. If in any school district there is a separate employee organization of certificated employees of a community college which organization shall, by secret ballot, have won a majority in an election to represent the certificated employees of the community college, as determined by a secret election, the representatives of the separate aggregation shall have the right, after using established administrative channels, to meet, confer, and negotiate with the board of directors of the school district or a committee thereof to communicate the considered professional judgment of the certificated staff prior to the final adoption by the board of proposed school policies related to, but not limited to, curriculum, textbook selection, in-service training, student teaching programs, personnel, hiring and assignment practices, leaves of absence, salaries and salary schedules, and non-instructional duties.

Sec. 5. Nothing in this act shall prohibit any certificated employee from appearing in his own behalf on matters relating to his employment relations with the school district.

Sec. 6. In the event that any matter being jointly considered by the employee organization and the board of directors of the school district is not settled by means provided in this act, either party, twenty-four hours after serving written notice of their intended action to the other party, may request the assistance and advice of a committee composed of educators and school directors appointed by the state superintendent of public instruction. This committee shall make a written report with recommendations to both parties within 20 calendar days of receipt of the request for assistance. Any recommendations of the committee shall be advisory only and not binding upon the board of directors or the employee organization.

Sec. 7. Boards of directors of school districts or any administrative officer thereof shall not discriminate against certificated employees or applicants for such positions because of their membership or nonmembership in employee organizations or their exercise of other rights under this act.

Sec. 8. Boards of directors of school districts shall adopt reasonable rules and regulations for the administration of employer-employee relations under this act.

Sec. 9. Nothing in this law shall be construed to annul or modify, or to preclude the renewal or continuation of, any lawful agreement heretofore entered into between any school district and any representative of its employees.

APPENDIX 2

1965 WEA Staff Organization Structure

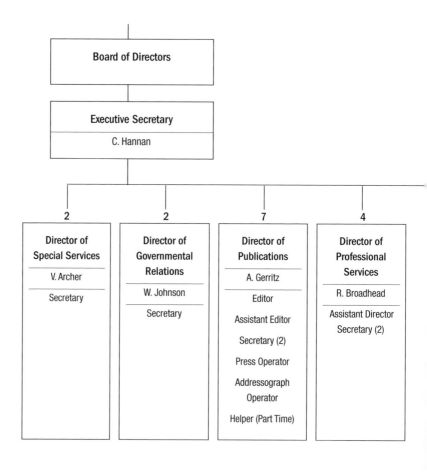

Board of Directors

Executive Secretary

C. Hannan

2

**Director of
Special Services**

V. Archer

Secretary

2

**Director of
Governmental
Relations**

W. Johnson

Secretary

7

**Director of
Publications**

A. Gerritz

Editor

Assistant Editor

Secretary (2)

Press Operator

Addressograph
Operator

Helper (Part Time)

4

**Director of
Professional
Services**

R. Broadhead

Assistant Director

Secretary (2)

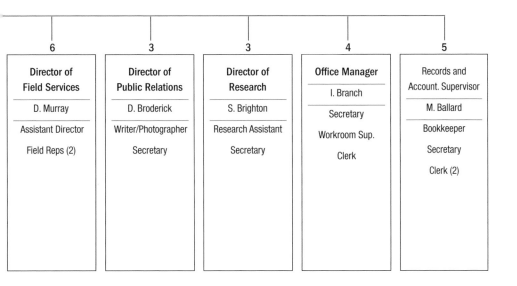

STAFF	
Professional	13
Semiprofessional	5
Secretary	12
Other	7
Ratio	0.94 to 1

6	3	3	4	5
Director of Field Services	**Director of Public Relations**	**Director of Research**	**Office Manager**	Records and Account. Supervisor
D. Murray	D. Broderick	S. Brighton	I. Branch	M. Ballard
Assistant Director	Writer/Photographer	Research Assistant	Secretary	Bookkeeper
Field Reps (2)	Secretary	Secretary	Workroom Sup.	Secretary
			Clerk	Clerk (2)

Present Salary Cost: $332,000

APPENDIX 3

1969 WEA Representative Assembly Motion for Tax Reform

It was moved that the WEA Representative Assembly direct the WEA Legislation Committee to prepare legislation designed to:

1. Establish a graduated net income tax having a range of five percentage points between minimum and maximum rates.

2. Establish a single rate net income tax on corporations and financial institutions.

3. Reduce the business and occupation tax.

4. Reduce the sales and use tax.

    (a) Relief from sales and use taxes for foods purchased and consumed off premises shall be provided through a tax credit.

    (b) Medicine sold on prescription or compounded by druggists, medical and dental aids or devices such as artificial limbs, eyeglasses, and dentures shall be exempted at the time of sale.

    (c) Tax credits for food shall be payable to individuals whether or not they have an income tax liability.

5. Establish a property tax base at 20 mils on 50 percent of true and fair value of taxable property.

    (a) The Washington State Department of Revenue shall by statute be required to take action to assure that counties collect taxes at 50 percent of true and fair value of taxable property.

    (b) All real property tax statements shall clearly state true and fair value of taxable property.

    (c) All real property owned or operated by presently tax-exempted institutions that is used for profit-making shall be placed on county tax rolls.

APPENDIX 4

Purposes of the WEA Office of Certification and Accreditation

Passed by the 1967 WEA Representative Assembly

It shall be the duty of the Office of Certification and Accreditation to:

1. Establish standards for professional certification and standards for accreditation of educational institutions and school districts.

2. Provide a continuing program of professional certification.

3. Provide a continuing program for the accreditation of educational institutions and school districts.

4. Select, with the approval of the WEA Board of Directors, employees to carry out the policies of the Office of Certification and Accreditation.

5. Prepare an annual budget for submission to the WEA Board of Directors.

6. Prepare an annual report of progress and recommendations for submission to the Representative Assembly.

7. Maintain a teacher placement service of professionally certificated educators.

8. Coordinate all activities of the WEA which are directed toward the development and applications of standards of educational performance, education, and facilities.

APPENDIX 5

WEA Mission, Goal, Objectives and Core Values

MISSION

The mission of the Washington Education Association is to make public education the best it can be for students, staff and communities.

GOAL

Our goal is to build confidence in public education and increase support for Washington's public school system.

OBJECTIVES

Our objectives are to:

- Increase WEA members' professional status and job satisfaction.
- Improve the quality of and access to public education for all students.
- Forge partnerships with parents, business and community groups.

CORE VALUES

WEA members believe in:

- Public education as the cornerstone of a strong democratic society
- The fundamental right of all students to have access to the best possible public education
- Life-long learning
- Individual and organizational integrity
- Respect for diversity
- High professional standards for members
- Personal and professional growth
- Continual improvement in the quality of public education
- Fair treatment for all people, including the right to due process and representation
- Shared decision making and shared accountability with the community for the quality of public education
- Academic freedom
- Safe learning and working environment
- Shared decision making and accountability for all constituencies within the WEA
- High expectations and performance standards for all students

Increase Followed by Decline in Washington's Average Classroom Teacher Salary Rank

WASHINGTON'S RANKING AMONG FIFTY STATES AND D.C., FIVE YEAR INTERVALS, SCHOOL YEARS 1970–1971 THROUGH 2000–2001

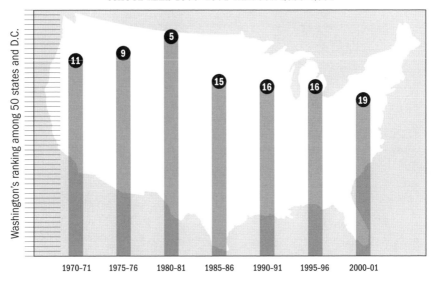

Source: NEA Rankings and Estimates. (Original source of salary data: state departments of education.)

Washington Education Association Membership Totals

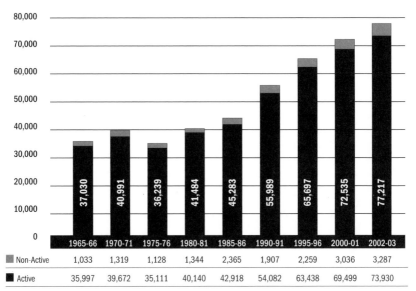

	1965-66	1970-71	1975-76	1980-81	1985-86	1990-91	1995-96	2000-01	2002-03
Non-Active	1,033	1,319	1,128	1,344	2,365	1,907	2,259	3,036	3,287
Active	35,997	39,672	35,111	40,140	42,918	54,082	63,438	69,499	73,930

APPENDIX 6

Washington Education Association Chronology of Events, 1965–2001

1965 Joe Chandler, WEA Executive Secretary since 1940, retires. Cecil Hannan succeeds him, but remains in the position for less than two years.

1965 Professional Negotiations Act is passed by the Legislature and signed by Governor Dan Evans. The PN Act gives Washington teacher organizations the right to "meet, confer and negotiate a wide range of school policies with their school boards."

1965 WEA creates its first political action committee, naming it PULSE (Political Unity of Leadership in State Education).

1967 Northshore is the first district to declare "Impasse" under the PN Act and ask for the assistance of a committee of educators and board members to help resolve the dispute. Association negotiator Bob Bell is thrust into the spotlight and is later hired by WEA.

1967 Cecil Hannan resigns as Executive Secretary to work for the NEA. Bob Addington from the California Teachers Association replaces him.

1968 Tacoma Association of Classroom Teachers bargains the first collective bargaining contract under the PN Act. Seattle follows in 1969. Bremerton had attained the first contract in the state under the AFT in 1954.

1968 On December 7 the WEA holds a special Representative Assembly at the UW's HUB Auditorium to hear the report of the Stanford Research Institute, hired by WEA to do a study of Washington's tax structure. The special RA passes a motion to seek reform of the state's tax structure, including seeking a constitutional amendment allowing an income tax. Other motions calling for statewide sanctions and a strike fail to pass.

1969 WEA opens an office in Olympia. Dave Broderick replaces Wally Johnson as WEA's chief lobbyist.

1969 In November HJR 42, to allow the state to levy an income tax for support of schools, fails badly at the polls.

1970 In July the NEA Representative Assembly in San Francisco passes the UniServ Program to provide trained staff for local associations all across the country. Washington's urban locals get funding the first year and pressure WEA to keep the program locally controlled. Other areas of the state have to wait a year to get into the program.

1971 Regionally formed UniServ Councils hire their first UniServ Representatives. This "freshman class" goes on to drive the greatest change in the WEA since it was formed in 1889.

1972 In May the first K–12 teacher strike takes place in Aberdeen.

1973 In May the second teacher strike takes place in Evergreen. Teachers there defy a court order to return to work. Three teacher leaders are jailed for over forty days. It is the defining teacher strike in state history. It is followed that year by strikes in Elma and Edmonds.

1973 Under pressure from elements on the WEA Board, Bob Addington resigns as Executive Secretary and is replaced by outsider Wendell Verduin whose title is now Executive Director.

1973 In October the WEASO, the employee union of the WEA, stages a seventeen-day strike over salaries and retirement benefits.

1975 WEA lobbies the Legislature to pass the Educational Employment Relations Act, a true teacher collective bargaining law that replaces the PN Act. Governor Dan Evans, signer of the PN Act ten years earlier, signs it. The law takes effect on January 1, 1976. The WEA gears up to bargain full-blown contracts in every district in the state.

1975 Pro–UniServ locals at the WEA RA in Spokane hold a proposed dues increase hostage until they are assured that a substantial part of it will go to support the UniServ Program. This emergence of the power of smaller locals ensures that UniServ and the "field" will dominate the WEA for years to come.

1975 Ten thousand WEA members stage a two-day march on Olympia. At issue is additional funding for levy-loss-ravaged school districts and a threat to change the 2 percent Teacher Retirement System. Some additional money is passed for levy-loss districts, and TRS II is passed to take effect for teachers hired after October 1, 1977.

1976 Led by Senate Majority Leader August Mardesich and abetted by teacher legislators Joe Stortini of Tacoma and Al Bauer of Vancouver, the Legislature guts the teacher Continuing Contract Law. The essential parts of the law are restored a year later.

1976 In a major policy address to the WEA RA, WEA President Jim Aucutt blasts the Legislature and other major power groups in the state for failure to financially support Washington's schools and for legislation gutting the Continuing Contract Law.

1976 Under WEA's new political action program headed by Steve Kink, WEA achieves unprecedented results in the November legislative races.

1977 Carol Coe becomes WEA president and begins restructuring WEA governance to provide for two-year terms and other reforms. It makes the presidency a stronger element in the WEA structure.

1977   Executive Director Wendell
Verduin resigns August 31
ending a stormy four years in
that position. He is replaced in
December by Gil Gregory, an
Association field staff manager
from Pennsylvania.

1977–78 As the push for collective
bargaining contracts gains
strength, the state experiences
peak numbers of teacher strikes in
these two years.

1978   Thurston County Superior Court
Judge Robert Doran rules that the
state's system of funding for public
education is unconstitutional and
orders the Legislature to "define
and fund" an adequate system of
basic education. The Legislature
responds by passing the Basic
Education Act, which shifts much
of the control of education from
local districts to the Legislature.

1978   In September the WEA, in
alliance with other public
employee unions, defeats Senate
Majority Leader August Mardesich
in the primary election. This
unprecedented show of political
power gains the attention of state
leaders as well as the news media.

1980   Under the leadership of Carol
Coe, the WEA gears up to take
over the state's Democratic
precinct caucuses to help assure
the renomination of Jimmy Carter
for president. In May the WEA
dominates the State Democratic
Convention in Hoquiam. In
September WEA-endorsed Jim
McDermott defeats incumbent
Governor Dixy Lee Ray in the
primary.

1980   The Reagan landslide rolls over
Washington. WEA is stunned as
Spellman defeats McDermott and
the Republicans take over the
House, with Democrats retaining
control of the Senate by one vote.

1981   On February 13 Democratic
State Senator Peter von
Reichbauer switches parties,
giving Republicans control of the
Legislature. With clear majorities
in each house, the Republicans
pass HB 166, limiting teacher
salary increases to "amounts
or percentages" passed by the
Legislature. This same Legislature
cuts back financial support for
Basic Education, thus setting the
stage for a second Doran decision
in a suit filed by Seattle and other
school districts. This time WEA is
a party to the suit.

1981   Seattle Teacher Association
President Reese Lindquist is
elected WEA President in a heated
contest with WEA Vice-president
Bill Miller. Terry Bergeson from
Tacoma is elected Vice President
in a tight race. This election sets
the stage for a decade of internal
conflicts within the WEA.

1982   WEA's Political Action Program
bounces back and helps return
control of the House and Senate
to Democratic control. However, in
a succession of legislative sessions
to follow, legislators fail to address
education funding or the repeal
or modification of HB 166.

1984   Booth Gardner, a personal friend
of Lindquist and endorsed by
WEA, is elected governor over
Spellman. He declares himself

the "education governor," raising WEA hopes that the state will give greater consideration to education issues.

1985   Terry Bergeson is elected WEA President in a bitter contest with Lindquist-backed candidate Bob Maier. Mead teacher Carla Nuxoll is elected Vice President. Camps within the WEA continue to split the Association.

1987   Edmonds teachers go on strike, largely over class size. The strike lasts thirty days and sets a record for the longest teacher strike in the state up to this time.

1987   In a major upheaval of the WEA led by Terry Bergeson, the WEA Board, in October, fires Executive Director Gil Gregory. Vice President Carla Nuxoll, who had been excluded from a series of secret meetings leading up to the vote, sharply criticizes the move. The WEA is deeply split. Bergeson is unable to get much else accomplished during the remainder of her time in office. In December the NEA assigns Jim Seibert from the Southeast Region to be an interim Executive Director. He eventually is hired permanently.

1989   Carla Nuxoll is elected WEA President. CT Purdom from Naches Valley is elected Vice President. The WEA puts behind it much of the division of the 1980s.

1989   WEA salary rankings among the states drop to twenty-third from a high of fifth in 1982. On April 27 the Northwest Region of WEA, along with the Central Region,

stages "Report Card Day" regional membership meetings to rate the performance of local legislators on salary and funding-related issues. A vocal membership calls for further concerted actions to force the Legislature to act. In August Western Washington members hold a planning meeting in Bellevue. Carla Nuxoll is invited. Members demand that she mobilize the WEA for action against the Legislature.

1990   Again led by the Northwest Region, locals across Western Washington stage a series of walkouts on February 13 demanding action from the Legislature. The focus of the discontent is Governor Booth Gardner.

1990   Mukilteo is on strike for thirty-three days, eclipsing the record set by Edmonds in 1987.

1990   During a meeting of the Education Commission of the States held in Seattle and chaired by Booth Gardner, over 6,000 WEA members demonstrate outside the meeting. The focus of the demonstration is a large hot air balloon. Banners read "No More Hot Air!"

1991   During eight days in late April, locals, virtually all from Western Washington, stage a "Multi-Local Strike" against the Legislature. Crowds in Olympia reach more than 20,000. It is the largest Olympia demonstration in the state's history. Gardner sends the Legislature home only to call them back in July. The Legislature does pass modest improvements over Gardner's objections. A year later the Legislature passes the largest salary and funding increases since the 1970s. These increases prove, however, to be an anomaly for most of the 1990s, as the Legislature falls back into a pattern of shortchanging the state's schools.

1991   The Legislature creates G-CERF to address issues of education reform and funding. It largely ignores teachers and does not deal with funding issues.

1992   WEA backs Mike Lowry for governor on promises he will address school funding issues.

1993   G-CERF makes its report to the Legislature and recommends creation of the Student Learning Commission. Terry Bergeson is appointed to head the commission. Their work leads to adoption of the state's Student Learning Objectives and the Washington Assessment of Student Learning (WASL) test.

1993   CT Purdom becomes WEA President and faces two revenue limitation initiatives, 601 and 602. WEA joins the campaign to oppose both. I–602 is defeated and 601 passes by a thin 51 percent. I–601 becomes the Legislature's excuse for not addressing education funding in the 1990s.

1995   Fife is on strike for thirty-seven days, over school board attempt to reduce their TRI pay schedule. Resolution is left to binding arbitration, which the FEA wins the next August. A new record for the length of strikes in Washington is set.

1996   The newly formed Evergreen Freedom Foundation (EFF), headed by failed gubernatorial candidate Bob Williams and backed by the National Right to Work Committee and other right-wing organizations, begins a series of attacks on WEA political spending. Challenges in the Public Disclosure Commission and the courts go on for the next three years and are largely resolved in WEA's favor.

1996   The WEA backs Gary Locke for governor on promises he will address salary and funding issues.

1997   Lee Ann Prielipp from Federal Way is elected WEA president.

1999   Going into this legislative session the WEA had experienced six years of no or minimal salary increases: 0 percent, 0 percent, 4 percent, 0 percent, 3 percent and 0 percent. The battle cry is "Catch Up and Keep Up." Members wear buttons reading "0, 0, 4, 0, 3, and 0." A concurrent public relations program gains considerable public support and a small increase from the legislature.

2000   The WEA gains over 330,000 signatures to put Initiative 732, guaranteeing school employees annual cost of living increases, on the November ballot. It passes by over 62 percent.

2001   Jim Seibert retires as WEA Executive Director. He is replaced by Armand Tiberio. Charles Hasse from Highline and Dave Scott from Edmonds are elected President and Vice President. The three form a completely new WEA leadership team.

APPENDIX 7

Washington Education Association Presidents

1965–2001

1964–1965	Frank "Buster" Brouillet	Puyallup
1965–1966	Jack Hill	Wenatchee
1966–1967	Gladys Perry	Seattle
1967–1968	Stan Jeffers	Central Valley
1968–1969	Ester Wilfong	Tacoma
1969–1970	Ken Landeis	Yakima
1970–1971	Jackie Hutcheon	Bellevue
1971–1972	Eugene Fink	Mead
1972–1973	Ken Bumgarner	Edmonds
1973–1974	Eugene Fink	Mead
1974–1975	Blair Patrick	Edmonds
1975–1976	Jim Aucutt	Cheney
1976–1981	Carol Coe (Gregory)	Northshore
1981–1985	Reese Lindquist	Seattle
1985–1989	Terry Bergeson	Tacoma
1989–1993	Carla Nuxoll	Mead
1993–1997	CT Purdom	Naches Valley
1997–2001	Lee Ann Prielipp	Federal Way
2001–	Charles Hasse	Highline

PERSONS INTERVIEWED

Sharon Amos: Aberdeen President and negotiator, WEA Board member, Interviewed 2/17/03.

Jim Aucutt: Cheney President, WEA Board, WEA President, NEA Board, UniServ staff in MidState and Eastern Washington. Interviewed 1/9/03.

Terry Bergeson: WEA Board, NEA Women's Caucus, WEA President. Interviewed 9/11/03.

Jack Beyers: Vancouver Education Association bargainer and high school vice principal, WEA Director of Field Services SW Region. Interviewed 2/12/03.

George Blood: UniServ staff in Soundview and Tacoma. Interviewed 1/31/03.

Box Bond: UniServ staff in Fourth Corner, WEA Grievance Administration and UniServ Manager. Interviewed 9/25/03.

Ken Bumgarner: WEA President, Summit UniServ staff. Interviewed July 2003.

John Cahill: Edmonds President, Edmonds UniServ staff, WEA Communications Field Representative, WEA Communications Division Manager, Tacoma UniServ staff. Interviewed 1/10/03.

Roger Cantaloube: Eastern Washington UniServ staff, WEA CPEA staff, MidState and Tacoma UniServ staff. Interviewed 8/14/03.

Bea Carlberg: WEA secretary and administrative assistant to executive directors. Interviewed 12/9/03.

John Chase: Chinook UniServ staff. Interviewed 11/26/02.

Carol Coe (Gregory): North Shore President, ACT President, WEA President. Interviewed 3/26/03.

Leona Dater: Eastern Washington UniServ staff. Interviewed 1/8/03.

Bob Fisher: Spokane President, WEA lobbyist, WEA Governmental Relations Manager. Interviewed 4/11/02.

Janet Genther: Renton President, Cascade UniServ staff. Interviewed 9/11/03.

Ron Gillespie: Central Kitsap President, Olympic UniServ Council President, WEA Board. Interviewed 1/28/03.

Bob Graf: Chinook and Tacoma UniServ staff. Interviewed 2/19/03.

Toni Jenner (Graf): Kennewick President, WEA Board, MidState and Soundview UniServ staff. Interviewed 5/23/03.

Julie Green: Edmonds President, Lower Columbia UniServ staff. Interviewed 1/29/03.

Gil Gregory: WEA Executive Director. Interviewed 9/8/03.

Bill Hainer: Highline UniServ staff, WEA Assistant Executive Director for Collective Bargaining, Field Services and Instructional and Professional Development. Interviewed 10/23/02.

Faith Hanna: WEA staff attorney. Interviewed 6/2/03.

Warren Henderson: Seattle President, Seattle Assistant Executive Director, UniServ staff in Tacoma and Edmonds, WEA CPEA staff. Interviewed 9/16/03.

Leon Horne: Tacoma President, WEA Board, NEA Board and Executive Committee. Interviewed 11/21/02.

Dick Iverson: Spokane President, WEA Eastern Washington field staff. Interviewed 3/24/02.

Stan Jeffers: Principal in Central Valley, WEA Board President, WEA President, Edmonds Executive Director, WEA Instructional and Professional Development staff. Interviewed 4/12/02.

Dick Johnson: Evergreen President, Riverside UniServ staff, WEA Communications Field Representative. Interviewed 4/19/02.

Don Johnson: WEA Board, WEA staff in Professional Rights and Responsibilities, UniServ staff, Assistant Executive Director, Deputy Executive Director, Chief Lobbyist in Governmental Relations. Interviewed 4/19/02.

Leslie Kanzler: North Thurston President, MidState UniServ staff, WEA Community Organizing Director. Interviewed 9/4/03.

Perry Keithley: WEA Director of Research in Governmental Relations and WEA Lobbyist. Interviewed 1/23/03.

Steve Kink: Lower Columbia and Olympic UniServ staff, WEA Political Action Director and Lobbyist, WEA Assistant Executive Director for Field Services, Temporary WEA Executive Director and WEA Deputy Executive Director. Interviewed 1/10/03.

Ken Landeis: Yakima President, WEA President-elect, WEA President, WEA Field staff, Southeast Washington UniServ staff. Interviewed 4/30/02.

Reese Lindquist: Seattle Teachers Association President, SEA President, WEA President. Interviewed 8/25/03.

Judith Lonnquist: WEA General Counsel. Interviewed 4/30/03.

Bob Maier: Mercer Island President, WEA Governmental Relations staff, WEA Manager and Chief Lobbyist in Governmental Relations. Interviewed 9/19/03.

Joann (Slye) Kink Mertens: WEA support staff, WEA Research staff, WEA Director of Research. Interviewed 7/29/03.

Teresa Moore: WEA Assistant Executive Director for Communications. Interviewed 9/4/03.

John Morrill: Everett President, Pilchuck UniServ staff. Interviewed 11/25/02.

Nancy Murphy: Seattle, Sammamish and Cascade UniServ staff, Seattle Executive Director. Interviewed 7/30/03.

Don Murray: WEA Field Representative, WEA Director of Training, WEA Director of Research. Interviewed 4/29/02.

Carla Nuxoll: Eastern Washington UniServ Council President, WEA Vice President, WEA President. Interviewed 1/8/03.

Mary O'Brien: MidState, Sammamish and Puget Sound UniServ staff. Interviewed 3/18/03.

Cory Olson: Kent President, Kent UniServ staff. Interviewed 6/24/03.

Steve Paulson: Evergreen President, North Central and Spokane UniServ staff, WEA Eastern Washington Network staff. Interviewed 1/9/03.

Bob Pickles: WEA ACT President, WEA Second Vice President, WEA Instructional and Professional Development staff. Interviewed 10/28/02.

Bill Powell: WEA Network Attorney. Interviewed 1/8/03.

Lee Ann Prielipp: Federal Way President, WEA Board, NEA Board, WEA Vice President. WEA President. Interviewed 8/21/03.

Patty Raichle: Fife President, Chinook UniServ staff, WEA Instruction and Professional Development staff, WEA Instructional and Professional Development Manager. Interviewed 8/21/03.

Jim Raines: Vancouver President, Vancouver Executive Director, WEA Field staff, WEA Director of Collective Bargaining. Interviewed 4/17/02.

Rod Regan: WEA Community Organizer, WEA Political Action staff, WEA Project staff. Interviewed 9/17/03.

Marline Rennels: Olympic UniServ staff, WEA UniServ Manager. Interviewed 9/4/03.

Wes Ruff: Seattle EA President, WEA Professional Negotiations staff, WEA Collective Bargaining staff. Interviewed 4/16/02.

Jim Russell: Olympic UniServ staff. Interviewed 5/7/03.

Ron Scarvie: Royal City President, Fourth Corner and Summit UniServ staff, WEA Collective Bargaining staff. Interviewed 11/15/02.

Mike Schoeppach: Fourth Corner and Bellevue UniServ staff. Interviewed 1/22/03.

Jim Seibert: WEA Executive Director. Interviewed 8/5/03.

Pat Steinburg: Port Angeles President,
        South Kitsap President, Puget
        Sound UniServ staff, WEA Special
        Education Field Representative,
        WEA Instructional and
        Professional Development staff.
        Interviewed 8/18/03.

Sheryl Stevens: Central Kitsap President,
        Olympic, Chinook and Riverside
        UniServ staff. Interviewed
        11/4/02.

D*oug Suhm:* Puget Sound, MidState and
        Tacoma UniServ staff. Interviewed
        4/11/02.

Dale Troxel: WEA Department of
        Classroom Teachers' staff,
        WEA Professional Rights
        and Responsibilities staff,
        WEA UniServ Program staff.
        Interviewed 4/17/02.

Jeff Wahlquist: MidState UniServ Council
        President, WEA Board, NEA
        Board, MidState and Eastern
        Washington UniServ staff, WEA
        Collective Bargaining staff.
        Interviewed 1/9/03.

John Ward: Marysville President, WEA
        Board, North Central and Summit
        UniServ staff, WEA Field Services
        Division Manager. Interviewed
        11/7/02.

Mike Wartelle: Everett President,
        Pilchuck UniServ Council
        President, Pilchuck UniServ staff.
        Interviewed 12/19/02.

Additional Questionnaires Submitted:

Mary Jo Baker: Southeast Washington
        UniServ staff

Darrell Puls: Southeast Washington
        UniServ staff

Carol Pursell: Pilchuck UniServ support
        staff

NAMES INDEX

INDEX OF SELECTED TOPICS

John Cahill and Steve Kink

JOHN CAHILL had a twenty-nine year career with the Washington Education Association, beginning as a UniServ Representative in Edmonds in 1972. In 1973, he helped organize Edmonds' first teacher strike. At WEA he was a Communications Field Representative, Assistant Executive Director for Communications and a member of the WEA Organizing Team. He served his last six years as a UniServ Representative for the Tacoma Education Association. He retired in 2001.

Prior to his career with WEA, Cahill was a teacher for seven years beginning in Bremerton in 1965, the year the Professional Negotiations Act, the state's first teacher bargaining law, took effect. From 1966 to 1972, he taught English and social studies at Alderwood Junior High in Edmonds. While there he served as Association President and as a member of the local's bargaining team.

STEVE KINK began his education career in 1966 teaching high school history in Florence, Oregon. He became active in the Association as a Building Representative and as a local vice president, an Oregon Education Association delegate and a Negotiations Commission member.

Kink's Association staff career started with the OEA in 1970 as one of the first and youngest staff hired in the National Education Association's UniServ Program. He moved to Washington state, starting the Lower Columbia and Olympic UniServ councils. In 1976, he became the Washington Education Association's Director of Political Action. Four years later, he joined WEA's management team as the Assistant Executive Director for Field Services and retired as the Deputy Executive Director of WEA. During his twenty-six-year career with WEA, Kink was responsible for implementing, creating, coordinating, directing or managing most of WEA's field programs.